To Henry – with all
best wishes,

Greg Whitcher

SMOKING THEM OUT

The Theft of the Environment and How to Take it Back

By
Greg Walcher

Smoking Them Out: The Theft of the Environment and How to Take it Back

Copyright © 2013 by Greg Walcher

International Standard Book Number: 978-1-938911-40-8

Published by American Tradition Institute
Denver, Colorado

Printed in the United States of America

TABLE OF CONTENTS

INTRODUCTION

The United States is quickly becoming the first country in the history of the world to adopt policies designed to ensure its own decline. Ours could be the first society ever purposely to plan its own bleak future. Sound melodramatic? Consider that our nation is actually adopting official policies promoting a lower standard of living for future generations, literally encouraging our people—through taxes, regulations, and higher prices—to travel less, live in smaller and less comfortable homes, give up their cars, and eliminate many other modern conveniences. No nation has ever even considered such a future, much less made it official public policy.

No nation has ever purposely burned its own food supply, yet that is precisely what the United States is now doing by subsidizing ethanol production at the expense of higher grocery prices, supposedly to save us from the evils of fossil fuels. In fact, we are rushing headlong into an official course of action based on the view that free enterprise is selfish, that prosperity is unequal and thus unfair, and that our people must stop much of their production, manufacturing, and especially consumption. We are headed in this bizarre direction because of the dubious theory that our pursuit of the good life is destroying our environment, if not the very Earth itself.

Issues related to our natural environment have been contentious for a long time, but this is different. This is new. Every society in history wanted the next generation to have it better than themselves, until now. This is not business-as-usual. And it is beyond comprehension to most Americans—who have done more to improve their environment than any people who ever lived—that their treatment of the environment is now being used against them.

This is not happening because Americans quit caring about the environment. Rather, the conservation movement has been hijacked —stolen by a huge industry of dishonest money changers whose agenda has nothing whatsoever to do with the environment. Instead, they are now using the popularity of the environmental cause to attempt the final destruction of our way of life.

Every day we see the growing use of environmental laws not *for* the environment, but *against* people. It is palpable across a wide array of issues—endangered species, public land management, clean air, wetlands, energy production, and the regulation of water. Ordinary people are denied the right to use their own private property. The rumored presence of mysterious species becomes a tool for stopping human activity. Public access to public land is increasingly limited. Law-abiding citizens are hauled into court and accused of outrageous violations, apparently presumed guilty until proven otherwise.

There are legendary cases in which property owners have been prevented from *removing* old tires and other trash because some bureaucrat declared the property to be "wetlands," or where rules changed *after* a property purchase were nevertheless used to stop the owner from building a house on his own land. Many Americans read about such abuses and assume they are just exceptions, rare examples of government run amuck. Unfortunately, they are becoming so common we are scarcely even surprised anymore. We have become so jaded that we are no longer offended when people are mistreated by a system that was supposed to protect us. Worst of all, because most of us continue to support strong environmental protection, we simply do nothing about it—not because we support such abuses of the law, but because we fear being accused of not caring about nature.

Over the course of a lifetime working on natural resources issues, it has always struck me as strange when working on environmental problems how often the environmental organizations fight the solutions that seem easiest. Just when you think there would be little controversy over restoring a dying forest, or installing solar panels, there is strong opposition from such groups. Political leaders are regularly accused by environmentalists of being "in the hip pocket of big oil," or being a "shill for the timber industry," or worse. They must either side with an ever-widening coalition of environmental groups or risk being painted as a corporate plunderer. Many politicians are unwilling to take that chance, regardless of the details.

The growth of this "us-against-them" mentality has replaced what was once almost universal support for environmental protection with contention, antagonism, confrontation, and litigation. Legislation, ballot initiatives, and lawsuits have taken the place of community discussion that might lead to consensus. Environmental groups raise and spend hundreds of millions of dollars on campaigns, nearly all of it on negative advertising—mostly against Republicans. These groups have thoroughly demonized leaders on one side of the aisle, especially conservatives and their allies in the business world. And most conservatives not only have no idea how to respond, in many cases they make matters worse, either responding incorrectly or not at all.

Most conservative leaders have chosen one of two approaches to environmental issues, both of them politically untenable:

- Some fight the proposals of environmental groups tooth and nail, making it even easier for the latter to label conservatives as enemies of the environment. Such leaders become easy targets, attract negative attention of the news media and the organized environmental lobby, and frankly, harm the reputation of all conservatives on environmental issues. The attacks on such leaders are often unfair, but nonetheless effective in convincing most voters that conservatives are not friendly to the environment.

- Others position themselves as conservative on fiscal and/or social issues, but more liberal on the environment, willing to cave in to interest group pressure periodically, hoping these groups will be supportive at the next election. It never works because, as we will see, the real agenda of those groups is not about the environment, and they will never support conservatives—no matter how many times they cave on these issues.

Many conservatives are sensitive about these issues, and bristle at the accusation that they are on the wrong side. They point out that the history of conservation has strong roots among Republicans over the past century, and they are right about that. They are often right about the unfairness of a media that consistently paints conservatives as environmental enemies. Still, the fact remains that if conservatives want to regain the high ground on these issues, a very different approach is needed.

The timing has never been better. Americans are increasingly skeptical of big environmental organizations because of their over-reach, and some pollsters claim such organizations are less trusted than ever before. For instance, many people are more skeptical today about man-made global warming than a decade ago, at least partly because of revelations that some scientists have falsified data. In addition, rising gasoline prices have made energy issues more personal than ever, leading to broad support for more domestic energy production. A Rasmussen poll in 2011 showed:

- Half of Americans believe the United States should produce more domestic oil by allowing drilling, even in the Alaska National Wildlife Refuge (only 35% opposed);

- 55% believe U.S. should produce more domestic oil by allowing increased production of oil shale (only 24% opposed); and

- By contrast, only 25% think we should cut back on energy use by returning to 55 mph speed limits (62% opposed).

Those are significant shifts in public opinion from previous years, and they illustrate that the time is right for a new approach to environmental issues in general. But no approach can win the hearts and minds of the American public unless it is perceived to be pro-environment. And let's face it—big environmental organizations are not going to relinquish the high ground without a fight, and the news media is not likely to help shift the focus. Rather, conservatives must begin to promote programs that are demonstrably better for the environment, and unquestionably so.

That means restoring healthy forests throughout the country, recovering endangered species by the hundreds, cleaning up our air and water, preserving habitat and open space, and providing better opportunities for the public enjoyment of public lands.

That does not require legal partnerships with the national environmental lobby, or giving government agencies control over private land. It does not require legislation, ballot initiatives, or lawsuits. Nor does it require increases in government spending or regulation. It requires a simple shift in thinking, based on one simple premise— we should improve our environment every way we can. That means working closely with property owners and the business community, not demonizing them. It means understanding that people are part of the environment and cannot be locked out.

The existing contentious approach has led to divisiveness, and dramatically increased the cost of environmental protection. And because that leads to an anti-business and anti-people regime, I simply don't believe Americans will tolerate it much longer. Some observers have expressed the opinion that America—the grand experiment in self government—is in the process of committing suicide. But I think our system and our people are more resilient than that. The abuse of the conservation movement is causing an immense national political backlash, and leaders who really care about the environment are well positioned to take back the high ground, re-assert their historic leadership, put an end to the nonsense, and build a more prosperous future with an even cleaner and healthier environment for the next generation of Americans. This book is about how to do that.

SMOKING THEM OUT

PREFACE

Thelma Hays stands in her back yard and wonders if there is any hope left for the country she loves. And she wonders why everyone else seems so complacent about it.

Thelma has lived most of her life in DeBeque Canyon, on the Colorado River in Western Colorado. The daughter of hard-working German immigrants, Thelma was the oldest of four children raised just a mile down the river in a little village called Cameo. Her family's farm—originally owned by her father and uncle, then by Thelma and her husband—offers one of the great scenic vistas in Colorado: a picturesque old farmstead with the Southwest's greatest river in the foreground and a backdrop of sheer canyon walls, etched by eons of wind and rain, and teeming with wildlife.

Today, however, that view is interrupted by a massive structure in the middle of the canal that brings water to the farm—a stainless steel and concrete monstrosity hundreds of feet long and taller than all the surrounding landscape features, oddly out of place in this relatively pristine setting.

Government officials told Thelma that it could not be located anywhere else but right in the heart of her farm and in the midst of her cherished view.

You might have watched a similar saga unfold over many months (as readers of the local newspaper did in this case). If so, you may have wondered, "why is the government doing this to these people?" The Hays case is a classic example of a conservation program that has been hijacked by people whose agenda has little to do with conservation.

Thelma Hays—Native Coloradan

Thelma Hays is not a troublemaker. She does not have millions to pay for expensive legal fees, and even if she did, suing her own government would be a foreign concept to someone like Thelma. She and her family worked hard and *earned* everything they have.

After high school, Thelma went to business school in Denver and met her husband, Herb Hays. In 1957, they bought her uncle's farm in the canyon. They had four children, so the work was hard and extra income was needed for their rapidly growing family. They worked day and night jobs, and ran the farm, too.

Before Herb's health began to fail, each of their four children became productive citizens, successful in their own endeavors. Herb and Thelma Hays created a legacy that not only includes children, grandchildren, and another generation on the way, but also one that employs hundreds of others throughout their community and touches the lives of thousands. Thelma would be quick to tell you their story is not unusual. There are millions of American families like hers, who have worked hard for what they have, and made their world better for it. Like other families, they also faced more than their share of tragedy. When Thelma's father and uncle both died while still in their 50's, she and Herb had to take over the farm while just beginning their own family. They lost their own beloved daughter Sandy, who also succumbed to illness much too young. And Herb himself began to face major health problems early. He suffered his first heart attack at the age of 45. Bypass surgery was yet experimental then, and it was only the beginning for Herb. He had another attack and a quadruple bypass 13 years later, and the ordeal left him unable to help with most of the physical labor. But Thelma did not complain; she just picked up the slack.

Despite often-difficult circumstances that might have led a weaker person to give up, Thelma Hays continued for years—and continues today, now in her 80s—running the family farm, selling its fruits and vegetables at her popular roadside market, and building on her solid reputation as a loyal and patriotic American.

So fighting the government, even when its actions seemed crazy, was not Thelma's first instinct. She always knew it was a battle she would never completely win. So she stoically deals with it the best way she knows how: she goes to work and tries not to think too much about it. But she also knows her farm will never look the same again.

The Government, the Fish Screen, and Common Sense

The giant structure on Thelma's farm is a fish screen, designed to keep endangered fish from entering the Highline canal, and it represents one of the most egregious examples imaginable of unadulterated government arrogance. The background story illustrates the worst kind of "command and control" bureaucracy, which for several years threatened to delay, if not completely halt, one of the most important elements of the Upper Colorado River Endangered Fish Recovery Program.

In a nutshell, the U.S. Bureau of Reclamation planned, as part of the fish passage structure at the historic 1912 Roller Dam, to install a fish screen in the Highline Canal, more than a mile downstream from the dam itself. In so doing, they were ignoring the strong advice of the State of Colorado and other independent experts.

Nevertheless, contrary to clearly defined provisions in the rules of the fish recovery program, the Bureau decided it needed to locate its fish screen precisely in the midst of this parcel of prime and unique farmland. Not only did officials want to displace an orchard which had existed for over 45 years, removing hundreds of profitable fruit trees in the process, they also tried to confiscate the century-old access to that property, and ran roughshod over one of the area's most respected families.

Perhaps worst of all, representatives of the Bureau never felt the need to justify their choice to locate the fish screen on Thelma's property. The canal runs for several miles without crossing any farms, so the screen easily could have been installed elsewhere without disrupting a soul. For the Bureau, no place else would do but the Hays' farm.

Forgive Us Our Trespasses

Legally, the issue was complicated. Since 1882, the land in question had been bought and sold several times, backed up by clear county property records. Thelma's family had grown fruit there for decades, never having any reason to suspect any ambiguity over their boundaries. No one from the government had ever attempted to inform the Hays family to the contrary.

It turned out that the government had built its Highline Canal across the Hayes property in 1912 a few feet off from the exact alignment purchased for building the canal. The records were old and incomplete, but apparently since 1912 the government's canal had crossed a few feet of Hays property it did not own, and so the Hays farm had been using a few feet of government land it did not own. And that situation had existed for over a century without any problems.

County property records did not reflect the fact that the federal survey was flawed, probably because nobody ever had any reason to re-check the original survey. Among neighbors with common sense, a simple land trade would have easily resolved this issue. (In fact, an old-fashioned hand shake sounded like the right answer to most people.) But there was no such common sense in dealing with the Bureau of Reclamation.

Instead, the Hays family was treated like criminal trespassers on their own property. They were told that regardless of past circumstances, the government now needed that land, and they were faced with a deplorable choice: The Hays family would either relinquish about half of the orchard (the most profitable part of the farm) and pay the government $1,700 a year to access the other half (for a mere five years)—or lose it all. They were told they could still manage the orchard remaining on the other half of the land, but only if they didn't plant trees, burn weeds or brush, or spray chemicals—making orchard management impossible. As a final affront, they were told they could no longer use the existing road to access their property, even though in that narrow canyon it is the *only* road to the farm (which was there before the government built its canal).

Adding insult to injury, the Bureau then asked the Hays family to allow disposal of 80,000 cubic yards of dirt on their property, with no compensation, and threatened to take out the remainder of the orchard if they refused. Worst of all, they were warned not to consult an attorney and given a whole 10 days to respond—even though the project's Final Environmental Assessment had not yet been completed, which made the alleged "urgency" of the warning very suspicious.

Thelma tried every way she knew to reason with the Bureau officials, even invited them into her kitchen, offering a homemade pie and fresh coffee. They came to her home, but only to explain their intractable position. And they rudely refused her homespun hospitality—as if they feared that someone might accuse them of being bought off with a cup of coffee.

The construction of the fish screen apparently had trumped any other consideration, including the future of people who depend upon the land and the canal. It had to be done, the Bureau said, because of its importance to the fish recovery program. And that was that.

Resolution—Partial But Poor

Operating in the background was the "Upper Colorado River Endangered Fish Recovery Program", a cooperative effort between four federal agencies, three states, electricity providers, and environmental groups since 1988. The program's activities include habitat development and management, in-stream flow acquisition, elimination of nonnative fish, research, public information, education, hatchery operation and endangered fish stocking. The Endangered Species Act requires any project that could affect the fish to be mitigated by a "reasonable and prudent alternative to avoid the likely destruction or adverse modification of critical habitat." In laymen's terms, that requirement all but prohibits most uses of the River and its water. Nearly all human uses of water modify the habitat—farming, irrigation, domestic use, power generation, even recreation—and mitigating that impact can be difficult, expensive and time-consuming.

This Recovery Program itself, however, serves as the "reasonable and prudent alternative," rather than requiring separate expensive mitigation from every single water user in seven states. That allows the continuation of farming and other water uses—and the continued existence of cities and towns—while the fish recovery proceeds. Without such a program, endangered fish and humans were headed for a showdown that is no longer necessary. Such a program is exactly the right approach to conflicts, and as Executive Director of the Colorado Department of Natural Resources I was proud of our role in an agreement by the Interior Department and three western governors for a ten-year extension of the program.

Nevertheless, despite its strong support for and involvement in the program, in 2002 the State of Colorado had to all but halt progress during the Hays property crisis. Previously, the program was a beacon of success in its ability to prevent potential conflicts between humans and endangered species. But the Hays situation, and others, indicated that the program was being misused, becoming a top-down federal command structure. And one example of this misuse was an attempt to stop farming and quite literally kick families off land they had farmed for generations.

The State of Colorado intervened on Thelma Hays' behalf, asking the Commissioner of Reclamation in Washington to "put a stop to this nonsense, delay issuance of the Final Environmental Assessment and instruct your staff to work with the State and the property owners to resolve this in a way that works for *everyone*."

To his credit, then-Commissioner John Keyes did get involved, personally visited the property, and worked through a year-long negotiation that enabled the Hays family to stay on the land it owned. He ordered the exchange of quit-claim deeds clearing up the boundary lines, and moved the construction activities out of the way of the farm. The Bureau agreed that after construction ended it would restore the field used for its "staging area" to its previous condition. As a result, the fish screen structure was eventually built so the program could continue almost on schedule. Cooler heads had prevailed, but was the final solution really the right outcome? In the end, the structure was built right in the middle of the farm, at a cost of millions, when far simpler and cheaper solutions were available. The Bureau still insisted that the Hays family had "trespassed," even though the government itself was responsible for the original mix-up. No amount of reasoning would change its single-minded determination.

Almost inevitably, the government has failed to keep its part of the deal it made with Thelma Hays. At her own expense, she had to remove rocks left behind in fields which are now compromised in their ability to grow crops. Even worse, the Bureau has still never exchanged deeds to clear up the property boundaries as promised. And guess what? The fish screen does not actually work. Engineered poorly from the outset, the screen frequently fills up with silt and must be bypassed—literally shut down—while being cleaned out. It has been bypassed more often than not since it was built in 2005, and has never yet become fully operational (the Bureau claims it has never been fully funded). Needless to say, not a single endangered fish has been screened from the canal and returned to the river.

Thelma's Story: Not Unique

Unfortunately, such stories are all too common. Thelma and countless other people are made to suffer financial or personal ruin because of bureaucratic overreach. How could that happen? The original purpose of conservation programs was to preserve our environment and conserve resources, so why do they create such disruption? If we can agree on the problem, why isn't it just as easy to agree on simple, cost-effective solutions?

That would be possible, if everyone at the table had the same goals. But many environmental activists have an entirely different purpose: they merely use the environment as a tool because they know the public generally sympathizes with environmental protection. How did we get so far off the rails before noticing that some scoundrel had hijacked the train? More to the point, how do we get it back? How can today's leaders recapture the traditional meaning of the conservation movement?

After decades of watching in dismay as more and more people like Thelma become victims of the government steamroller, this book seeks to answer those questions. My own experience engaged in environmental reforms at both the state and federal levels suggests that it *is* possible to recapture the high ground of leadership without alienating different interest groups, or shutting down businesses. It is possible to improve environmental protection in a manner that also preserves freedom and protects human interests. It's possible to bring together groups with divergent views. It is even possible for private citizens and private companies to improve the environment without government involvement. Believe it or not, it all boils down to: "Put the environment first."

Environmental causes will always be popular with voters.

Leaders who propose and implement simple, cost-effective solutions will always surpass those with other agendas. When the environment is the top priority, the political impacts will take care of themselves. Political leaders who do the right thing for the environment will never want for followers.

Thus, across the range of environmental issues, the only real debate ought to be about *what is the right thing* for the environment. Unfortunately, this focus has become the exception rather than the rule. The debate is far more often about the process, the rules, the power, and the players—not about the desired outcome. As a result, a tremendous vacuum for leadership on these issues has emerged.

People like Thelma Hays have suffered for too long at the hands of environmental extremism and government overreach. It's time for new leaders—in government and in business—to occupy the moral high ground, fill the leadership void, and recapture the proud legacy of conservation.

Today, the government's fish structure overwhelms the view of the Hays farm

CHAPTER 1

THE GREAT DIVIDE

The best-laid schemes of mice and men
often go awry,
And leave us naught but grief and pain,
For promised joy!
                    —Robert Burns

There should be mice. There should be eagles. They don't play nicely together, but without the one there might not be the other. The diversity of life on the Earth not only makes our lives more interesting, it quite literally sustains us. That gives mankind a profound responsibility to do no harm to our fellow creatures, even to reverse damage done by our ancestors. We have not always lived up to that responsibility.

The Endangered Species Act (ESA) was written in 1973 with one simple goal: to preserve and recover species that were about to be lost forever. Reports about the vanishing grizzly bear, peregrine falcon, alligator, whooping crane, and the symbol of America itself—the bald eagle—distressed Americans. In 1963 there were only 417 nesting pairs of bald eagles known in the United States, and their decline was said to be man's fault.

Pollution and pesticides killed off some of our favorite fish, birds and animals, with others hunted nearly to extermination. By the early 1970s, Americans wanted something done, and Congress responded. The new law was designed to stop the killing and preserve habitat, so these species could recover their earlier glory days. It contained two important new legal protections. The first was a series of measures to outlaw killing or "taking" of species listed as threatened or endangered. The second was a complex process for protecting the habitat of such species from human activities that could diminish the chances for long-term health of the nation's variety of plants and animals.

This new law represented two fundamental priorities—conservation and recovery. Protecting habitat was considered critical to reversing the demise of some of our favorite birds and animals. We certainly would not be happy with only 417 pairs of bald eagles forever. All generally agreed that such species had to be recovered; perpetuating the status quo was not good enough. The new law specifically stated, "The purposes of this Act are to … provide a program for the conservation of such endangered species and threatened species… and develop and implement *recovery plans* for the conservation and survival of endangered species" (emphasis mine). In other words, we were to remove the causes of the endangerment, *and* to put into action plans for recovery.

In the years since the law passed, our system has evolved into a national obsession with the first priority (habitat conservation). The second (recovery) has been mostly ignored. The system that has evolved is largely based on the theory that mankind can do nothing to recover lost, or nearly lost, species. The best we can hope for, according to that theory, is to do no further harm—but we will never recover the rich biodiversity we once had. Stephen Meyer of MIT summed up the theory in his book, *End of the Wild*, in which he wrote:

> *The broad path for biological evolution is now set for the next several million years. And in this sense the extinction crisis—the race to save the composition, structure, and organization of biodiversity as it exists today—is over, and we have lost.*

Therefore, according to such pessimists, we can only stop the damage—invariably through government regulations that seek to minimize human activity. Is it any wonder that nearly all the discontent is about seemingly arbitrary bureaucratic land management decisions rather than common-sense steps to recover an endangered species?

Today the 35-year-old Endangered Species Act represents a major contradiction in public policy: the most powerful environmental law ever passed, and yet one of the most dismal failures in the history of government. It is often considered the most important environmental law because the American people had finally prioritized a healthy environment over the economy—and all other priorities. But it is a dismal failure because the government has done virtually nothing to recover any of the hundreds of endangered species, and in most cases has made the situation worse.

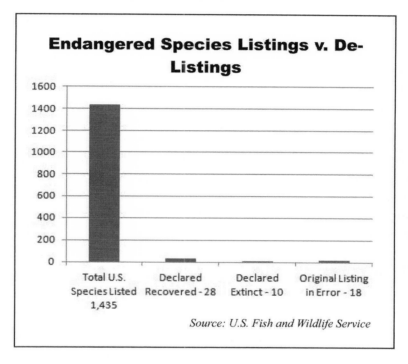

Some observers compare the endangered species list to the Hotel California, where "you can check out but you can never leave," because the government adds species to the list but never takes them off. Clearly, when it comes to recovering endangered species, the federal regulatory approach is not making progress, despite vast expenditures of tax money and the ever more intrusive control of private land for habitat conservation. As a nation we condone this approach because we have lost sight of the original goal: recovering species. The obsession with habitat conservation has become an end in itself, rather than a means for recovering endangered species, and thus success is often measured in acres rather than wildlife. This emphasis on habitat conservation leads the federal government into a routine policy of controlling property and resources, and denying multiple uses of public and private land, whether that results in actual species recovery or not. If you think that is overstated, read on and find out how our nation has lost sight of its original environmental goals and is using the vast power conveyed in the Endangered Species Act for other goals, alienating potential allies in the process and failing to restore endangered species sufficiently to take them off the list and declare them "recovered."

This badly-broken system leaves local officials and concerned citizens throughout the country—especially in public land states—with two stark choices: we can attempt to recover these species ourselves and get them off the list, or we can live with the other alternative, the federal regulatory approach, which isn't working. To state and local leaders concerned about unfunded federal mandates, that ought to be a no-brainer. The federal government has a mandate to regulate, backed by those who don't live in the West but want to control its resources, but as you will see, state and local leaders can do more than they may think.

The Great Divide

Everywhere political leaders go they are plagued by questions, complaints and frustrations about environmental laws. Pollsters assure us that environmental protection remains popular in every part of the country. Yet invariably, at every campaign stop in the West, politicians hear about citizens' frustrations with such legislation, especially the Endangered Species Act, which capriciously threatens to limit access to public lands, and even the use of private property, without any proof that such action actually restores the numbers of endangered species. One cannot escape the conclusion that somewhere, just barely beneath the political radar screen, there is a growing mistrust of the entire environmental movement.

These issues, especially for many people in the West (because government owns so much of the land), has evolved into a great divide, almost a holy war, between people with completely different views of the same situation.

I have known many of the leaders of the major environmental

organizations, at the state and national level, for a long time. They are not stupid. It is simply not possible for that many credible leaders to be completely out of touch with reality. They all drive cars, live in wood houses, buy reams of paper, use electricity and eat agricultural products. Further, most are true believers convinced their approach is right for the environment, not sinister hypocrites with a secret plan to repeal the Bill of Rights.

Similarly, I have known most of the leaders of the private property rights groups, and many people involved in multiple uses of public lands: oil and gas executives, cattlemen and woolgrowers, loggers, miners, off-road vehicle groups, hunters and anglers, the ski industry and the chambers of commerce. The traditional us-against-them picture doesn't fit there either. These people do not hate the environment. Their very livelihood depends upon good stewardship of the land and especially upon sustainability of the resources. Some of them talk with a nearly religious fervor about the beauty of the land they call home, and most are avid outdoorsmen. Like environmental leaders, they are also true believers who think they are helping create a better world, not fat robber barons intent on bulldozing the wilderness for bloated windfall profits.

How could this debate have become such a ferocious good-bad-ugly argument among people in the same community, who share so many common values and dreams, and profess such a universal love of the natural world? Not that this is brand new—the conservation ethic has always been somewhat divisive. President Theodore Roosevelt did not have unanimous support for creation of the national park system or the national forests. These issues are not black-and-white, right-or-wrong, yes-or-no, up-or-down issues. This bitter pitting of one interest against another, the accusations and epithets hurled in recent years at both sides, by both sides, and the constant lawsuits, have polarized into factions who call each other "eco-terrorists" and "enviro-nazis" or "wilderness rapists" and "plunderers." The language is different now.

How did Americans allow the lofty goals of conservation to become so polarized as to prevent us from doing what is right for the environment? Understanding how the original conservation movement, truly motivated to protect the environment and restore wildlife, descended into this extreme state requires a review of how the environmental movement evolved.

How it All Started

Though modern conservationists trace their roots back as far as Thoreau, Emerson and Audubon, it was not until the homestead era in the mid-19th Century that Americans began to realize how truly magnificent much of the country was, and began to think about the need to protect some of it from overuse. The expeditions to survey, map, and photograph the new western territories gave the public its first actual view of spectacular places like Yellowstone, the Mount of the Holy Cross, and the Grand Canyon. They resulted in the first permanent designation of public land to be preserved forever (Yosemite, 1864), the first national park (Yellowstone, 1872), and the evolution of a political movement.

By the end of the 19th Century many of America's great forests had been cut for railroad ties, mine timbers, and towns. Congress had reacted by creating the first national forests. Concern about the vanishing Bison had become a cause among hunters who founded the Boone and Crocket Club to ensure survival of game species. But the most powerful embodiment of America's newfound love of the great outdoors and its resources was the great conservation movement led by Theodore Roosevelt. Conservation was a central component of his philosophy of life, and immediately became part of his national agenda as president. It had three essential themes:

- Resources should be used to create a more prosperous society;
- Resources must be protected so their use can be available for future generations;
- Social justice requires that resources benefit all the people, not just a few private interests.

The first two themes are alive and well in today's environmental arguments (preservation vs. use). The third has unfortunately been lost in the debates of the modern era. That is sad, because it is an enormously important point, as we shall see.

From Consensus to Contentious

During the progressive era of the early 20th Century, Congress created a nationwide system of national forests, national parks, and wildlife refuges. Presidents for the next 75 years added to our collection of protected places, now including millions of acres in every part of the country. And for a long time, nearly all Americans shared a view of the importance of saving these places for future generations to use and enjoy.

By the late 1960s, national conservation policy had become so universally popular that both parties endorsed federal regulation of clean air and water and protection of endangered species. Today Congressman John Dingell (D-Michigan) is dean of the House of Representatives and one of its more liberal members. He sponsored both the National Environmental Policy Act (NEPA) and the Endangered Species Act (ESA), the first in 1969 as Chairman of the Subcommittee on Fish and Wildlife, the second in 1973 as Chairman of the Energy and Commerce Committee.

Dingell's father, a Congressman himself for two decades, helped create one of the nation's premier conservation laws, the Federal Aid in Sportfish Restoration Act (the Dingell-Johnson Act). The law allocates excise taxes on boats and fishing equipment to sport fish restoration and management. Even more important, it prohibits legislatures from diverting fishing license revenue to any purpose other than administering the state fish and game agency. That requirement was also in the earlier Pittman-Robertson Act of 1937, which uses federal funds from the sale of guns and ammunition to protect state hunting license revenue from diversion to non-wildlife purposes. These laws have prevented considerable legislative mischief for many years. So the younger Dingell's support for environmental causes came naturally to him, though these issues were not especially partisan during those years. Indeed, Dingell helped shepherd these new environmental laws through an overwhelmingly Democratic Congress, but with the Republican Nixon Administration pushing them every step of the way as well.

Richard M. Nixon signed into law more environmental legislation than any other president in history—far more, even, than

Theodore Roosevelt. Ironically, he is not especially noted by history for this contribution, though he spoke, wrote and talked about it often. Watergate and Vietnam, of course, eclipsed what might have been an honored place in history based on these accomplishments. By the time Gerald Ford completed Nixon's second term, the list of environmental protection laws enacted would include virtually all of what modern activists call the "cornerstones" of environmental policy:

- National Environmental Policy Act (NEPA), 1969
- Clean Air Act, 1970,
- Occupational Safety and Health Act, 1970,
- Clean Water Act, 1972,
- Federal Environmental Pesticide Control Act, 1972,
- Ocean Dumping Act, 1972,
- Endangered Species Act, 1973,
- Safe Drinking Water Act, 1974,
- Resource Conservation and Recovery Act (RCRA), 1976,
- Toxic Substances Control Act, 1976, and
- Federal Land Policy Management Act (FLPMA), 1976.

Perhaps the single most significant change, though, was Nixon's establishment of the Environmental Protection Agency (EPA), which he created by executive order just 18 months after moving into the White House. Despite the Vietnam War, rising inflation, and Watergate, his leadership on environmental protection was supported by large majorities of voters, and by congressional leaders on both sides of the aisle.

These cornerstones of environmental protection were almost universally popular only 30 years ago, but today no environmental issue crosses the partisan aisle. What happened to change the spirit of cooperation in a common cause? How have these issues become so bitterly partisan? How has federal environmental protection become such an East/West battle? Why have these issues fostered such an "us-against-them" attitude? The answers can be fully understood only in the context of two absolutely pivotal events: the Carter water project "hit list," and the appointment of James Watt as Secretary of the Interior.

The Carter Hit List

Environmental issues were not a significant factor in the election of 1976, but they might have been if western voters had known what was coming. Largely because of the political fallout from pardoning Nixon, Gerald Ford lost the election in his own right to Jimmy Carter. Just weeks after his inauguration, Carter stunned the West by announcing what became known as a "hit list" of western water projects authorized by Congress that he wanted de-authorized. He was flabbergasted by the political firestorm it caused, and ended up despised by many in the West. As the Environmental Defense Fund's Dan Lueke wrote in *High Country News* in 1990,

> *Virtually every elected official west of the 100th meridian, including members of his own party, attacked him savagely for his failure to understand Western water and the political realities of a semi-arid region.*

The projects on the "hit list" included some that westerners had sought for decades. They were part of several long-standing and very delicate agreements among western states. Water projects had become the most powerful tools of the most powerful Congressmen, who had made deals for projects that would require generations to complete.

Carter's announcement called for initial de-authorization of 19 projects, with another 13 to be re-evaluated, mostly in the South and West. The initial list even included the Tennessee Tombigbee Waterway, the Central Arizona Project and several others already under construction. Some were projects Congress had negotiated for 20 years, compromise forged over long and bitter struggles. Congress rebelled almost immediately and while Carter eventually got his way on several projects (he wasn't completely wrong; some of them clearly should never have been built), he paid a heavy price in several ways.

Carter's relationships with individual members of Congress from the West and South, regardless of political party, suffered badly. They were offended not to have been consulted, and angry that the Administration would take such extreme action without a better understanding of the complex deals that had been reached. Carter clearly did not understand the importance of these projects to the arid West. But while history has already nearly forgotten the bad tempers and ill will generated by the controversy, along with the names of most of the ill-fated water projects, it will record a nearly complete political shift on environmental issues that began during that time.

Many members of Congress, governors, and water leaders felt blind-sided by the attack on long-standing agreements, and defended their projects. They explained that the original "Pick-Sloan" plan to tame the Missouri River was still only 60% completed. They pointed out that Colorado had only agreed to the giant Central Arizona Project (to take Colorado River water to Phoenix) in exchange for several projects in Colorado that had not yet been built, including Animas-La Plata, Dallas Creek, Narrows, San Miguel, Savory Pothook and others.

Carter had misread public sentiment to some degree, perhaps understandably. On June 5, 1976 the brand-new Teton Dam, a 305-foot high earthfill dam in Idaho failed, setting off a growing chorus of concern about the safety of large dams. It dumped 260,000 acre feet of water, some 80 billion gallons, down the Snake River, flooded Wilford, Sugar City, Rexburg and parts of Idaho Falls, and killed 14 people. It was covered on national television in the same way Hurricane Katrina was in 2006—saturation of the news to the exclusion of all else for days.

A sympathetic news media covered a growing opposition to continued federal funding of large projects throughout the 1970s. So it may have seemed natural for Carter to assume the sentiment represented a geographically broader area than it did (after all, the Teton Dam flood occurred right in the middle of his presidential campaign). In fact, many viewed his "attack" on water projects as an attack specifically on the West and the South, and not really just about water, but more broadly about the economy and prosperity of rural America. Since water has always been the lifeblood of the arid West, an attack on water must surely be an attack on life itself in the West, or so it seemed to many westerners.

During those same years, those regions became strongholds of the Republican Party, a 25-year shift that is now a matter of history but at that time was still unsettled. Westerners and Southerners began to feel that Carter simply did not care about them, so they felt abandoned and forced into the other camp—by the millions. Thus, these divisive East-West, North-South issues began to break down along more partisan lines than before. They contributed greatly to Carter's defeat when he ran for re-election in 1980. In fact, some scholars including Marc Reisner (author of *Cadillac Desert*) argue that this issue played as much of a role in his defeat as the Iran hostage crisis and double-digit inflation. Except for his home state of Georgia (and Hawaii), Carter lost every single southern and western state, and the entire Mississippi River Valley. It was ironic because Carter's own roots were rural, small-town and Southern. Yet too many rural Americans had come to believe that he didn't care to understand their rural cultures, lifestyles and needs. It became a regional and cultural division. The fact that environmental issues were at the center of it was incidental at first. But the stage had been set for the most divisive era in the history of conservation.

James Watt v. the Environmentalists

When Kipling wrote, "*Oh east is east and west is west, and never the twain shall meet, 'til Earth and sky stand presently at God's great judgment seat*," he could well have been writing about the divisive "wedge" issue the environment was to become. Shortly after his stunning upset victory over Carter, President-elect Ronald Reagan announced his intention to nominate James G. Watt as Secretary of the Interior. Virtually nothing about the environment has achieved a bipartisan national consensus ever since.

James Gaius Watt was more than just a radical departure from the type of men who had previously served in this vitally important job. He was more than just a westerner with a different perspective, though he often wore cowboy boots with his suits. He was a character, in every sense of the word. He would quickly become a caricature. On January 8, 1981, before Reagan had even been inaugurated, Watt was lampooned in a cartoon in the *Los Angeles Times*. The Steve Greenberg cartoon, still copyrighted and now legendary, pictured Watt yelling "When I'm Secretary of the Interior you environmental extremists are gonna tow the line!" The extremists he was yelling at: Johnny Appleseed, Smokey the Bear, Woodsy Owl and Bambi. It was an eerie prediction of the relationship with the news media that would plague the brief remainder of Watt's public career.

Watt grew up in Wyoming and became a highly educated lawyer. He founded the Mountain States Legal Foundation in the 1970s and began to build a national reputation as a critic of environmental activists and federal land management. Many westerners have always been sensitive about the fact that the government owns so much of the land, and have always resisted easterners determining their destinies through management of public lands. Watt had built an impressive career and reputation not only playing to those sensitivities, but helping lead them. So when Reagan saw how Carter's water project hit list had alienated the West, he rewarded the mountain states for their support by appointing Watt.

Watt not only knew he would be controversial; he intended to be. He even warned the new president that he planned to "take on the environmentalists" and make significant changes, and that he planned to push the envelope every step of the way, even predicting that if successful he wouldn't last 18 months in the job. Reagan liked his style and appointed him anyway, despite the already-underway media onslaught.

Watt quickly laid out an ambitious agenda to bring major change to the nation's conservation structure and policies that had been a century in the making. He cut funding for endangered species programs. He proposed removing some federal environmental regulatory powers and replacing others with economic incentives rather than rules. He proposed delegating some federal land management decisions to state and local governments. He tried to eliminate the popular Land and Water Conservation Fund, which uses offshore oil revenues to add land to state and national parks and forests. He even proposed opening some wilderness areas to oil and gas drilling. He stopped all further study by the BLM of potential new wilderness designations in Alaska. Each of these issues became a major cause for harsh criticism from environmental activists, and each in turn created a virtual feeding frenzy in the media. One of the biggest firestorms came when he began a program to sell some federal lands. Though they were mostly small tracts of land not needed by BLM nor connected to parks or wildlife refuges, the concept of selling off public lands will never be popular, as Watt soon learned.

Watt's policies themselves were contentious and divisive enough, but what damaged him most was his own reaction to the fierce controversies they created. Far from backing down in the face of stiff opposition, Watt didn't even want to explain the details or justify the proposals in some instances. Instead, he went on the attack, challenged the credibility of opponents, and labeled critics in unflattering terms (he frequently referred to environmental activists as "extremists" or "radicals," sometimes even as "Nazis" or "Bolsheviks"). He made the battle personal for environmentalists and for many members of the press. He actually appeared to enjoy the negative publicity. He was reported to have told an interviewer in talking about his plans for the new job, "We will mine more, drill more, and cut more timber." He enjoyed goading his opponents, and sometimes purposely created controversy about one issue, thinking he could focus on another more desired goal while his opponents were distracted. This all too clever strategy is often tried in politics but rarely with success. In Watt's case, the criticism simply never calmed down during his tenure, because he never stopped pushing the envelope long enough to allow it. He told _Newsweek_ how he felt about the press: "They kill good trees to put out bad newspapers." He was quoted by another paper responding to a critic by saying, "A lie can run around the world before the truth gets its boots on," paraphrasing Mark Twain, but not to the amusement of the reporter.

Perhaps the largest flap was over Watt's supposed view of environmental protection issues through the perspective of his Evangelical Christian views. He was once said to have quipped in a speech (it was not recorded) that "We don't have to protect the environment;

the Second Coming is at hand." Whether Watt ever really said it—or whether he was joking or not—remains uncertain to this day. In his Senate confirmation hearing he responded to a question about it by saying, "I do not know how many future generations we can count on before the Lord returns, but whatever it is we have to manage with a skill to leave the resources needed for future generations." Some members of the press seized upon the sensational accusation that Watt believed because of the Second Coming, environmental protection was a low priority. Bill Moyers used a similar quote erroneously attributed to Watt and was forced to issue an apology later (turning him from a critic into a dedicated enemy). In any event, the media and environmental groups continued an almost-uninterrupted two-and-a-half-year "field day." James G. Watt continually fanned the flames—on purpose.

Even First Lady Nancy Reagan felt the need to intervene in 1983 when Watt banned rock and roll music during the July 4 celebration on the National Mall, after hearing the Beach Boys were again scheduled for a third consecutive year. Watt said he feared rock music "attracts an undesirable element" unwelcome on public property and demanded more pro-family entertainment. Saying simply, "I like the Beach Boys," Mrs. Reagan got the White House to overrule him and a concert went ahead (though the Beach Boys had already been booked elsewhere). She publicly apologized to the band and invited them back the next year (they were semi-regular fixtures for years afterwards), but a serious wedge had been driven between Watt and the new generation of young Republicans who had been crucial to Reagan's election. Much of the Washington establishment branded Watt as out of touch with real people because of the incident, and began to distance itself from him.

Many of Watt's policies, but especially his combative and dismissive manner, made him unpopular with both Republicans and Democrats in Congress. He further undermined congressional support with his 1982 speech joke, "I never use the words Democrats and Republicans. It's liberals and Americans." Several environmental organizations started petitions seeking his removal from office. The Sierra Club reported that over 1.1 million signatures had been gathered in just a few weeks. Several senators drafted a resolution calling for his dismissal, but before it could be acted upon, Watt himself delivered the last straw on a silver platter.

In the most cynical display yet of his contempt for political correctness, he made a speech at the U.S. Chamber of Commerce September 21, 1983, in which he boasted about the formation of a new federal advisory committee, saying the group included "every mixture you can have. I have a black, a woman, two Jews and a cripple. And we have talent." It was enough, even for the White House, which had steadfastly defended both the man and his policies every step of the way, though with ever-decreasing enthusiasm. Following almost two weeks of non-stop fodder for comedians and editorial pages alike, Watt resigned on October 9, having served as Secretary of the Interior for just over 30 months.

Some Republicans believe those 30 months set back the GOP a century in its legacy of leadership on environmental issues. Others say Watt changed the nature of environmental politics, much to the GOP's disadvantage. Both views are right. Many environmental activists think of him as the best thing that ever happened to the movement. They're right, too. Watt's tenure at Interior was too short to accomplish much of any agenda, or to bring about any substantial changes in policy, but the nature of his character and the controversy it stirred gave many environmental organizations something completely new—an enemy with a public face, and a world-class fund-raising tool. Membership in the Sierra Club, for example, had risen from 114,000 in 1970 to 200,000 when Reagan took office in 1981, respectable growth by any standard. But it increased to 325,000 after just 2 years of Watt's tenure at Interior and more than doubled before Reagan left office.

Nor did Watt ever lessen his "in-your-face" approach, even after his resignation. In fact, even ten years later—after his indictment for perjury and conviction of withholding documents from a federal grand jury—he made news with another of his trademark outbursts. In front of a 1991 dinner of the Green River Cattlemen's Association, Watt said, "If the troubles from environmentalists cannot be solved in the jury box or at the ballot box, perhaps the cartridge box should be used." For many environmental organizations dependent on a constant "enemy" for their fund-raising, Watt was a gift that just kept on giving.

Environmental organizations had always fought big businesses and corporate polluters, and occasionally tried to stop government activity, such as the Hetch Hetchy dam proposal and the Tennessee Valley Authority. But they had rarely been given such a chance to take on the U.S. government so directly, and best of all, to paint the picture of a losing battle to the public. Clearly if Watt and his fellows were not stopped, wilderness that Americans had worked so hard to protect would be lost forever, so the argument went. The progress clock would actually be turned back. Rivers and streams would again be so polluted they could catch fire. Endangered species could vanish from the Earth forever. Our irreplaceable forests would be bulldozed for parking lots, and the public lands turned into cash registers for greedy corporate tycoons. Even worse, these public treasures might be sold outright. It must be stopped before it's too late, they warned; join the cause now—and send money.

The ability to demonize an enemy effectively is a Godsend to non-profit organizations. Their success hinges on the ability to generate awareness, activism, involvement, notoriety, membership and, most importantly, money. During Watt's tenure, Americans joined environmental organizations in unprecedented numbers, and fund-raising skyrocketed. That growth has not significantly slowed since. Watt had plainly helped turn environmental organizations from a political movement into a flourishing industry.

In accordance with Newton's law that every action produces an equal and opposite reaction, the opposing sides polarized relatively quickly. The harshness of the environmentalists' often-shrill attacks on Watt angered many conservatives, especially in the West and South. They thought the environmentalists were being unfair, inaccurate and unprofessional. Thus, they reacted, often in kind, and the gulf grew wider and wider. Policy-makers at every level began to choose sides, and the battle moved beyond the regional and into the partisan. Many Republicans felt the need to defend a Reagan cabinet member under attack (whether they agreed with him or not), so as the volume became louder, the divide became more partisan.

Where environmental disagreements had often been seen as cultural misunderstandings between diverse sections of the country, they now became bitter partisan battles. Environmentalists supported increased federal control, regulation and continued additions to the system of protected lands. Where the first environmental revolution (under Theodore Roosevelt) had been based largely on protecting and saving beautiful places, the second (1960s and 1970s) was based primarily on restricting or stopping damaging human activities. By the early 1980s, those who opposed such federal control increasingly included people whose livelihoods depended on various uses of public lands: ski areas, cattlemen and woolgrowers, oil and gas drillers, loggers, miners, hunters and anglers. Small communities throughout the West began to lose these battles to overwhelming public opinion in larger and more urban states. They began to fear the permanent loss of a way of life they had known for a century. It became an us-against-them battle for both sides and the stakes were high.

During the 1980s and 1990s the environmental movement went through two subtle but significant changes. First, this unprecedented rapid growth caused the movement to expand beyond its original focus. What had been a relatively small number of organizations dedicated to specific environmental causes became a sophisticated industry—a huge industry as we will see. Second, the focus of much of the movement's activity shifted from political action, publications, meetings and other traditional activist strategies to direct legal action.

Today the conservation movement is radically different than anything its founders would recognize, and it frequently takes positions with which they would not agree. It has become a massive coalition of groups that represent not an old-fashioned love of the great outdoors and a desire to protect it for future generations, but something else. Its primary goal is not to do what is right for the environment. Indeed, to many people, it has become a disruptive and obstructionist approach that must be respected and feared (with all the good and bad that implies), leaving in its wake anger, bitterness and resentment.

CHAPTER 2

ENDANGERED SPECIES

*"I can never fear that things will go far
wrong where common sense has fair play."*
—Thomas Jefferson

In early 2000, at a conference of the Western Governors Association, Colorado presented to the other states its new approach to endangered species—based not on regulation but on actual recovery and removal of endangered species from the federally protected list. Then-Governor Bill Owens proposed a resolution that began with the innocuous "whereas" that the goal of the Endangered Species Act (ESA) is to recover endangered species. To the amazement of nearly everyone present, four states objected to that statement. They made impassioned pleas against upsetting the apple cart and offending federal officials and environmentalists, citing the vitally important federal funding of dozens of important programs. These four states declared the purpose of the Endangered Species Act was to allow the continuation of human activities *in spite of* endangered species, not to actually recover them. What an eye-opener.

This extraordinary revelation leads to some perplexing questions. How bizarre have our environmental debates become when actually solving an environmental problem is not the goal? Is federal funding of pilot programs, demonstration projects and partnerships more important than the problems they were intended to fix? Unfortunately, as we will see, much of today's debate about the environment is a false debate, not really about the environment at all. In fact, some of today's environmental agenda is actually bad for the environment.

One State Puts Its Own House in Order

When I became Executive Director of the Colorado Department of Natural Resources in 1999, our state faced a series of major problems as a result of federal failures in endangered species. With the strong support of a new Governor and allies throughout the state, the Department began an entirely new approach that stirred up a hornet's nest of a national debate about returning to the original intent of the ESA. For the first time, a state took a leading role in the actual recovery of endangered species, causing a sea change in environmental politics.

States can deal with endangered species problems better than the federal government for several reasons. A state can quickly put more resources "on the ground," especially professional biologists and dedicated funding, than distant federal agencies can. With programs designed for specific local species, state wildlife departments almost always have more expert biologists, can dedicate protected funds for biological and technical research, and promote more tangible success on the ground, in the water and in the sky. States also own considerably more facilities and equipment at the local level, and are much less prone to killing good ideas with endless committee meetings and bureaucratic obfuscation.

Wouldn't everyone agree that a state interested in recovering endangered species should be honored, or at least supported? Environmentalists should be pleased, right? Wrong—as we soon found out in dealing with the endangered fish program.

The Ah-Ha Moment

Colorado has sometimes been called "the nation's rooftop state," because all the water flows outward. Its rivers not only supply water to Coloradans, but also to residents of a dozen other states, based on legal agreements that are delicate, divisive and sometimes contentious. Needless to say, Colorado is profoundly involved in every issue that affects its water, including aquatic species conservation efforts. Yet the state's first notable dust-up with the federal government on that issue was the new plan to recover four species of endangered fish while allowing for future use of Colorado River water to which Colorado is legally entitled.

The "Upper Colorado River Endangered Fish Recovery Program," created in 1988, is a partnership of 4 federal agencies, 3 states, and 6 non-profit organizations, as mentioned in the preface. By the year 2000 the program had spent nearly $100 million and had another $100 million promised over the next few years. As one might expect it has a biology committee to determine the habitat needs of the fish. However, this elaborate program also supports a management committee with little to manage, an implementation committee that actually governs the program, and even an "information and education" committee. The latter has spent thousands of dollars educating congressional staffers and reporters, including printing refrigerator magnets with pictures of the fish. But after all this effort and money, the fish themselves remained brainlessly unaware of all this activity on their behalf, and were headed the way of the Dodo.

Astoundingly, the program had never bothered to determine how many of these fish once occupied the river, nor had anyone come close to defining what would constitute recovery. How will anyone know when the program has succeeded, you may ask? That is precisely the right question.

Colorado could not wait forever while federal committees met interminably to talk about ways to increase federal control over the water in the Colorado River. Any approach to the fish recovery that concentrated entirely on controlling water was, by definition, a potential threat to Colorado water rights. This program not only concentrated on controlling water, but with an enormous budget and all the power of the Endangered Species Act.

The recovery program's website in 2000 included the statement that "the short-term recovery goal is to prevent extinction in the wild," but included no long-term goal, no plan for recovery at all—as if preventing extinction with no thought about recovery is good enough! Colorado began by advocating the adoption of recovery goals for the four fish, measurable criteria that would determine when the fish would be considered recovered, and taken off the endangered list. The program's lead agency—the U.S. Fish and Wildlife

Service—resisted, of course, as did the environmental groups represented as "stakeholders" on the program's governing committee. Predictably, they argued the lack of sufficient funds and staff, so the state of Colorado offered to staff the program and do the research at the state level. Fish and Wildlife responded that states could not be entrusted with federal responsibilities, even claiming that the law prohibits it, now a common theme of the Obama Administration. They maintained that recovery goals were impossible (some even said irrelevant), at least before the program's congressional authorization was to expire within two years. They proposed another ten-year re-authorization and said recovery goals could eventually be addressed, after the more urgent renewal agreement was in place. Why did they want to postpone everything until after the reauthorization? The truth was that if the States had agreed to a re-authorization, they would have had no leverage at all to force the issue later. The federal government's need for the States' agreement before re-authorizing the program gave Colorado a legal "hook" it might never have again, and they knew it. The time was ripe for a State to use this temporary advantage to demand true conservation, that is, quantifiable recovery *and de-listing*.

Colorado state officials continued to insist on such "goals" as a condition of Colorado's continued participation, and the discussion was often contentious. Before 2000, mostly scientists and biologists, who should know what constitutes a healthy fish population, debated recovery issues. That's where those debates belong, of course, not with political leaders. But the federal resistance to recovery goals (and Colorado's insistence on them) became so exasperating that some members of the governing committee cynically asked me— at a very public meeting—what I thought the goals should be. I expressed a simplistic view: that the goal is to recover the fish, take them off the endangered list, and abolish the program. And I said that if anyone had a different goal they ought to announce what it is. Then something remarkable happened. Every person in the room instantly professed agreement, despite their months of resistance to the whole idea.

Years of wrangling over water flows had led to strongly held views among most residents of Western Colorado that the program was really all about water, not fish. It also seemed clear to many of us that the idea of abolishing the program was anathema to members of this committee, whose jobs the program supported. Yet whatever the real agendas were, with a simple goal so plainly stated, not one person dared to articulate any other goal—at least not in a public meeting. There was some nervous laughter and clearing of throats, but no one could disagree that the program's purpose was to *recover* and *delist* the fish so it could *abolish* the program. At that moment it became clear that we can achieve a completely new approach to endangered species recovery—an approach that does not question the purposes of the ESA, but embraces them.

If the whole endangered species debate can be focused on actual recovery, the battle against federal control of lives and property is moot. After all, who is prepared to say they really support some other agenda? Who will speak to a crowded room of westerners and say, "I don't really care about the fish; I just wanted to control your water?" Who can admit that, "For me this is not about those birds; I just want to stop people from riding snowmobiles?" Whatever the various hidden agendas might be, very few can admit to them publicly. Thus, if a state (or anyone outside the federal government) leads an effort to recover a threatened species and remove it from the protected list, who will oppose it? Answer: no one, at least not publicly or with any credibility. That would put citizens, property owners, and state and local governments squarely where they should be: leading the effort to improve our environment.

This twist of circumstances proved pivotal in the case of the fish program. Despite the federal government's resistance to publishing recovery goals, the state had a unique and powerful hole card: the Colorado River Endangered Fish Recovery Program's congressional reauthorization (originally set to expire in 2000) depended on renewed agreement of the original three states. Without that agreement, the program's funding could evaporate along with its legal authority. While Colorado supported this important program and never threatened to withdraw its agreement, the state insisted that it would come only after recovery goals were written, adopted and published. So with the whole program in jeopardy, the U.S. Fish and Wildlife Service (after almost 2 years of wrangling) finally published recovery goals that are measurable, enforceable and will be attained. For the first time, the program had a light at the end of the tunnel that did not need to involve complete and permanent federal control over state water rights. And with the agreement of all three states, the program was extended for another decade. In the end, that guarantees water decisions can be made locally while the fish are being recovered. They are already well on the way to recovery as a result, and that will undoubtedly influence the discussion on whether to continue the program in the future.

It is impossible to overstate the importance of separating this fish recovery process from the touchy water issues that are so central to everything in the West. Colorado River water supplies over 25 million people in 7 states, and is carefully allocated under a very delicate Interstate Compact and a complex series of related agreements, as well as a century-old system of complicated state water laws. The fastest-growing part of the United States (the Southwest) is also its driest region, with only one major river system, the Colorado. Its scarce water is delivered to cities and towns, businesses and farms through an elaborate system of reservoirs, canals, pumping stations and pipelines. The entire system obviously has a direct impact on the habitat of the fish, but do suckers and chubs mean more to us than the lives of all the people in Denver, Phoenix, Las Vegas and Los Angeles, or the thousands of square miles of small towns and farms in between?

The powerful Endangered Species Act does not permit such a question—the fish matter more than anything under the law. Thus, unless the fish are recovered and delisted, the West faces inevitable new federal regulation of its dams, reservoirs, pumps, pipelines and river flows for the sole benefit of the fish. You may think the government would never actually shut off the aqueducts and tunnels that supply Los Angeles and Denver, but the law is clear and the courts have demonstrated their willingness to enforce it. No state could take that chance, and all seven Colorado River states have taken the position that recovering these fish does not require surrendering the water to federal control. Clearly, it does require putting the fish back into the river—and that is what Colorado decided to do.

Bigger Fish to Fry - the Hatchery

In pursuing the goal of putting the environment first, Colorado used the endangered fish issue to pioneer a new no-nonsense approach to recovery. With recovery goals in place, the state wildlife division built the first state-owned "native aquatic species hatchery" in the United States. Similar to hatcheries used for a century to raise trout for mountain streams, this hatchery instead raises endangered species, and species some experts think might become endangered. Located near Alamosa, Colorado, it quickly became a wildlife tourist attraction, visited by many officials from other states intrigued by the possibility of actually raising endangered fish to be put back into the wild.

Officials continually tour the site to see how it works, and to discuss the state recovery initiative with Colorado's wildlife professionals, who are among the nation's foremost experts in their fields. At various times visitors have observed

Humpback Chub

nearly every aquatic species of concern in the region—Colorado River pikeminnow, razorback sucker, bonytail chub, humpback chub, Arkansas River darter, Rio Grande silvery minnow, boreal toad and many others. It includes indoor tanks for hatching eggs, grow-out ponds for raising fish to a survivable size, and is in every way a state-of-the-art facility like no other in the country. Colorado spent about $5 million building this unique facility, putting its money where its mouth is and dedicating several of its best biologists to staffing the place. The state also acquired a similar facility for reintroduction and rehabilitation of threatened and endangered birds and mammals.

The goal is simple: if these species are to be recovered they must be put back into suitable habitat in sufficient numbers to sustain a viable population. All species work *begins* with habitat. But the federal system is consumed by an entrenched tradition and mentality which assumes that the work also *ends* with habitat. This history has illustrated very clearly that the *only* agenda has been about controlling land and human activity, rather than about recovering endangered species—only part of which is about habitat. In the case of the Colorado River system, the program worked on habitat for 20 years, restoring and preserving wetlands, recreating flooding ponds important to the spawning habits of these fish, protecting stream flows under state laws, and constructing expensive fish passages around dams. Still, at the end of all the successful habitat work, without the efforts of hatcheries, bonytail chubs would still be extinct in the Upper Colorado River. Eventually, someone has to put the fish back or they will never be there again.

The same situation exists all over the country with many species that can never recover by themselves because there aren't enough left in the wild. An endangered Arizona fish called the Gila Trout was all but extinct in most of its historic range. A 1990 Tonto National Forest fire destroyed virtually all life in Dude Creek, but presented an opportunity for artificial reintroduction of the species, since no non-natives remained to compete for food. The State of Arizona, in partnership with Trout Unlimited, re-stocked the fish (4 years before the federal government approved any recovery plan) and the population is well on the way to recovery. In fact within 6 years after the restocking began, the government "down-listed" the fish from "endangered" to "threatened," concrete proof of the success of a recovery effort fueled by artificial reintroduction.

The idea of raising endangered species in captivity for restocking the natural habitat should not be controversial. Nature is filled with all kinds of non-native wildlife brought in by man, very often to the detriment of native species. No one argues that stocking trout in mountain streams won't work. No group claims that the catfish and bass competing for habitat throughout the West got there by themselves. Some argue that introducing non-native species is a bad idea, but very few can deny that it works. If man can introduce everything from kudzu to wild pigs and they thrive in non-native habitats, why should we doubt our ability to reintroduce native species to their own natural habitat with equal success?

If it seems like an obvious part of the solution, think again. A substantial portion of the environmental lobby and many federal regulators are unalterably opposed to the idea, though many leaders have great difficulty explaining why. Some opponents argue that the genetic and environmental implications of re-introduction are not well understood (we should fund more studies). Others argue that species raised in captivity do not have the survival skills parents normally teach offspring in the wild and so cannot survive. Still others argue against any intervention whatsoever by mankind in natural processes. That is the silliest argument of all, since man has unquestionably altered the natural environment already, and we should at least feel some obligation to reverse damage we have done.

In opposing salmon stocking in the Pacific Northwest, American Rivers' staffer Amy Kober put it this way: "Counting hatchery fish the same as wild fish not only does not pass scientific muster,"— her degree is in creative writing and literature—"it would be a huge setback to efforts of citizens across the Northwest and California who are really trying to recover salmon." If the citizens she mentions oppose putting fish back into the river, how exactly are they trying to recover them?

In the case of the Colorado River fish, the federal government officially argued that reintroduced species are not the same (genetically) as wild ones—though that was easy enough for the biologists to disprove. The confirmation of a hidden agenda on the part of these opponents lies in the inconsistency of their argument. Some of the same people who push to reintroduce wolves in the Southern Rockies argue there is something impure about reintroducing fish— presumably because the former supports their political agenda and the latter does not. Still, *if* the real purpose of these programs is to recover endangered species, reintroduction must eventually be part of the effort. That's a big *"if,"* but it shouldn't be.

See How They Run

While Colorado received widespread support for its "radical" new approach, it also confronted some rather confounding challenges. One such challenge involved a plan to re-introduce the Canadian Lynx to the Southern Rockies, to the dismay of some Coloradans.

Farmers and ranchers feared (with good reason) that the lynx would become the latest endangered species to be used as leverage to stop grazing on national forest lands. Loggers feared that the "threatened" listing of the lynx would be the final nail in the coffin of already-declining federal timber sales. Recreationists worried that all their favorite roads and trails would be closed. Colorado's multi-billion dollar ski industry was extremely concerned that a new federal designation called "lynx corridors" would be (not coincidentally) in the same area where all the ski area expansions were planned. Off-road vehicle groups, environmental organizations, skiing and timber interests, wildlife advocates and some of the state's top sportsmen's groups were irate and complained loudly.

After hundreds of meetings, letters, e-mails and other messages coming into the Department, the Governor's office and the Legislature, an extraordinary picture emerged. We all realized that none of the complaints were about the lynx. Hundreds of messages and letters opposed the lynx re-introduction plan, but not one single message contained any complaint about the animal itself.

Not one person alleged any negative interaction between lynx and people. Lynx do not eat lambs or calves, and they do not carry children away from campfires during the night. They don't even tear up people's gardens. Not one single complaint even mentioned any problem with the lynx itself. All the voices blended into one clear message: the endangered species is not the problem. These complaints were about interpretation and enforcement of the Endangered Species Act by the U.S. Forest Service. All of the concerns voiced were not about lynx, but about federal land management decisions people knew would follow the presence of an endangered species. There is a vast difference.

The lynx had been declared threatened and protected, and all national forests in the Rocky Mountain Region had been ordered to rewrite their management plans based on that new listing. All the land managers, communities and stakeholder groups had to determine what it meant to them. So discussions inevitably centered on whether to close roads and trails, ban snowmobiles and ATV's, discontinue logging, stop oil and gas exploration, limit ski area expansions or eliminate grazing; in short, to eliminate the public from public lands. It was about everything but the lynx. Apprehensive local citizens understandably focused on the almost-certain regulatory actions of federal land managers, and the land managers necessarily concentrated their efforts on ways to allay these public fears. User groups were angry that the agency might use this excuse to stop such activities, and environmental groups were angry that it might not do so. And no one was talking about the future of the lynx.

Listening to the voices of concerned people all over the West—and to common sense—led to the obvious need for a very different approach to endangered species. Colorado decided to go ahead with the lynx re-introduction program, but decided in favor of a new approach to the local problems brought about by what so many in the state had come to see as a heavy-handed oppressive federal system when it came to the management of public lands. The state embraced the lynx project and sought funding to continue the re-introduction over the next four years.

The author helps Colorado Wildlife Commission Chairman Rick Enstrom with Lynx releases, 2003

After the introduction of about 218 of the animals to the Colorado Rockies, they are well on the road to a spectacular recovery and one of the great conservation success stories (at least 141 kittens have been born in the wild), not because of government regulation and certainly not because of any of the Forest Service's management plans. It was successful because a state insisted on the original intent of the Endangered Species Act: to recover species we might otherwise lose. Lynx were not endangered because of habitat loss; they live primarily at high altitudes where man has not developed towns. They were endangered simply because they have beautiful fur and our ancestors trapped them for it. For a time, the government tried to blame the loss of lynx in Colorado on shrinking snowshoe hare populations caused by timber harvest and fire suppression, but ultimately research proved the animals were extirpated from that State by entirely natural factors.

The high Rocky Mountain habitat remains intact, so replacing the lynx was the simple answer, and it worked. It is unclear whether the federal system would ever have reintroduced the animals without the state's leadership, even though it is the obvious solution for recovering such a population—and for avoiding heavy-handed federal land use control. The Colorado Division of Wildlife has now declared victory in the program, calling the lynx population self-sustaining (reproducing faster than they are dying).

However successful the lynx program has become, there remains an ominous footnote. Absent clearly defined and legally enforceable recovery goals (such as obtained for the fish), the lynx still remains on the threatened list despite its successful recovery in Colorado—no matter how many of the cats there may be. That counterintuitive response is the way the ESA has evolved, to such an extreme that the actual status of a species is not the determining factor, and many environmental groups and federal agencies have a self interest in making sure it stays on the list. The Colorado approach is creating the first prospect of changing that.

Information is Power

In some ways the lynx was an unlikely animal to become a national cause in the first place. By habit, it is too shy a species to attract all the attention it received in Colorado, but nearly every detail of the lynx re-introduction was front-page news for over two years. It was filmed by National Geographic and covered by the *Los Angeles Times* and *The New York Times*. By all accounts, the program could have been called a failure and abandoned early in the process, because a number of the first cats brought to Colorado did not survive the first few weeks.

The first effort wasn't even well received by the very federal agencies that wanted the lynx protected. U.S. Fish and Wildlife Service officials generally oppose any "artificial" reintroduction of species by people, but argue that if people are to be involved in such efforts they certainly should be federal officials. The state sought a separate designation from the federal government—called a "non-essential experimental population." That designation would have ensured that the state's activities would not be affected by the national "threatened" listing of the lynx, at least not with respect to the re-introduced cats themselves. That request had been denied, leaving open the possibility of federal regulatory action being taken because of the very animals the state brought in with the best of intentions. In addition to that problem, some animal rights activists claimed that the program was cruel and called for its termination. A number of state legislators openly opposed the reintroduction, and several tried to cut the budget to stop the program.

At first the effort was tragic because so little was known about a species that had not inhabited Colorado for generations, so it required lots of guesswork. The first lynx were transplanted from the Yukon and Northwest Territories, northern British Columbia and Alaska. No one knew how they would react, what they would eat, where they would go, and especially how they might deal with a state populated by almost 5 million people. The Colorado wildlife staff flew the cats in from Canada, took them to the selected release area in the San Juan Mountains and released them as quickly as possible, and in front of dozens of onlookers and flashing cameras. So the lynx—hungry, scared, lost and disoriented—began their new lives by running as fast and far as they could go. They scattered to the four winds trying to get away—running away from the carefully selected habitat where the best food supplies were located. Some showed up hundreds of miles away, several starved to death, a few were shot and some were hit by cars and in numerous other ways met with sad fates that were very discouraging.

In fact, there were many reasons to consider ending the program, but something extraordinary happened instead. As biologists in the Colorado Division of Wildlife were allowed to do their research, track the animals, learn from mistakes, adjust release protocols and update monitoring methods, they also began to learn more about the lynx—and what they learned was surprising and important.

The next time around, they held the lynx in captivity in Colorado until they acclimated to the area and were calm, healthy and more accustomed to people. Not a single animal brought in during the second year under the new protocol starved because, aside from learning a better way to re-introduce these animals, monitoring their behavior provided a great deal of information that was previously unknown. Additionally, it actually proved that the assumptions of the U.S. Forest Service (USFS) were wrong in many areas.

Because the Forest Service used lynx as a tool to require rewriting the management plans for all the national forests in the state, that agency made numerous assumptions on which to base management decisions. This was especially ironic in light of the U.S. Fish and Wildlife Service's conclusion that Colorado is *not* important to the species' prospects for recovery. Even after a careful review, the latter agency revised the "critical habitat" designation for the lynx in early 2009, again leaving the entire state of Colorado out, with this explanation:

> *We recognize that this reintroduction has been an effort to recover the lynx in Colorado; however, the Southern Rockies contain marginal habitat, are on the southern limit of the species' range, and have not been shown to support a breeding population of lynx. Therefore, we find that habitat in Colorado is not essential to the conservation of species.*

Despite this important finding by the agency charged with knowing such facts, the Forest Service remained determined to use lynx as a management tool. Early USFS information on lynx was based entirely upon their behavior in Canada and Alaska, where they are common. The last lynx documented in Colorado was in 1973, but even before that they were extremely rare in the Southern Rockies—fewer than 20 were ever documented in Colorado's history. Thus, very little was known about how they would behave in the southern Rockies, such as what they could eat and whether they could survive, primarily because the climate and environment are so different than Alaska or the Yukon Territory (where they had been studied carefully).

Federal documents said the San Juan Mountains were the southernmost limit where lynx could live, yet several migrated farther south, even into New Mexico. Forest Service officials once claimed lynx would not cross open areas greater than 100 yards because they live only in dense wooded habitat. Yet several Colorado lynx that were introduced in Southwest Colorado crossed enormous areas of wide-open spaces on lengthy migration routes. One was actually trailed to Nebraska, several across the San Luis Valley, still others north of Interstate 70—some 200 miles north of their release. In early 2007 another one crossed 5 counties into Kansas before being recaptured south of Wakeeney, a distance of 375 miles (more than half of it across the open space of the Great Plains). Others have roamed north as far as Montana, but the ultimate traveler was a lynx labeled BC-03-M-02, which after 4 years in Colorado headed home to Canada, only to be killed by an Alberta trapper—1,200 miles from his Colorado release site. So much for the Forest Service theory that lynx will not cross open areas greater than 100 yards. In fact, it turns out that lynx regularly travel enormous distances and establish huge territories because of the need to roam far and wide for food and for mates.

The USFS also said the lynx ate only snowshoe hares, yet Colorado lynx have eaten a much more varied diet including squirrels, prairie dogs and birds. Some federal officials said lynx were threatened by ski areas, yet at least one was monitored actually living in a ski area during the busy winter ski season.

That close monitoring will eventually change the way lynx decisions—and related land management decisions—are made. Here's why: there is a vitally important phrase in the Endangered Species Act called "best available scientific information." Contrary to popular myth, the Act does not require good science. It does not require sound, peer-reviewed science, or even accurate science. It merely requires that decisions be based upon the "best available" science. Sadly, there is no legal definition of "best available science," so in every case it is a subjective judgment influenced by such human factors as the fear of lawsuits, peer pressure, concerns about next year's budget, concerns about retaining one's job, and the private political views of civil servants.

For that reason, state wildlife experts need to have the best possible information on endangered species in their state (or the many species being considered for listing). That is why the lynx program became such a fascinating study for so many. Perhaps for the first time, a state government was in a position to direct decision-making on a nationally listed species precisely because its experts accumulated the "best available science."

Even without clear recovery goals, to the extent that it knows precisely how these animals are doing, Colorado will eventually drive the decisions: whether to de-list a recovered species, what places should be designated as its critical habitat, what land management practices cause adverse impacts, and others. For now political leaders should let the biologists do their jobs and collect that information in a scientifically credible manner. In the end Colorado's lead will result in a better outcome—for the economy, the environment and the lynx—than if we had left the animals' future to the perpetual debates of federal committees.

If it's Broken, Fix It

The State of Colorado's decision to undertake a new state-leadership-based approach to endangered species was grounded in three virtually undeniable premises. *First, the Endangered Species Act is among the most powerful laws ever passed by Congress.* It supersedes nearly every other legal enactment except, perhaps, the Constitution (some westerners argue that point). Essentially, if an endangered species is listed, it trumps everything else, including any other law, presidential directive or even court order. Congress may direct a bridge to be built, but if an endangered species is discovered there, the ESA overrides even the more recent Act of Congress. No other federal agency may do anything that might adversely affect a listed species (and they are required to ask if they think there might be a chance), and the Act is enforced against other federal agencies, state and local governments, and private landowners alike. The law does not even permit nature itself to eliminate a species—the boreal toad was endangered because of a natural virus. Any species endangered is legally presumed to be mankind's fault, and the regulations are triggered *whether or not* the cause is manmade or completely natural.

Second, there is little chance of any significant change in the Act in the foreseeable future. Congressional attempts to *revise* the law have invariably been portrayed by a skeptical media as efforts to *weaken* it. Congressmen who make the attempt are portrayed as anti-environment, sometimes at the peril of their office (note the 2006 defeat of House Resources Committee Chairman Richard Pombo, whose attempt to reform the law was at least partly to blame for his loss after 14 years in Congress). Quite simply, the public overwhelmingly supports the protection and recovery of threatened and endangered species. The Endangered Species Coalition cites polls showing 90% public support for the ESA (virtually all polls show similar results: a 2006 Decision Research poll placed public support at 86%). Democratic governments are not in the habit of repealing programs that are popular, nor should they be. Hoping the ESA will be repealed, or even significantly reformed, is pure fantasy.

Third, the federal record of recovering endangered species is pathetic. In the years since the ESA was passed in 1973, the federal government has added over 1,435 species to the protected list, while removing 56 (3.9%). Currently pending lawsuits and petitions seek to add almost 700 more, and new petitions are at an all-time high. That is a gross failure by any standard, but even the number 56 is unfortunately misleading. 18 were delisted because the original listing information turned out to be wrong, and 10 became extinct (with no recovery plans in place). That leaves a grand total of 28 species (out of 1,435) that are listed as *recovered* since the Endangered Species Act became law. And six of those species were delisted only in part of the country, but remain listed elsewhere, so the real number is probably 22, and federal activity is responsible for almost none of those (state and private efforts are more often credited). Despite the ESA's uniquely powerful provisions, the federal government can only claim recovery of half of one percent of the endangered species it has listed. The enormity of that failure is staggering.

Half of all the species on the endangered list have been on that list more than 20 years and barely a third of the total have a recovery plan of any kind (many such plans remain in "draft" stage after years of meetings). In the first year of the new law (1973), seven U.S. species were put on the list—of those, one has been declared extinct, and the other six are still listed. In short, getting on the list is easy; getting off is nearly impossible. That is the core of the problem.

In practice, the system used to get a species listed is fairly simple and routine. Environmental groups regularly file petitions with the U.S. Fish and Wildlife Service (or in some cases the National Marine Fisheries Service) asking for new species to be added to the protected list, and the agency has 90 days in which to respond.

As a matter of course, the Fish and Wildlife Service almost routinely adds species to the list because, if it fails to do so, petitioning groups often file lawsuits, whereupon federal judges frequently order the listing anyway. Taking the path of least resistance, the Service has simply found it easier over the years to list a species than not to do so. There is no downside for the agency. For instance, three years of study that led to a conclusion not to list the wolverine were ignored with very little discussion by a federal judge who overturned the decision and ordered the Service to take "a closer look." The lesson to federal officials from countless similar examples is to do what the petitioner asks, or a judge will order you to do so. Though oversimplified, this is essentially how the process has evolved. Court orders now dictate such a high percentage of the Fish and Wildlife Service's activities that it has very little discretion over its own budget and priorities. Even its recent effort to devise a system for prioritizing listings so limited resources could be used on the most at risk species resulted in a lawsuit and—predictably—a court order disallowing any such prioritization.

By early 2011, Fish and Wildlife Service Chief Rowan Gould told Congress that the agency has no hope of working through the backlog of petitions for new listings. He testified that his agency's work is driven largely by lawsuits, and that the budget is further decimated by having to pay legal fees for the plaintiffs. Almost in exasperation, the Obama Administration asked Congress to cap the amount of money that can be spent to process petitions. Thus, the government could argue in court that it had done all it could before running out of money. In other words, the agency has completely lost control of a process Congress intended it to manage for the benefit of endangered species. Despite this proposal, the agency was forced in May 2011 to settle its largest lawsuit (filed by WildEarth Guardians) by agreeing to act on over 250 listing petitions within 3 years—and to pay millions in legal fees to the plaintiff organization. In a similar action, the agency agreed to act on over 750 listings requested by the Center for Biological Diversity within seven years, in exchange for the organization's agreement to limit its lawsuits.

Despite that agreement, that same organization filed another petition in late 2012 to list 53 more species. So, since Congress continues to provide inadequate resources for recovery programs, new listings are the past, present and future of that agency—not recovery.

Once a species is added to the list, however, it generally becomes a problem for others inside and outside government to deal with. Because Congress rarely gives the Fish and Wildlife Service the financial resources for recovery programs, the "listing" becomes a problem for the U.S. Forest Service, the BLM, the Bureau of Reclamation, the Corps of Engineers, the National Park Service, state wildlife departments, farmers and ranchers, county road departments, local governments and private property owners throughout the habitat area.

The City Mouse and the Country Mouse

There are plenty of federal impediments to dedicated, responsive and service-oriented state and local government. In town meetings, campaign rallies and coffee shops in every corner of the land, people vociferously complain about their frustrating dealings with federal agencies. The Endangered Species Act comes up as often as any example, especially throughout the West. It is aggravating that the ESA has imposed huge costs and obligations on many state agencies, local governments and businesses, while achieving so little in actually recovering species.

Colorado wanted a different outcome. By giving the green light to the lynx re-introduction plan, building the fish hatchery and taking a recovery-oriented approach to all species issues, Colorado began to change the political landscape. So much state activity is dictated by federal endangered species rules, it is clear that the essential business of species recovery ought to be a high priority for any state.

Believe it or not, it can be credibly argued that the ESA pervades nearly all aspects of government services and human activities. Whether working on long overdue road improvements, continuing historic farming practices, providing critical water systems, enhancing outdoor recreational opportunities, or simply building a house, states and citizens are invariably challenged and often thwarted by an endangered species issue.

Colorado's proactive stance began with creating a new Office of Endangered Species Coordinator to oversee all state government activities affected by endangered species issues. The primary object of this office was to put the state in the lead on species recovery, with the ultimate goal to take species off the federal list. Colorado has 15 federally listed species, and another 15 "candidates" for listing in the foreseeable future. Some states have many more, but one is enough to put the issue on the front burner for any state.

In addition to those already listed as threatened or endangered, there are hundreds of "candidate species" and the government regularly receives petitions for new listings. Former Interior Secretary Bruce Babbitt once bragged that he had told Fish and Wildlife Service employees that their strategy should be to add 1,000 new species to the list. In fact, during Babbitt's tenure (1993–2001), the Department of the Interior added 486 species to the list—nearly half of Babbitt's original goal.

As effective as he was in pushing new listings, however, recovering species was never among Babbitt's goals. He wrote a book in 2005 entitled *Cities in the Wilderness: A New Vision of Land Use in America*, in which he proposed, among other things, to amend the Endangered Species Act to use it to identify, conserve and protect landscapes, watersheds and ecosystems whether or not any endangered species happens to be there. Making a parallel with preventive medicine, he argued the ESA should promote the protection of open space and ecosystems before the downward spiral to extinction begins. Using the ESA to further the objective of federal control of "land use in America" has nothing to do with endangered species recovery, and is a completely inappropriate use of a powerful tool never intended for such purposes.

By contrast, Colorado's goal was to successfully recover and take off the list all 15 listed species in the state, while also working to ensure that no new species ever need to be added to the list. Many natural resources leaders around the country have a very different perspective than Bruce Babbitt, though clearly sharing many common goals. Indeed, it seems counter-intuitive that anyone could look at the listings themselves as a measure of success. Rather, we should look at every single new addition to the endangered species list as a call to implement a measurable recovery plan and get it off the list as soon as possible.

Colorado created an Interagency Management Team, with all the departments and divisions whose activities potentially affect endangered species, to enhance the state's efforts to recover threatened and endangered species. The Team—in cooperation with local governments, other public and private landowners, and federal agencies—was charged in the authorizing legislation with "developing and implementing a strategy for the recovery and de-listing of all threatened and endangered species in Colorado, as well as identifying funding and staff needed for these efforts."

Not surprisingly the creation of this team brought even more recognition to Colorado's new leadership role on the ESA. By bluntly calling "recovery and delisting" the main goal, this approach recognized the sheer practicality of putting the state, which has citizens with a stake in the game, in the lead on such programs. It sidestepped the burdensome federal regulatory superstructure. More importantly, it focused on actually protecting the environment.

Moving the Cheese

Colorado's new approach was everything we had hoped for, and less.

Has this state-leadership approach caught on with all the other states? Sadly, no. However, the national government has accepted the states playing a lead role on its previously federal turf, though only to a limited extent. Positively, it has resulted in collaborative efforts and interdepartmental cooperation. And absolutely, some previously endangered species have recovered.

As envisioned, state and federal agencies are working together on numerous projects aimed at species recovery and de-listing. Under Colorado's more recent Governors, Bill Ritter and John Hickenlooper, the management of this program has become more institutionalized and routine, mostly delegated back down the line to wildlife experts (where it really belongs). The program remains a forum where agencies communicate endangered species concerns across departmental lines, and form strategies to enhance conservation and recovery. The Colorado Division of Wildlife is now routinely called upon by other states and federal agencies alike to lend its expertise to species recovery problems, especially those where its expertise is unassailable, such as the lynx or endangered fish programs (after all, state wildlife agencies have been the repositories of biological research and application since long before the federal Endangered Species Act was passed).

This team approach shattered the walls that once separated the work of different agencies. Suddenly, the Department of Transportation spearheaded prairie dog relocation efforts because of the need to mitigate habitat loss caused by the expansion of Interstate 25. Colorado State Parks worked closely with transportation officials to provide a home for the relocated prairie dogs, and in the process created popular new public educational opportunities. The Department of Public Health and Environment stepped up its monitoring of sylvatic plague in prairie dog colonies throughout the state as part of the same educational effort.

These collaborative efforts led by the state have changed the setting in Colorado forever, in ways future generations will notice. The successful recovery of the peregrine falcon and bald eagle are well documented in the West. But Colorado can also boast of several other historic recovery programs:

- The greater prairie chicken, whose population went from a low of 600 birds in 1973 to over 12,000 today (a recovery so thorough that hunting is once again allowed);

- The river otter, once trapped out of existence in Colorado, now returned to its historic (low) population and headed toward delisting;

- Moose, which had been hunted to extinction in the state, were reintroduced so successfully that there are now three separate thriving populations;

- Desert bighorn sheep, also completely gone from Colorado by 1970, were successfully transplanted and today more than 100 roam the Western Slope;

- The black-footed ferret, widely considered the most endangered mammal in North America and thought by many to be extinct 30 years ago, is now reproducing in the wild and well on the way to recovery;

- Columbian sharp-tailed grouse are doing so well in Colorado because of state-of-the-art mined land reclamation efforts that they can easily sustain a regular hunting season;

- The boreal toad, nearly wiped out by a natural virus, is now recovering throughout its range with the help of Colorado's native species hatchery;

- The Greenback cutthroat trout, thought to be extinct in 1937, was ultimately down-listed from endangered to threatened because of state biologists' efforts;

- The lynx population re-established not just by reintroduction, but also reproduction in the wild, now to a permanently sustainable level.

All of these efforts were accomplished by the state, more often in spite of the federal government than in partnership with it. The relationship between the two remains a significant problem. Unfortunately, as Theodore Roosevelt warned, sometimes the carrot must be accompanied by a stick. Not all state efforts can concentrate only on recovery and delisting because the ESA has evolved into a punitive system, not based on incentives or partnerships. My experiences convince me that the federal system simply does not trust state or local governments, nor does it rely on the good will of its own people. Thus, in addition to doing the right thing for the species, sometimes it is necessary to stop the federal government from doing the wrong thing.

Plagued With Prairie Dogs

The clearest case in point is a prairie rodent called the black-tailed prairie dog. Historically, it lived all across the fruited plain west of the Mississippi River, from Mexico to Canada. Although there are fewer today than the "infinite" number described by Lewis and Clark, and they do not occupy every acre they once did, they are clearly not endangered. Yet communities throughout their range have been facing a potential endangered listing for several years.

More often than not, species are listed as threatened or endangered because the organization filing the listing petition has the "best available" scientific information. In many cases the petition contains the *only* available science on species that have been little known and never studied previously.

When the National Wildlife Federation filed a petition to list the black-tailed prairie dog, like most western states, Colorado knew very little about them. Because they had always been considered a nuisance by farmers, and listed as a pest species in wildlife law, Colorado had never spent any resources studying them. Everyone knew there were hundreds of thousands of them, occupying thousands of acres across the plains from New Mexico to North Dakota, but absent any scientific evidence of those facts, the "best available" science was contained in the petition, and a listing became almost inevitable—almost.

Black Tailed Prairie Dog

Colorado wildlife officials had numerous meetings with federal officials about the silliness, on its face, of calling an animal "endangered" that is so common. Federal officials claimed their hands might be tied by the "evidence" in the petition, which claimed 99% of all prairie dog habitat had disappeared (99% of the Great Plains gone!) with the resulting decline in population. The petition, as it turned out, was based more on computer modeling than any actual knowledge of prairie dogs, so the state spent over $75,000 on a contract to do something really radical—count the prairie dogs to find out how many there were. It found, predictably, that many times more of this species live in just one state than the petition alleged live in the entire country. In Colorado alone they occupied more land (630,000 acres) than the petition claimed they occupied nationwide. Overall, there are more than 30 million prairie dogs in their ten-state habitat.

In spite of better "available science," the government insisted that it might have to go forward with a listing, privately expressing the understandable fear of a lawsuit automatically filed by environmental groups when an animal may not be listed. Because the fear of lawsuits motivates so much federal decision-making, Colorado Attorney General Ken Salazar and I (on behalf of the Natural Resources Department) cosigned a letter to the Fish and Wildlife Service threatening to sue if the prairie dog were listed, using that fear of lawsuits to turn the tables in the name of common sense. Miraculously, the Service declined to list the species as endangered, opting instead for an in-between status called "warranted but precluded." In fact the species was not only "sustainable" but on the rise. Four years later, its occupied acres in Colorado alone had grown from 630,000 to 788,000.

Other states had also joined the effort; notably South Dakota and Colorado both banned the sport shooting of prairie dogs and took other actions that eliminated almost every argument the proponents of listing had used. Several states helped with better information on existing populations and acreage, and by 2004 the government had revised its national estimate from 636,000 acres to over 1.8 million.

Counting the animals in the field ought to be an obvious first step, but it is very rarely done. Consider that for more than 30 years "experts" thought the population of western lowland gorillas in Africa was declining, to a total population of 100,000 in 1980 and perhaps half that number by 2000. Yet in 2008 when a field census was undertaken by the Wildlife Conservation Society (based at the Bronx Zoo), more than 125,000 previously unseen gorillas were found in one part of the Congo alone—a discovery that doubled the known population of the animals. Why did it take so long for someone to go count them?

Western states used our field inventory to eventually remove the black-tailed prairie dog from the "candidate species" list altogether—a final conclusion that the species is not endangered and is not likely to become endangered. This important victory for the plains states shifted the debate to focus on the species itself. Environmental groups saw protecting the habitat (again calling into question their real motives) as a powerful tool to control urban sprawl in cities like Denver, Cheyenne, Wichita and Oklahoma City. While that may be a laudable goal on which all the states have spent considerable effort and resources, it has nothing to do with recovering species—the purpose of the Endangered Species Act. Moreover, it is just plain wrong to attempt federal control over such obviously local issues.

The Mouse that Roared

In taking a new approach to recovering endangered species, Colorado also had to overcome the natural skepticism among landowners who have trouble trusting that the state wants to balance their right to use their own land with the goal of recovering endangered species. Landowners are not insensitive to endangered species, but they have experience in how an overly aggressive bureaucracy can limit the use of their own private property. The good news is that they are realists who certainly understand that species conservation should be addressed early before the regulatory burden accompanying "threatened" or "endangered" listings becomes their burden.

One classic case of this frustration involves a "subspecies" the federal government calls "Preble's meadow jumping mouse," whose habitat is believed to be in riparian areas (ditches and streams) along the Front Range of the Rockies from Colorado Springs to Cheyenne, an area where open space is disappearing at an alarming rate because of urban sprawl. In 1998 the government listed the mouse as threatened throughout its entire range, estimating that the listing would cost the economy roughly $180 million. That cost estimate will increase another $52 million if a proposal to double the critical habitat is approved, and communities have already spent millions reacting to various forms of government over-kill. For instance, the city of Colorado Springs was once prevented for months from replacing a washed-out culvert on an existing city street because it might be habitat for the mouse (no actual mice lived there).

Following a "threatened" designation, the federal government must publish rules outlining when the incidental "take," or death, of a species can be allowed in the course of normal operations like farming. Colorado wildlife officials worked for several years with the federal agencies (while farmers remained in limbo) to craft rules to help preserve farming practices in the least disruptive manner. Those activities were successful only because many landowners voluntarily participated and shared their expertise. Most were more than willing to do so, at least in part because they understood the alternatives would be far worse.

The case of "Preble's meadow jumping mouse" was so contentious that six years later factions were still debating the particulars of the "incidental take rule" that would finally accompany the listing. One initial draft suggested that farmers who burn their ditches are destroying Preble's habitat, and perhaps killing the mice themselves. The first draft proposed to prohibit agricultural burning in critical habitat. Without the state's immediate intervention, the federal agency might have overlooked a critical point: You can't farm in the arid West without burning ditches. In the Mid-West and the East "dry-land farming" does not require irrigation (because there is enough rain), so there is no need for irrigation ditches. But in the West they are prerequisite to farming and they must be kept clear of weeds for water to flow—a fact that federal officials who wrote the first draft evidently didn't know.

With help from the landowners themselves, the feds crafted a rule that avoids a heavy-handed regulatory approach, permits incidental take during periods when burning is necessary, and recognizes that habitat is actually created or improved by some farming activities. The result does more than just free farmers from an impossible dilemma—it promotes the recovery of the species.

All the activity on behalf of this particular species would seem like outstanding progress were it not for one awkward reality: there is no such thing as a "Preble's meadow jumping mouse."

Farmers had been saying for years that the "subspecies" is no different than the ordinary field mice that hop all over the northern plains, elsewhere called "Bear Lodge meadow jumping mice" and technically just "meadow jumping mice." Several years into the program, a respected geneticist named Dr. Rob Roy Ramey, Curator of Vertebrate Zoology at the Denver Museum of Nature and Science published DNA-based test results proving the farmers right. His findings showed that the mouse had been protected based on guesswork and outdated science, and that it is genetically identical to the common Bear Lodge mouse. These findings did not criticize the earlier researchers, who did not have DNA technology, but simply demonstrated that the earlier science was wrong.

The Ramey study, prepared in cooperation with the University of Wyoming and the Wyoming wildlife agency, was subjected to intense peer review. Skeptical experts at the Colorado Division of Wildlife spent months analyzing the findings, which contradicted several years of previous work. They solicited and received 9 independent peer reviews. The U.S. Fish and Wildlife Service had the report reviewed by 7 more scientists it trusted, all at taxpayer expense. Although the 16 reviews (as is predictable among scientists) were not unanimous, the availability of new genetic scientific technology proved conclusive to a majority: most found Ramey's methods scientifically correct, and none was able to disprove his conclusion. Perhaps most significant of all, the very scientist who had originally classified Preble's as a subspecies, Philip Krutzsch, recanted his findings. The Preble's mouse had been classified as a subspecies based on a review of only three adult specimens, and the original science simply could not hold up under more modern technology. This is a common concern with "subspecies"—there are actually ten different mice on the endangered list, including 6 "different" southern beach mice, Key Largo cotton mouse, Pacific pocket mouse and salt marsh harvest mouse. That makes it important to get the science right, but whether the Preble's mouse is real or not, a great deal of political capital has been spent using this "subspecies" as a tool to control growth, and the government

Meadow Jumping Mouse (USFWS)

has no interest in giving that up. Several years of meetings, debates, public hearings, political activity and lawsuit threats followed the Ramey/Wyoming research.

In 2005 the Interior Department finally relented in the face of compelling scientific evidence (and congressional oversight hearings), and proposed to delist the species. It was to be the first time in history a species would be delisted because better information proved it never existed in the first place. That would have set a new standard for defining "new" species and subspecies. But environmental organizations and Fish and Wildlife Service bureaucrats working as the "Preble's Team" were not about to be defeated, demonstrating that the process mattered more to them than the species. They tried to discredit Ramey, criticized his work and his "behavior" in e-mails and press releases, and threatened his reputation and future funding of the world-class Denver Museum of Nature and Science where he worked. Eventually they decided to commission yet another study. This one was written specifically to refute the Ramey/Wyoming data and came almost out of nowhere—not from Fish and Wildlife Service biologists, nor from the leading experts in the Colorado or Wyoming wildlife agencies, nationally-known biologists or other academics, but from the U.S. Geological Survey (USGS) in Washington, D.C.

Commissioned in violation of the Fish and Wildlife Service's own standards for peer review, the only thing USGS researchers had to do was make sure their study was larger and more expensive than the previous evidence, making it virtually impossible for any federal judge to sort out the conflicting science. The "Preble's Team" had found a way to defeat the top scientists in the field, both state governments involved, and their own boss, the Secretary of the Interior—and the Department was forced to withdraw its proposed delisting. Instead, in a 2007 attempt to forge a compromise that left no one happy, Interior de-listed the species in Wyoming but left it listed in Colorado (where there is far more urban sprawl to be controlled), which illustrates the unintended consequences of putting politicians and interest groups in charge of science that can deny them power or money.

This outcome was especially ironic for Colorado because the same agency had refused to consider Colorado's previous request to treat the lynx in Colorado differently than those in other states. At that time, Colorado was told that delisting in one state while listing in another was illegal, but apparently that was wrong (at least 6 other species have been delisted in some places and not others). The public was left to wonder whether the mice know where the state line is any better than the lynx do.

The entire 10-year episode plainly demonstrates why all species decisions should begin with sound science. It also speaks volumes about the impact of such decisions on communities and private landowners, whose livelihoods are at stake while scientists, bureaucrats, politicians, lobbyists, lawyers and the media argue.

Grousing about Private Land

Much of the new approach to endangered species must involve private landowners for one simple reason: they own most of the habitat. Even in the West where so much land is federally owned, wildlife—like people—tend to inhabit the valleys and river basins rather than the deserts or mountaintops. Those valleys are mostly private land so the conflicts between man and wildlife are constant.

A general awareness is growing that if the government expects property owners to manage their lands differently, especially for the sole benefit of endangered species, they should be compensated to do so. This awareness stems not from a desire to subsidize private businesses, but from an understanding of the obvious: the overwhelming majority of endangered species habitat is on private lands, so government simply cannot do it alone.

Aldo Leopold's famous essay on "Conservation Economics" warned of "the time-honored supposition that conservation is profitable." His carefully reasoned thought about how to deal with private land that is also critical habitat bears repeating. He concluded that conservation becomes *possible* on private lands when it also becomes *profitable* for the economic and other goals of private landowners. In 1934 he wrote simply *"that conservation will ultimately boil down to rewarding the private landowner who conserves the public interest."* A heavy-handed system that won't even consult landowners can never get there.

As Interior Secretary, Bruce Babbitt recognized that reality and placed heavy emphasis on "habitat conservation plans" and other programs, in part to better involve landowners. Hundreds of such plans are now in place. This approach works in many areas because it promises landowners "no surprises" later if they participate in the habitat planning. Property owners cannot fairly be expected to make agreements with federal agencies if a new Administration or a new discovery might change the deal. In many instances that has happened and landowners have reason to be skeptical. Ranchers should be able to agree to careful management practices and allow access to their land for wildlife officials, in exchange for promises that any species found will not be used against them. That was Babbitt's sound concept. But the promise has far outshone the performance.

Colorado has invested millions in conservation easements to preserve ranchlands in the Gunnison Basin, a legacy to be proud of for many reasons. Besides preserving the historic character of a majestic mountain valley, it is a crucial part of the effort to preserve the Gunnison sage grouse, another species that environmental groups have sought for years to declare endangered. The Colorado Division of Wildlife in 2005 completed an agreement with the federal government that allows landowners to enroll in a program of protective habitat management, with the assurance that their farming practices will not get them into trouble if grouse nests are accidentally disturbed. The agreement represented exactly the right approach, but its completion was in doubt for several years.

The skepticism of ranchers in the area came down to one final and difficult question: can we trust the government to do what it says? This is a clear example of a common irony: because the focus is on land management instead of recovery, adding a species to the endangered list can actually harm the species. That is precisely because its habitat is mostly on private land. If landowners' participation in the preservation effort is purely voluntary, then anything that might cause them to pull the plug could sound the death knell to the species. And that is precisely what some ranchers threatened when it seemed that despite their best efforts the government might list the grouse as endangered anyway. They knew such a listing would bring on the requisite regulation of human activity that the entire program was designed to avoid while preserving and improving habitat. Colorado state officials were able to convince the Fish and Wildlife Service— at least for a time—that a listing would almost certainly result in at least some ranchers refusing to enroll in the habitat conservation plan, and even further, might refuse to negotiate conservation easements to protect the open space. Such refusals could only result in eventual development of their land and loss of grouse habitat.

Wildlife management agreements are an especially useful tool to ensure that farms do not destroy important habitat or unnecessarily kill wildlife. Thousands of acres throughout the country are successfully managed to everyone's benefit under such agreements. They give wildlife professionals access to the otherwise closed private land, so they can monitor populations of threatened and endangered species, keep tabs on air and water quality, trap and tag wildlife for better tracking, inventory and study nests, and many other activities important to their duties. And for the landowner, these agreements provide assurances against policy changes and other "surprises." They are often called agreements "with assurances," meaning the landowner received "assurances" from the government that he will not be penalized for his normal management practices if future endangered species are found on the property, if he agrees to certain "best management practices" designed to protect habitat reasonably.

The most important advantage of working closely with landowners—instead of against them—is that it changes the culture over time. In the past, many landowners have been so worried about potential government control of their property that they dared not admit to finding an endangered species on their property. Many ranchers refer only half-jokingly to the old "triple-S strategy: shoot, shovel, and shut up." But management agreements with strong assurances are beginning to change that culture, as government managers learn that there are alternatives to regulation and punitive actions. This "cultural shift" is vitally important to both sides.

In *A Sand County Almanac*, Aldo Leopold wrote, "We abuse land because we regard it as a commodity belonging to us. When we see land as a community to which we belong, we may begin to use it with love and respect." That is the cultural shift we see when private landowners work with management agreements, conservation easements, and other programs to save both agriculture and wildlife. An equally important cultural shift happens with the regulators. To paraphrase Leopold, we abuse landowners because we regard them as the enemy of the land, but when we see them as partners in conservation, we create love and respect for both the land *and* each other.

Happily, Gunnison sage grouse population is increasing. Still, ultimate success remains elusive. Some environmental organizations simply will not give up on the federal "command-and-control" approach that has served their purposes so well, and the biggest weapon they wield is the Endangered Species Act. Predictably, several sued the Interior Department over its decision to remove the Gunnison sage grouse from the candidate list, and forced a reversal. If the money spent on that one lawsuit could instead be spent on habitat improvement and conservation easements, recovery could be achieved even sooner. This is obviously a more effective approach, *but only if recovery is the goal.*

Here is further proof that the goal is often something else. The National Center for Public Policy Research wrote about the case of Viola Allen, a 72-year-old widow confined to a deteriorating old house and hooked to an oxygen tank, and her 82-year old neighbor, Delila Gribble. These ladies had agreed to sell their combined 18 acres to a housing developer, so they could move to homes that were easier to maintain. Local environmental activists opposed to

Gunnison Sage Grouse

the housing development (or any housing development) went to court to stop Viola Allen from selling the land she had owned for 44 years, because of a little stream called Tunnel Creek, which is barely a trickle in the winter and completely dry in the summer. They claimed the creek was essential to the habitat of federally protected Chinook salmon. It took over two years to resolve an annexation dispute between the city and county, followed by the lawsuit of a group called Citizens for a Natural Habitat (CNH). Several studies were completed, proving that Tunnel Creek is not capable of supporting salmon. There has never been a salmon in that creek. No matter, Mrs. Allen and

Mrs. Gribble were stuck with substantial legal fees, and prevented from selling their land during the years-long dispute. Ironically, the entire episode was all about stopping a housing development and had nothing to do with the endangered salmon. However, the fish provided the most powerful legal hook for the CNH, which would otherwise have no business in these ladies' business.

Sowing the Seed

The movement toward state-led recovery programs has slowly gained some traction in other states. Shifting the fundamental assumptions of a 30-year-old program, however, comes gradually at best. First there have to be arguments. Pioneering this new approach, Colorado Governor Bill Owens returned in 2001 to the Western Governors Association (WGA), calling for state leadership of recovery programs, and placing the emphasis on recovery and de-listing. The resolution touched off a fascinating debate, in which three governors again argued that recovery of endangered species is *not* the primary goal of the ESA. They argued that *federal funding* of programs is the major priority. Obviously that must be their personal goal. Incredibly, they believed the ESA's purpose was to fund state and local government activities *in spite of* endangered species, not actually to do *anything* to recover the species.

Amazingly, our national thought process on this issue has veered so far off track that many can't even remember why the Act was passed in the first place. In the end, however, 12 states agreed with Colorado's position, and WGA adopted a strong policy advocating state leadership of recovery efforts–and insisting on recovery goals.

The strategy of state leadership of recovery-based programs also made for enlightening conversation among my counterparts in other states, revealing many common frustrations in very diverse places. We formed a national organization of natural resources cabinet secretaries in 2000 (I was proud to serve as its first president) and our national meetings provided opportunities to share ideas for state leadership on important environmental issues. The Endangered Species Act was a frequent topic, and cabinet secretaries from around the country offered their particular local insights—always with remarkably common experiences and frustrations. Despite great conversations and several notable success stories, however, most states continue to view endangered species recovery as a federal problem.

Species recovery and de-listing—and state leadership—should be primary goals for all ESA reform advocates across the nation, not only because the public supports and expects it, but also because it is the Achilles' heel of a federal primacy approach that is clearly a demonstrable failure. The dismal record of federal recovery programs, and the property theft of American citizens left in the wake of these programs, cannot be denied and frustrated citizens everywhere know there must be a better way. There is.

Success in the politically charged arena of species conservation can be measured in many ways, but it requires a substantial departure from the 40-year-old practice of reliance on federal land use enforcement alone. It requires people at the local and state level, and especially landowners and private businesses, to take ownership of endangered species recovery. That may be new thinking for many, but it was the accepted practice for generations before there was a federal species law. The American Bison was recovered by hunters, not by federal bureaucrats or courts. But in recent years, people more often turn toward Washington, D.C. shaking their fists in anger and calling for changes in the way federal agencies enforce the law. The more realistic approach is to recognize the ESA's enduring popularity, and work to fulfill its original intent—without waiting for federal agencies to stop acting the way they inevitably act.

Colorado's intense advocacy to force federal officials to publish workable recovery goals for the Colorado River endangered fish— and its construction of the hatchery to make recovery a reality—is a model of how a better approach can re-center a government program that has lost its bearing. It proves the right approach can work. It is impossible, however, to overstate the importance of defining recovery as the foundation of this approach. We cannot determine whether we succeed unless we have first defined what success is.

The road to recovery can be dark and fraught with peril and delay, without a clear roadmap. Recovery programs will only work with a requirement that de-listing criteria be published in addition to simply adding species to the endangered list. Clear goals must not only be forged by scientists with no political stake and accepted by the various players, but also published with the force of law. That is the only guarantee that when the populations of various species reach a certain level, and have reproduced in the wild for a defined period, and live in a habitat protected to an agreed standard, they *will* be taken off the endangered list.

That is the light at the end of the tunnel: an assurance that the program itself is not eternal. It should also be the clear direction for Congress.

Those who have spent years trying to amend the Endangered Species Act to fix every perceived problem with a badly broken system will never succeed as long as the public support for protection is so inviolable. Massive reform proposals have always died of their own weight in congressional committees, and some politicians have paid a dear price for pushing such far-reaching reforms (e.g., Richard Pombo). What Congress ought to enact instead is a very simple and small quick-fix that would not be complicated: require recovery goals for all listed species. New species should not be added to the endangered list until de-listing criteria is established so everyone knows what is required. That would refocus the goal squarely where it needs to be and would be very difficult to oppose.

A simple bill would require de-listing criteria as a precondition of new listings, and also require such criteria within a reasonable time for all the species already on the list. That would change the debate because it would replace a shotgun blast approach to a wide range of issues with a rifle shot at the crux of the problem. It would garner overwhelming public support and smoke out the hidden agendas of opponents who don't really support recovery of endangered species. Instead of driving the debate by obscuring the goals, their counterproductive approach would be marginalized and trivialized.

The heart of the issue is an environmental industry that no longer puts the environment first, but rather uses the popularity of endangered species to push other agendas and generate vast sums of money. Most of their supporters are well-meaning people who want to do their part for the next generation; they have been misled without understanding the unintended consequences of these policies. And to protect their own property, landowners have often been forced to oppose environmentalists, and the federal laws they abuse, even though they also care about recovering endangered species. Such divisiveness can only harm the species.

Absent some proof of success, how long will the public continue supporting the most powerful environmental law ever passed? The public is often made to feel that if they do not support the environmental industry's agenda without question, they are anti-environment or anti-nature. We should all fear for the future of endangered species if the public ever decides this whole experiment was a mistake.

Building a Better Mousetrap

Initiatives like that in Colorado provide a new model where endangered species can be dealt with as they should be. Actual recovery programs can respond to citizen concerns, give state and local agencies a means of dealing with ESA problems, and provide unparalleled expertise with predictable and dedicated funding. Perhaps most importantly, they actually result in the recovery and protection of species considered to be in danger.

Species recovery (which includes habitat restoration and protection) should be the only objective, something to be advocated on an aggressive timeline and actively pursued as the end goal. It is not only a way to get people out from under the federal regulatory thumb, though there is certainly merit in that. It is not just a means for restoring endangered species so people can continue to live and work and raise their families in areas also occupied by wildlife, though that is a laudable goal.

In the final analysis, it is quite simply the right thing to do for the environment.

CHAPTER 3

POLAR BEARS AND THEIR PLANET

"Be worried–be very worried. Climate Change isn't some vague future problem—it's already damaging the planet at an alarming pace. Here's how it affects you, your kids and their kids as well."
—*Time Magazine cover, April 3, 2006*

A cover story in a 2008 issue of Audubon Magazine featured a photo of a polar bear swimming in the water with no land in the picture. The caption said, "Although polar bears are superb swimmers, paddling in open water for too long can make them vulnerable to exhaustion and cold, rough seas." The implication was that the poor polar bear in the photo might have to tread water forever because all the ice is gone! The article's opening salvo leaves no doubt of the author's agenda: *"With the clock running out in January, the Bush Administration, ignoring the concerns of its own scientists and possibly breaking federal law, looks to open a vital stretch of Arctic habitat to offshore oil and gas drilling. So much for saving endangered bears."* The article, called "Polar Distress," was written by a Colorado environmental activist, not a climate scientist or arctic biologist.

It was just one of thousands of news stories over the past two decades giving such coverage to the ultimate environmental issue: the very survival of the planet itself. The sensational worldwide press coverage goes beyond anything the conservation movement has ever previously known or hoped for. If people have advanced so far they now have the ability to alter the globe itself, perhaps we have planted the seeds of our eventual destruction, and the destruction of everything on Earth. If that doesn't provide an excuse for serious government regulation, nothing will!

A Bigger Hammer

The problem with the global warming phenomenon is that it has not continued unabated, as many scientists claimed it would. Global warming essentially stopped a decade or so ago, which is why its advocates began calling it "climate change" instead. And as the "climate-gate" scandal embarrassed some of the top advocates of man-made global warming theory, many people began to be increasingly skeptical of the science. So, unable to convince Americans to adopt the disingenuous cap-and-trade schemes and other draconian approaches to global warming, environmental groups have fallen back on a more tried-and-true apparatus they know works—the Endangered Species Act (ESA). If the international hammer of the United Nations cannot stop the use of fossil fuels in the United States, perhaps the Endangered Species Act can get the job done. Remember that the ESA is among the strongest laws ever enacted, trumps nearly everything else, and does not require absolute scientific proof before triggering very onerous requirements.

That makes ESA the perfect tool for controlling human activities, as we have seen. Beyond that, however, consider the ramifications of a species being listed as threatened or endangered specifically because of global warming. That would, indeed, be a complete new tool in the toolbox for the environmental organizations and their friendly government regulators. For the first time ever, that would permit the ESA to be used to control activities *regardless of their location*. In other words, anything that contributes to greenhouse gas emissions could be a threat to the survival of the listed species—whether or not the activity is anywhere near the species. Nothing more perfectly fits that objective than the polar bear.

If the polar bear could be listed as threatened or endangered—specifically because of global warming—then federal agencies could stop development of power plants, timber harvests, public land grazing permits, coal mine or ski area expansions, oil and gas exploration, airport and highway construction, and many other projects throughout the United States. Projects would not have to be anywhere near the polar bear's critical habitat because any greenhouse gas emission could be said to contribute to global warming, and thus contribute to the demise of a listed species.

Previously, projects had to have a direct impact on a listed species or its habitat in order for the ESA's enforcement actions to be triggered. But any species that could be listed because of global warming would change that. Suddenly there would be a listed species whose critical habitat was essentially the whole world. For those reasons, environmental groups began mentioning the polar bear early in the crusade.

The UN's International Panel on Climate Change (IPCC) painted the most dismal picture in a March, 2007 report. The document contained dire warnings of the effects of global warming during this century:

- Tens of millions of people could be flooded out of their homes each year,
- Tropical diseases like malaria will spread,
- Pests like fire ants will thrive,
- By 2080 hundreds of millions of people could face starvation,
- More than 3 billion will face water shortages,
- Smog in the U.S. will worsen,
- Ozone-related deaths will rise by 4.5%,
- Half of all plant species in Europe will be vulnerable, endangered or extinct by 2100,
- Polar bears and other animals will exist only in zoos.

One of the report's authors said, "We truly are standing at the edge of mass extinction." Once the environmental organizations decided upon this strategy, there was really never any doubt that the government would fall into line. The public could easily be persuaded of the need to protect a species as cute and cuddly and the polar bear, much easier to "sell" than an obscure snail or an unknown cactus plant. Nor was there ever any doubt that the Fish and Wildlife Service wanted to add polar bears to the endangered list. Several years were spent studying the various climate models, and the polar bear's habitat and behavior. All the studies were designed to conclude that if sea ice diminishes over time, the bears will die off. Having reached that conclusion early in this century and created lots of "studies" to prove it, the bureaucrats faced the challenge of overruling their bosses (the Bush Administration had said it would oppose listing the polar bear). They resorted to a trick perfected earlier when Interior was on the verge of de-listing the Preble's Meadow Jumping Mouse (the non-existent sub-species mentioned earlier) and overturning the Fish and Wildlife Service—get another study from another agency.

In early 2007, the Fish and Wildlife Service asked the U.S. Geological Survey (USGS) to perform additional analyses of the polar bear and its sea ice habitats. In seven months, USGS prepared nine separate reports on the issue, with one central conclusion: "[p]rojected changes in future sea ice conditions, if realized, will result in loss of approximately 2/3 of the world's current polar bear population by the mid 21st century." The Fish and Wildlife Service and the USGS work in the same building and they are hardly strangers, much less disinterested peer reviewers. They are friendly colleagues. Nevertheless, the appearance was that experts from completely unrelated agencies had examined the situation and independently reached the same conclusion: global warming is killing off the polar bears.

The process played out the way it nearly always does. The "Center for Biological Diversity" filed the predictable petition for listing. The Interior Department dragged the review process out for months beyond the required legal deadline. Congressional committees held oversight hearings, environmental groups threatened to sue Secretary Dirk Kempthorne for the delay, and more congressional hearings were held. Finally, Interior added the species to the threatened list, knowing if it did not do so a federal judge would order it, and the end result would be the same anyway.

During the months of internal debate at Interior, officials tried to find a way to head off the radical environmental strategy of using the polar bear to stop anything in the country. They knew they would eventually be required to add the species to the list, but they did not want it to be used to stop energy production. Environmental groups were already using polar bears as a prime excuse to oppose drilling in the Arctic waters north of Alaska—drilling the Administration supported. Interior knew the environmental leaders wanted to use the same tool to stop other energy projects throughout the country, so Kempthorne looked for ways out of that box. His staff debated whether the Department could add a species to the threatened list without naming the cause of the threat. They reasoned that it might be difficult for environmentalists to criticize a decision to add polar bears to the list, even if the listing did not give them the tool they needed to stop development.

The fact that Interior even discussed such a strategy was inevitably leaked to the media and Capitol Hill, environmental leaders went ballistic, and there were more oversight hearings in Congress. Outraged Congressmen predictably personalized the issue, blaming the Bush Administration and demanding to know why Kempthorne was delaying the decision. Interior officials responded to hundreds of letters from politicians, phone calls, e-mails and petitions from "concerned citizens" around the world, and fielded a flood of inquiries from reporters with a nose for news.

In the end, Interior tried to establish a new precedent and touched off a new round of lawsuits that will keep attorneys employed for years to come. The misguided strategy was to list the polar bear as threatened, blame the threat on global warming melting the arctic sea ice, but also issue an accompanying rule that essentially waives the enforcement side of the law—the part the environmental organizations most wanted: Section 7.

The Endangered Species Act has a provision called Section 7, which requires any federal agency to "consult" with the U.S. Fish and Wildlife Service before taking any action on any project that could possible "adversely affect" a listed species. After such consultation, the Fish and Wildlife Service must either determine that an agency action will or will not adversely affect the species. If it will, the agency may not proceed, which gives the Fish and Wildlife Service effective veto power over innumerable other federal agency actions. These "Section 7 Consultations" are a primary delay tactic in holding up hundreds of permits across the nation, and they are a source of tremendous frustration to other federal agencies. Importantly, they are also a giant hammer environmental groups frequently use to stop energy, agriculture, land management, forest health, and transportation projects. If an agency fails to consult, environmental groups will sue. If the Fish and Wildlife Service issues a "not likely to affect" decision, they will sue. No activity under Section 7 happens without the close scrutiny of these groups.

In the case of the polar bear listing, the Fish and Wildlife Service essentially added a species to the threatened list, and simultaneously adopted a rule that waived the Section 7 Consultation requirement for projects outside the bear's immediate vicinity. Although the ploy was too clever by half, there was some legal basis for the distinction the agency tried to make. The memo from the U.S. Geological Survey to the U.S. Fish and Wildlife Service–while concluding that 2/3 of all polar bears would disappear by 2050—also hedged on the direct link to greenhouse gas emissions. It quoted yet another government report stating:

> *"In an ideal world, there would be reliable quantitative estimates of all climate forcings—both natural and human induced–that have made significant contributions to surface and tropospheric temperature changes. We would have detailed knowledge of how these forcings had changed over space and time...Unfortunately, this ideal situation does not exist.*

The memo went on to explain why no system exists for measuring the impacts of a single source of greenhouse gas emissions on a particular climate impact somewhere else:

> *"The final conclusion that can be reached from this information is that human-induced global warming can be observed and verified at global to continental scales where cumulative GHG concentrations can be measured and modeled. Climate impacts, however, are observed at specific locations, at much more specific and localized scales—incongruent with the global scale of the aforementioned measured and modeled climate forces. It is currently beyond the scope of existing science to identify a specific source of CO2 emissions and designate it as the cause of specific climate impacts at an exact location."*

In other words, both the USGS and the USFWS had said they had no way to link individual greenhouse gas-emitting projects elsewhere in the U.S. to melting sea ice in the polar bears' region. So the Administration seized on that "opportunity," made the listing decision, and simultaneously issued the accompanying rule. The idea was that the polar bear would be protected under the Act from threatening activities in its immediate vicinity, but *not* by power plants, logging, or other activities in distant states. But the environmental organizations are much too sophisticated for that strategy to work, at least without a fight, and it began immediately.

The very day after the listing decision was announced, the same environmental groups that had petitioned for the listing, and sued to force an earlier decision (Center for Biological Diversity, Natural Resources Defense Council, Defenders of Wildlife, and Greenpeace) sued the government over the rule accompanying the listing. The new suit said that by refusing to use the ESA to regulate greenhouse gas emissions throughout the United States, the government had provided inadequate protection for polar bears. Within a week, the State of Alaska had also filed suit—on the opposite side of the issue—claiming the unwarranted listing would stop economic activity that does not threaten the bears, especially oil and gas production.

Environmentalists were quick to make clear that stopping such development was, in fact, their agenda. The director of a group called Pacific Environment whined that "things are happening so fast in the Arctic that we need to take a timeout from further offshore oil development in the region." Happening so fast? The process for scrupulously regulating offshore mineral leasing includes test permits, exploration, environmental scoping, public comments, environmental analysis, permitting, appeals, administrative hearings, lawsuits, court proceedings, and congressional hearings—all of which has taken more than a decade already. One wonders how many years these groups think are needed to review and study a project that could substantially alter the nation's dependence on foreign oil. In any case, how the listing will be used to regulate human activity will not be determined by the hundreds of people who spent thousands of hours involved in the process, or even by the general public or their elected officials.

Earthjustice vowed to "thoroughly evaluate" the new rule, and said at least three ongoing lawsuits (all seeking to stop oil and gas production) will remain unchanged. That is because the lawsuits are not really about polar bears; they are about stopping oil and gas production. There was never much doubt what the outcome of these various lawsuits would be: a federal court ruled that the government needed to conduct a more thorough review and sent officials back to the drawing board. Eventually courts will determine that the rule violated the ESA and throw it out, leaving the full force and power of the ESA available for lawsuits against any project in the U.S. that can be shown to contribute greenhouse gases. It is as predictable as night following day.

As with all other endangered species, the debate ought to be about the polar bears. There are plenty of available forums for discussion of our national energy policy. Whether or not we should drill offshore, and even whether or not we should produce American oil instead of importing middle-eastern oil, are legitimate disagreements that reasonable people may ponder. But they are not about polar bears. If we are truly concerned about the fate of polar bears—and I am—we should study them, know how many there are and where they live, understand their habitat and keep tabs on their populations. Perhaps most important, if we think they are in danger of extinction, it would make more sense to stop killing them on purpose.

Hunters pay $30,000 to $50,000 for the privilege of participating in trophy hunts in Canada, and the U.S. government specifically allows importing polar bear carcasses legally hunted in Canada. And of course, we allow Alaska natives (Eskimos) to engage in what is called "subsistence hunting." It is an antiquated concept because there are no Americans who are forced to depend on bear meat for their very survival. It is really "traditional hunting," but "subsistence hunting" sounds more defensible so we call it that. But far beyond those local traditions, we also allow these trophy hunts to continue every year on a large scale. Over the past 10 years, more than 800 polar bears have been killed under this legal system to decorate American homes.

To be clear, I am an advocate of hunting. In fact, Boone and Crocket Club members have demonstrated for more than 100 years that hunters are the most ready source of time and money to maintain populations of game animals. They are the wellspring of the most effective conservation of hundreds of species throughout the world. Here, my only point is that if we really thought polar bears were in danger of becoming extinct, one of the first things we would do is stop killing them.

There is an easy explanation for why we have not banned hunting polar bears—they are not endangered. The most ironic aspect of the decade—long battle over polar bears and global warming is that the species itself is not only viable, but in the midst of a dramatic re-surgence. Population studies showed the species had declined to about 5,000 animals after World War II. Hunters (not governments) advocated limits in order to save the population, playing the conservation role so common to hunters. The population had stabilized by the 1960's and there were as many as 10,000 bears by 1970. Today there are an estimated 25,000 polar bears in at least 9 different regions, according to most surveys. In addition, it is now known that polar bears evolved some 200,000 years ago, meaning they survived the last major warming period when average global temperatures were 10 degrees warmer than today and there was probably no polar ice at all. Al Gore says sea ice was the lowest ever measured in 2007, but satellite measurements only go back 30 years. In fact, we know the Northwest Passage, clogged with ice today, was free of ice and open to shipping in 1945, and that Roald Amundsen passed through it in a sailing ship in 1903. Yet polar bears were there then, despite the shortage of ice.

This is not business as usual. This may not be the first time in the history of endangered species protection that a species has been added to the threatened or endangered list that is known to be both vigorous and increasing. But unlike many other species in dispute, in this case there is no significant disagreement about that fact. Rather, this is a purposeful expansion of the scope of the Endangered Species Act. The government's justification for the "threatened" listing is not that the bears are in decline, but speculation that they *may decline in the future* as a result of global warming. No species has ever been listed on such a basis before. On that dubious speculation alone, the Endangered Species Act is now to be used as a tool not to recover a species in danger of extinction, but to regulate air pollution. The latter has always been the job of the EPA under the Clean Air Act, and the U.S. Supreme Court recently ruled that the EPA has authority to regulate carbon dioxide as a pollutant. Still, environmental leaders know that the ESA is a much more powerful tool, so it will again become the primary means for stopping anything anywhere. And the primary enforcer will not be the EPA, but the Fish and Wildlife Service.

Just so there is an insurance policy in case the courts ever rule against using the ESA to protect a species that is not really endangered, the environmental lobby has insurance in the form of other species waiting to be listed. The same groups have also petitioned to list several species of walrus, seals, and whales—also because of the dangers of global warming.

It is almost redundant to ask if this abuse was ever really intended by the authors of the Endangered Species Act. Perhaps Interior had no choice but to list the polar bear as threatened or endangered. Several Canadian provinces had already done so and the political pressure was relentless. But caving in to that pressure, while attempting to withhold the power of the ESA, was never going to work. The better solution would have been to rely on the "best available science" to know more about polar bears than the petitioners or the federal courts.

The government could have done a much more thorough job of documenting the polar bears' dramatic increase in numbers, declined the listing petition, and published a scientific, peer-reviewed, credible study explaining why the species is not in any danger. In addition to better information on the growing population of polar bears, it could also have documented the incredible rebound of the sea ice during the winter of 2007-2008. Reports from the National Oceanic and Atmospheric Administration (NOAA) showed that nearly all the "lost" ice had recovered. A 2008 NOAA report showed that ice levels, which had shrunk from 5 million square miles in January 2007 to just 1.5 million square miles in October, were almost back to their original levels by February of 2008. Newer studies also show that polar bears are more resilient than previously thought; we now know they survived a period of global warming thousands of years ago that melted nearly all sea ice. These new studies may not be conclusive, but they certainly point to the absurdity of calling a species threatened or endangered that is clearly not.

Plainly, the government had other options in dealing with the polar bear listing petition. Of course, had the petition been denied, environmental groups would have sued. But they did so anyway, so the government gained nothing, and spent time and money in court defending the indefensible. The right response for the government would have been to deny the petition based on sound science, and to focus its efforts away from lawsuits and onto polar bears. Dare we say, the government could even be so proactive as to raise polar bears, reintroduce them into the wild, and ensure an even larger population in the future. That would make sense *if* the agenda were really about polar bears. But it isn't.

So What About the Planet?

Every period in Earth's history has experienced climate changes with alternating periods of warming and cooling. Global warming is thought to have been one of several factors that led to the extinction of the woolly mammoth some 6,000 years ago. We also know that ice ages have caused extinctions of other plants and animals—that is nature. So while rising, falling, or steady temperatures can be documented, it is pure folly to pretend they are conclusive proof of impending apocalypse. And it is dishonest to pretend scientists have accurate historical data going back thousands or even hundreds of years, when in fact they have hypotheses based on educated guesses, extrapolated from ice cores, tree rings, and mostly computer models.

My grandpa used to occasionally talk about the unprecedented amount of change he had seen during his lifetime. He was born and raised before there were cars, telephones, radios, televisions, or computers. He lived to see men on the moon, interstate highways, jet airplanes, even cordless phones. Though I used to marvel at such an extreme change in human progress that occurred during his lifetime, think about what we have seen during ours. We have gone from the world's smartest scientists warning of the coming ice age to dire predictions of catastrophic global warming—all in the space of about

30 years! Is it a coincidence that so many people have also gone from unquestioned respect for scientists to widespread skepticism about their expertise, and even their motives?

Throughout the 1970's, climate scientists and their studies attracted worldwide press coverage with suggestions that the Earth was cooling dramatically, putting the productivity of agriculture in peril and signaling the possibility of a new ice age. Articles appeared in Time, Newsweek, the New York Times, even National Geographic, with varying degrees of sensationalism. The New York Times wrote *"A Major Cooling Widely Considered to be Inevitable."* Newsweek Magazine worried about the impacts on agriculture, reporting that meteorologists were *"almost unanimous in the view that the trend will reduce agricultural productivity for the rest of the century."*

Even today a Google search for "coming ice age" produces over a half-million articles, and clearly the theory is still alive and well. A similar Google search for "global warming," however, produces over 56 million articles, so it is clear where most of the writing and publishing today comes down on the matter. How do they reconcile the apparent about-face? Many of these writers simply claim that the coming ice age will be caused by global warming–no matter how counterintuitive that may sound. It enables some to be on the politically-correct side of the global warming debate without admitting they were wrong about the coming ice age. As Greenpeace activist Steven Guilbeault put it, "Global warming can mean colder. It can mean wetter. It can mean drier. That's what we're talking about." (Translation: "Name a weather phenomenon and I'll blame it on global warming.")

A group of 16 scientists summed up this strategy in a letter printed in the Wall Street Journal.

"The lack of warming for more than a decade—indeed, the smaller-than-predicted warming over the 22 years since the U.N.'s Intergovernmental Panel on Climate Change (IPCC) began issuing projections—suggests that computer models have greatly exaggerated how much warming additional CO2 can cause. Faced with this embarrassment, those promoting alarm have shifted their drumbeat from warming to weather extremes,

to enable anything unusual that happens in our chaotic climate to be ascribed to CO2."

Note the number of news reports in late 2012 that blamed the damage done by "Super-Storm Sandy" on climate change. The subsequent debate in December at the annual UN Global Climate Change Conference (this time in Doha, Qatar) saw proposals to make the U.S. and other developed countries pay for damages throughout the world caused by natural disasters—an idea President Obama has already hinted might be acceptable to his Administration.

Despite the radical shift in scientific opinion during the past 30 years, many advocates for strong laws restricting human activity because of global warming argue not only that the warming itself is no longer debatable, but that man is causing it. It is "settled science," they say. But is it?

Al Gore and other proponents of manmade global warming have consistently argued over the past decade that the claimed scientific "consensus," is so settled that governments should proceed with heavy taxation and rationing of hydrocarbon energy now. They say we cannot and should not wait for further discussion of the "settled science" upon which the legislative action should be based. That theory alone should prompt real scientists around the world to want more research, since the very purpose of science is offended by the concept of a complex matter so "settled" that further discussion is unwarranted.

True scientists are, in fact, offended by the notion of "settled science." Because these claims have not yet convinced the U.S. government to initiate energy rationing, the United Nations has held a series of international meetings attended by a group of about 600 scientists and a large number of bureaucrats and other non-scientists from environmental, business, and political organizations—about 2,000 people at most of these annual gatherings. These conferences have attracted tremendous worldwide press coverage with two primary messages: the United States should be pressured to ratify the Kyoto Protocol (which took effect in 2005 without the U.S.), and there should be no further time wasted arguing about the "settled science." The clear goal is to convince the world media that the "consensus" of scientists backing the theory of man-made global warming is so overwhelming that further examination of the science is not only unnecessary, but probably dangerous, fiddling while Rome burns.

It is worth noting that throughout history, scientists have often united behind a popular theory, only to be proven wrong by better research, often by a single scientist whose work was roundly criticized by peers. When Galileo demonstrated that balls weighing different amounts dropped from the Leaning Tower of Pisa hit the ground at the same time regardless of their weight, he was accused by his own university colleagues of rigging the test. He was also convicted of heresy and placed under house arrest for the remainder of his life for supporting Copernicus' view that the Sun, not the Earth, was at the center of the galaxy. Virtually all scientists once believed diseases were caused by bad air, until the discovery of viruses and bacteria. Before the 19th Century most scientists believed ice only formed near land, so there would be no ice at the North Pole, and thus a navigable sea route existed there. History is full of colorful examples of "settled science" which was discredited by further study.

In this case, the public has become increasingly skeptical as the facts simply do not continue to bear out the dire predictions. As a result, western governments are losing public support for the most draconian tax-and-regulate measures that seemed almost inevitable a few years ago.

Plan B: The Polar Bear

It is an unfortunate sign of the times that popular species like polar bears have become the tool of choice for other purposes. It is sad because so many of us actually care about polar bears, and other environmental issues, and so are easily misled into active support for policies that are counterproductive. Rank-and-file members of conservation groups around the world have no idea that their leaders are really pushing some other agenda, which in this case has nothing to do with polar bears. The agenda of those pushing the theory of man-made climate change is quite simple. They want to stop the use of fossil fuels.

It may seem ironic that the polar bear would become a symbol of the fight against carbon dioxide emissions, since they exhale as much as the next animal. In fact, burning fossil fuels is probably not the largest contributor to carbon dioxide emissions. All animals have developed the bad habit of breathing. Grade school children learn that all animals, including polar bears and humans, breathe in oxygen and exhale carbon dioxide—which plants absorb  while giving off oxygen. The average person and most animals exhale 2.2 pounds of carbon dioxide a day. There are 6.6 billion people and another 3.3 billion cows, sheep, goats and pigs, in addition to the billions of non-domestic animals over which mankind has little control. Many observers have done the math and concluded that more carbon dioxide comes from animals than from fossil fuels. You may remember during the 1990's the press was filled with articles about cow flatulence damaging the Earth's atmosphere.

Some global warming proponents argue that animals generate carbon dioxide in a "closed system," meaning they can only breathe out what they eat from plants or animals that had eaten plants. So they argue that we are merely recycling already-existing carbon dioxide, where burning fossil fuels "liberates" additional carbon dioxide that was absorbed by plants millions of years ago. While that is technically true, it is a minor distinction because in both cases carbon dioxide is merely being moved between the air and land "reservoirs." Our use of energy changes the timing of that cycle, but it does not make new elements that weren't there.

Even the UN thought the role of animals was worth studying. A 2006 report by the UN Food and Agricultural Organization entitled "Livestock's Long Shadow" studied the "damage" done by livestock, which the report said are responsible for 18 per cent of the greenhouse gases that cause global warming, "more than cars, planes and all other forms of transportation put together." It also said burning fuel to produce fertilizer to grow feed, to produce and transport meat, and clearing vegetation for grazing, produces 9 percent of all carbon dioxide emissions.

Most of the report and others like it focused on cows, since every single cow on Earth pumps out as much carbon dioxide every day as a standard-sized SUV driving 33 miles. These reports also concentrate on another greenhouse gas, methane, because livestock around the world produce about 80 million metric tons of methane a year. Methane is only about 5% of the total greenhouse gas so it doesn't really matter, but the IPCC says it is 20 times better at trapping heat in the atmosphere than carbon dioxide. So IPCC makes a big deal of the fact that the "six million tons of methane that North American cows burp annually are equivalent to 36 million tons of carbon dioxide." Put another way, livestock is responsible for 50 percent more greenhouse gas than the worldwide transportation sector. One result is that millions of government research dollars in many countries are being spent looking for better feed and other ways to keep cows from breathing, burping and otherwise passing so much gas into the air.

You might think advocates so determined to stop all the carbon dioxide and methane emissions possible would focus considerable effort on getting rid of livestock. You would be wrong. When some government officials in New Zealand proposed a tax on flatulence as a way of reducing its carbon footprint, environmentalists in the Green Party immediately announced they would not support it. A party leader said the only point in taxing greenhouse gas emissions is to provide an incentive to reduce them, but "there is no way of reducing methane from cows and sheep except by reducing their numbers." Indeed, if one really wanted to reduce greenhouse gas emissions, wouldn't one support such an incentive? "The last thing we want to do as an economy dependent on agriculture is to put financial pressure on farmers to cut back the numbers of sheep and cows when they have no alternatives." She told the press. "We should focus policy on the emissions which are easy and cost effective to reduce like energy use and on those growing fastest like transport and electricity generation. A carbon tax on fossil fuels could help…"

In other words, do not propose limits to the number of cattle, because that would be so unpopular it might endanger public sympathy for the entire global warming movement. People might be willing to drive smaller cars, ride buses to work and install fluorescent light bulbs, but they are not about to stop eating. Thus, the cadre of groups pushing man-made global warming would henceforth ignore a large portion of the emissions they identified as a problem, and stay carefully focused on the burning of fossil fuels—and on new ways to levy taxes. In its second term, there is virtually no doubt that the Obama Administration will focus considerable attention on a proposed carbon tax.

A 2007 UN climate conference in Bali, Indonesia helped illuminate the real agenda of a number of man-made global warming advocates. Attendees urged a global tax on carbon dioxide emissions "to help save the Earth from catastrophic man-made global warming." One panel encouraged adoption of a tax that would represent "a global burden sharing system, fair, with solidarity, and legally binding to all nations." Who would collect the tax? The UN, of course—an organization that has never had (but always wanted) direct taxing authority to fund itself. At long last, the UN could free itself from the tiresome burden of having to rely on the good will of member nations for its annual budget.

One advocate of the global warming tax said the amount should generate at least $10-$40 billion dollars per year, and wealthy nations like the U.S. would bear the biggest burden based on the "polluters pay principle." The U.S. and other wealthy nations need to "contribute significantly more to this global fund," he said, adding that "It is very essential to tax coal."

Interestingly, the proposed tax actually generated some push-back from the UN's own scientists. More than 100 scientists, including many members of the IPCC, signed a letter saying the global tax and other aspects of the UN's attempt to control the Earth's climate was "ultimately futile." The scientists wrote, "The IPCC's conclusions are quite inadequate as justification for implementing policies that will markedly diminish future prosperity. In particular, it is not established that it is possible to significantly alter global climate through cuts in human greenhouse gas emissions." This last revelation should be shocking, but was hardly mentioned in press reports about the Bali conference. One hundred of the very scientists upon whom Al Gore and his friends rely—the same ones who say human emission of greenhouse gases is causing global warming—were now saying reducing such emissions would diminish prosperity and might not even help the planet!

The UN and other man-made global warming advocates reacted to this stunning statement by ignoring it. Undeterred, they simply continue to press the agenda, because it is not really about whether climate can be controlled. It is about money. It is about a massive redistribution of wealth. These are goals freely admitted by at least some of the attendees. As the environmental group Friends of the Earth made clear in Bali, the agenda is the transfer of money from rich to poor nations. "A climate change response must have at its heart a redistribution of wealth and resources," said Emma Brindal, a "climate justice campaign coordinator" for Friends of the Earth.

As with so many other aspects of the environmental agenda, those issues ought to be debated on their own merit. There are policy makers around the world who genuinely believe in redistribution of wealth as an important social cause. Some believe it is an affront to justice that so much wealth has been accumulated in the U.S. and other industrialized countries. Those are legitimate issues for philosophy, literature, and even politics. But those debates are *not about the environment*, and they most certainly are not about polar bears.

Before beginning any discussion about any environmental issue, the first step is to make sure we're in the right debate. If we set the reference point for discussion on the environment, those with some other agenda will always be left behind. And we must make sure decisions are based on sound science, not about some other issue, but about the issue of the moment. If the policy being debated is whether to list polar bears as endangered, the scientific evidence needed is about polar bears, not climate change.

Despite all the bad feeling and hysteria the global warming debate has engendered (on both sides), the environmental industry persists because the issue provides a potential tool to control everything everywhere. If everything mankind does on the planet can be said to affect the climate, then climate regulators would be able to regulate everything mankind does.

The tool is already being used to control development in nations where the Kyoto agreement is legally enforceable, but the man-made global warming advocates have not yet been able to use it to control the big prize—the United States (because the U.S. has never ratified the Kyoto agreement). That is why classifying the polar bear as threatened was so important to the environmental industry. It will enable use of the powerful Endangered Species Act to accomplish what the White House, Congress, and united efforts of hundreds of environmental organizations could not—the complete regulation of all emissions from all sources in the country.

Close and careful study of actual data—not computer models—should govern scientific conclusions, whether the issue is counting prairie dogs in Colorado or determining what is happening to the global climate. But sometimes the pesky facts just do not support the conclusions sought by political activists. And make no mistake; there are activists who seek drastic changes in our world, from its global economic systems to the governance of entire continents. They are not seeking a cleaner and healthier environment, or a rich diversity of plant and animal species. Those are merely the tools they use to gain public support for their policies. Unfortunately, the policies they pursue are often bad for the environment.

CHAPTER 4

MANAGING THE FOREST

"Men argue; nature acts."
—Voltaire

Long before the talk about global warming, before the relationship between trees and carbon dioxide was understood, before anyone cared about the difference between new trees and old growth, people always had an instinct about the importance of forests. Henry David Thoreau even thought he could learn from trees, at least in a metaphorical way. His publication of *Walden, or Life in the Woods* in 1854 became the lightning rod for debate about a simpler lifestyle among the elite of his day. Thoreau spent two years, two months and two days in a crude cabin he built at the edge of the woods near his real home, and proposed to live primitively, growing his own food and making his own shelter and clothing. His original goal was to study society by living apart from it, but in the end he wound up studying and writing more extensively about nature and the forest.

I went to the woods because I wished to live deliberately, to front only the essential facts of life, and see if I could not learn what it had to teach, and not, when I came to die, discover that I had not lived.

Today Thoreau is considered one of the indispensable pioneers of the conservation movement because his work gave voice to a never-ending love affair Americans have with the forest. When the early settlement and growth of the country led to massive clearing of trees across the continent, most Americans recognized that fact as a problem. Saving the remaining forests from decimation and ensuring our progeny productive forests formed the basis of the conservation movement more than any other single concern. Decades later the movement would also take on the challenges of defending wildlife, and protecting clean air and water from pollution. But initially, it was all about the forests. For many people, it still is.

Theodore Roosevelt wrote that "to waste, to destroy, our natural resources, to skin and exhaust the land instead of using it so as to increase its usefulness, will result in undermining in the days of our children the very prosperity which we ought by right to hand down to them amplified and developed." He was talking about the need to preserve the nation's forests, and his work with Gifford Pinchot in designating National Forests, and creating management systems to protect them, began a recovery that was nothing short of miraculous. Less than a century later, our generation of Americans inherited a land with more trees than were here when Columbus landed in the New World in 1492. Yet during the past two decades, our generation has all but stopped the professional management that Roosevelt and Pinchot began. Now these precious forests are paying an appalling price. We are now witnessing the disease, death, rotting, collapse and burning of *billions* of trees covering *millions* of acres of previously healthy forest lands. Some of these devastated landscapes will not recover their former beauty in our lifetimes, and some will never again provide the same habitat for wildlife, or the same quality water supply they once did. Dead forests contribute significantly to the decline of species with nowhere else to go. For example, the Mexican spotted owl and the mountain plover are both birds that depend on healthy forest habitats in the southern Rockies, and both are endangered because of the loss of that habitat. Our generation did not purposely set out to squander this historic trust; it happened gradually over a period of years while most Americans (who do not live near the national forests) simply didn't notice.

As a society, we have made a colossal mistake in the stewardship of our national forests. We should admit it, and correct it.

Fooling Mother Nature

Nature has its own way of managing large forests in the absence of mankind. For centuries the forests of North America enjoyed a state of natural balance, which is easily upset when people and cities also inhabit the land. So our job as stewards of the land is to mimic the role of nature as closely as possible, and thereby to maintain the most natural conditions possible. We have failed miserably in recent years. The current situation is very complex, but in a nutshell, here is what has happened:

- Nature had always kept the growth of forests in check with periodic fires, sparked by lightning. These natural fires burn the shrubs and brush and grasses on the forest floor, also destroying saplings and small trees so the forest does not grow too dense, but mostly leaving the older and larger trees undamaged.

- After Americans began to settle the forested areas in large numbers, and to depend on the forests for the wood and other resources they needed, they understandably viewed forest fires—natural or not—as a crisis. Vast resources were spent putting out forest fires and for over a hundred years, fire suppression has played a dominant role in the culture of forest management.

- In spite of that man-made activity, the forests still did not grow overly dense because in the early years of professional management, the natural role of fire was replaced with a steady program of forest thinning. National forests were logged to provide lumber for commercial activities, to promote forest recreation, healthy watersheds, species protection and management, and to prevent wildfires.

- Then in the late 20th Century, logging became unpopular with the American people, and the cutting of trees was all but stopped. And we replaced that management tool with—nothing.

The result is a massive unnatural overgrowth not only of large trees but of brush, grasses, weeds and smaller trees creating a tinderbox that, when ignited, obliterates the landscape. Our political leaders react with money, committees, planning, studies, more documents and more meetings. And while American political leaders have debated forest management for the past generation, nature has begun to run its inevitable course.

A Death in the Family

Many environmental leaders do not seem to understand a central truth about forests—plants either grow or die. Some activists seem to think if we stop all activity in our national forests, they will be there forever in the same condition, as if we can preserve a snapshot for all time. Some even argue that since today's leaders are deadlocked in their differences over forest management, we ought to leave the forests alone and let some future generation figure out what to do. At least, they say, we will not have done any further damage. They could not be more wrong. Leaving the forests alone—neglecting them—is a death sentence.

Mankind has the ability to destroy forests in more ways than one. Clearing all vegetation from entire landscapes—skinning the land, as Theodore Roosevelt called it—can cause destruction that may take a forest a thousand years to recover. So will doing nothing, allowing the vegetation to grow to such overcrowding that a fire will destroy everything, clearing the land just as thoroughly and destroying the forest for just as long.

All the plants in our forests continue to grow while we look the other way, not just the large old trees we all love, but also the grasses, weeds, brush and small trees that make an inevitable tinderbox of the entire landscape—dooming the large old trees, too. These landscapes are not static snapshots, because the trees keep growing. Our national forests produce eight times more *new growth* than managers remove every year. If the amount *grown* and the amount *removed* are not similar, no snapshot can be maintained; instead, the situation will worsen every year. That is exactly what is happening across vast landscapes of the American West—literally a tenth of the entire United States. Most people do not know how large our national forests are, so when they see forest fires on the nightly news, there is no context for understanding the magnitude of the problem. Thanks to the miracles of today's instant communication, people in New Jersey can watch California's unprecedented wildfires on TV, but do they really understand that the size of those fires equals more than the entire state of New Jersey?

America's 155 national forests cover an area as large as Connecticut, Delaware, D.C., Hawaii, Indiana, Kentucky, Louisiana, Maine, Maryland, Massachusetts, New Hampshire, New Jersey, Ohio, Rhode Island, South Carolina, Vermont, Virginia and West Virginia *combined*. These forests—just those owned by the public— cover over 223 million acres, nearly every acre covered with hundreds of trees and other plants. Believe it or not, that is the problem.

In their natural historical condition, the ponderosa pine forests in the western mountains grew in stands of 20 to 55 trees per acre, constantly kept in check by small natural fires. Today those same forests grow in densities of 300 to 900 trees per acre, and this overcrowding is not just an aesthetic problem—it is deadly for the forest and the wildlife that inhabits it. Worse yet, since these stands of trees often grew in the place of earlier fires or logging projects, they are almost all trees of the same age and species—one of the most unnatural and unhealthy conditions imaginable in nature. Think about a city where the entire population consists of people in their 70s and 80s, with every single person of the same race, size and appearance, and more than 60% of them sick and dying. Obviously that city cannot sustain itself much longer. That is exactly the condition of most national forests, and they cannot survive much longer in that condition, either.

If you are skeptical about this bleak picture, consider this: the U.S. Forest Service officially classifies more than 60% of the trees in our national forests as unhealthy, at risk, diseased, dead or dying. In many national forests that number approaches 90 percent. The same agency whose mission is to manage these resources for the public says more than 60% of its domain faces abnormal fire danger, including almost 90 million acres rated at "high risk" for catastrophic wildfires—an area larger than New York and all of New England. Agriculture Secretary Tom Vilsack, whose jurisdiction includes national forests, has said as many as 100,000 dead trees fall down every day, and will do so for the next decade. Yet his Forest Service Chief, Tom Tidwell, told an audience of Conservation Districts in July, 2011 that he is more worried about the future of private forest land than national forests, because private lands are more vulnerable to "development," and because private lands converted to commercial uses become more "fire prone." Ninety million acres of *national forests* are at risk of catastrophic wildfires, and the Chief is more worried about how *private* owners are managing *their* land? As a result of this lack of attention, the Forest Service and its huge team of professional foresters are doing almost nothing about it—not because they don't want to, but because they are not allowed to, as we will see.

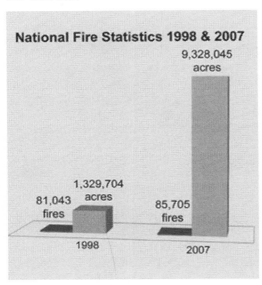

National Interagency Fire Center

As a result, right on cue, our national forests are dying and burning at a rate unparalleled in recorded history. Over the past ten years alone, wildfires have ravaged 68 million acres of our prized forests. That does not mean we have more forest fires than before (in fact there are fewer fires than there were in previous generations). But these fires burn unnaturally due to the overgrown state of the forest, burn far more acres than natural fires historically have, and are far more destructive. A comparison of wildfires in 1998 and 2007 demonstrates this difference; notice that there were almost the same number of fires, but those in 2007 burned nearly ten times the acreage of the earlier fires. During the 1960s, most years saw nearly twice that number of forest fires, but still burning only a fraction of the acreage common in today's wildfires.

Understand: today's massive forest fires are not natural. They are a direct result of two particular conditions—both manmade—converging at the same time to create the perfect storm. One is the absence over the past generation of any systematic thinning program. Logging was used for this purpose by forest managers for years, but not anymore. Logging in the national forests has plummeted over the past 20 years by an incredible 84%—from 12 billion board feet per year in the 1980s, to about half that amount in the 1990s, to about 2 billion board feet since 2007.

The second factor leading to these catastrophic and unnatural wildfires is the worst infestation of tree-killing bugs in history.

Ladies and Gentlemen: the Beetles

Billions of evergreen trees, covering millions of acres in a dozen states and 5 provinces, have died in the past ten years. They have fallen victim to a beetle smaller than a kernel of corn.

Mountain Pine Beetle Range: USDA

The pine, spruce and fir forests that cover the mountains from New Mexico to Alaska, dominating the Sierra Nevada and Rocky Mountains, are literally dying in front of our eyes. The infestation of bark beetles is like nothing ever before seen in the history of nature, turning the green mountains into rusty red jungles, interspersed with fallen timber and giant stretches of dead trees blown down like matchsticks by the wind.

At first, the epidemic was most prevalent in northern Colorado and southern Wyoming, though it has quickly grown all across the western half of North America. The spread of these beetles is also faster than ever seen before. In 2006 the Forest Service reported that there were a million acres of dead trees in Colorado and Wyoming, growing to 1.5 million acres in 2007 and over 2 million acres in 2008—literally doubling in two years. The 33-million-acre lodgepole pine forest that covers most of British Columbia and Alberta is now almost completely dead, as are millions of acres of Douglas-fir forests throughout the American northwest. One species of these bugs, called mountain pine beetles, look like a small black grain of rice. But their size belies their destructive capacity—they are rapidly killing virtually all the lodgepole pine forests in the Rocky Mountains. In Colorado that is 5 million acres—an area the size of the entire state of Massachusetts.

Residents of the hundreds of towns that populate the mountain west can see the result from their own windows. Home-owners from Vail, Colorado to Coeur d'Alene, Idaho are sur-rounded by forests of dead and dying pine trees. Entire moun-tainsides are now covered with the rusty red trees, their once evergreen needles now proof of a new death in the family. The first year the needles turn red, the second and third years the

Discolored needles show early infestation of bark beetles in Lodgepole Pines - USFS

needles fall off, leaving nothing but a forest of dead sticks where there used to be a blanket of green. The appearance of these dead and dying forests is evident to everyone who looks. But the dirty little secret, not so readily evident without further study, is that failed management by people—not nature—is responsible.

The beetles themselves are fairly complex creatures, and can be extremely effective killers. The beetle bores a hole through the bark of a tree and lays its eggs inside. When the larvae hatch, they eat the layer of wood right under the bark, which contains the most important nutrients for the tree. Trees have natural defense mecha-nisms against such pests. The trees respond to holes by moving sap to fill the hole, which can drown the larvae. Not to be outdone, these bark beetles inject a fungus to stop the movement of tree sap. As a second back-up system, the trees then emit a white waxy substance into the holes, which can simply trap the beetles in place and starve them.

In a normal, natural forest, the trees usually win this battle. Just enough trees will succumb to keep the beetles from becoming extinct, and to continuously turn over the tree population, but never enough to kill the forest. That is the balance of nature. That is the balance that mankind has interrupted.

When the beetles mate, and when they sense danger, they send out a signal (a scent) that attracts other beetles—literally calling for reinforcements. More beetles will then swarm into the same

Mass infestations of bark beetles
kill an entire forest
(Prescott National Forest, Arizonia)

tree, which simply cannot produce enough of the waxy substance to defend itself against overwhelming odds. Once a tree dies, it no longer produces the juice needed to grow larvae into adult bugs, so they move on to the next tree, then the next, with alarming accuracy, efficiency and speed. In the course of only a season or two, they can kill the entire forest.

An entire forest ecosystem, operating almost as one giant organism, also defends against such an infestation—if it is healthy. Trees can produce much more of the waxy resin and beetles lay exponentially fewer eggs, if the trees are stronger, healthier and spaced farther apart. There are two reasons for that. First, trees are stronger if they have more water, so when the forest is badly overcrowded and trees face more competition for water, they are weaker and more vulnerable and cannot produce the resin needed to fight the beetles. This is especially true during drought years, making thinning even more vital to the survival of these forests. Second, like all living things, trees are stronger and weaker at different ages. When the entire forest of trees is of similar age (as most are in our National Forests), the entire forest becomes vulnerable at the same time. So rather than perform their natural thinning function, the beetles simply kill all the trees at the same time. There is nothing natural about this event.

Once entire forests have completely
died, the resulting tinderbox
is a catastrophic fire waiting to happen

Forest managers have several tools for fighting this outbreak. On a small scale, for instance, tree owners attach "pheromone inhibitors" that confuse the bugs' sense of smell and thus hinder reinforcements from showing up. These are commonly used in orchards and tree nurseries to fight many different species of beetles, and they can also work in forests, though they are expensive on a large scale. Trees can also be sprayed with various pesticides and such treatments have been used very effectively, though also on a small scale. Spraying a back yard fruit tree is one thing, but spraying an entire forest of trees 75 feet tall is quite another. On a landscape scale, the cost is simply prohibitive, and in densely overgrown forests the spray often cannot reach the bottom half of the tree anyway.

Lodgepole pines grow at the higher elevations in the western mountains and they were the first trees to be hit hard by the beetle outbreak. But today the bugs have moved on into many other species, too. Ponderosa pines, which grow at lower elevations closer to the cities and towns of the West, are now infested, too, and are dying just as quickly, creating even greater danger that forest fires will destroy not just trees, but homes, too. Beetles also have moved into the white bark pines in the Northern Rockies and Pacific coast, and the spruce and fir forests across the Southern Rockies and Sierra Nevada.

The one thing managers can do on a landscape scale is to thin the forest back to its natural level of density, strengthening the remaining trees and returning a more natural condition that will recreate the balance of nature. We stopped doing that a few years ago, so the beetles continue unchecked in their Shermanesque march across the forests of North America.

Some foresters say this beetle plague will only be checked when severe winters bring temperatures of 30 below zero, which has not happened in several years in much of the Rocky Mountains. In fact there have been dozens of other natural cycles of warmer winters in the past, but never accompanied by swarms of beetles that killed forests the size of entire states. That is because during those earlier times, these forests entered warmer cycles in a much healthier condition than today, not with the dense overgrowth that has resulted from 20 years of continuous fire suppression with no harvesting or other thinning. When "experts" today say nothing but colder winters can stop the bugs, what they are really saying is that they do not plan to do anything about it. In fact, the Forest Service has a web page dedicated to the mountain pine beetle problem in the Medicine Bow and Routt National Forests, which states flatly that "this infestation cannot be stopped."

One environmental blogger recently posted this gem of an explanation: "Scientists have concluded warmer temperatures that reduce snow pack and prolong drought are killing forests." Even Forest Service Chief Tom Tidwell told Congress in March, 2012 that a warming climate is responsible for the severity of both the beetle outbreak and catastrophic forest fires. That is a good example of the extremes to which some activists will go to avoid any discussion of thinning—blaming the dead trees, at least by inference, on global warming. Clearly temperatures and snowpack levels did not *cause* this infestation of beetles, though they might make it worse. Even more incredible, some have argued that beetles are actually good for the trees. One University of Wisconsin ecology professor recently published a study claiming that by thinning forest crowns the beetles actually reduce the risk of fire—completely ignoring the elementary reality that dead wood burns more readily than green wood. Even the author admitted that the conclusion is "really counter-intuitive." In fact, it is just plain wrong, again glossing over the fact that the magnitude of the current beetle infestation is unnatural, whatever you think the impact on wildfires may be.

The point is that an almost complete lack of management led to this crisis, and thinning the forests to a more natural level would end it. Yet as we will see, today's environmental lobby would rather watch all our national forests die than entertain any discussion about allowing any tree to be cut anywhere. These are people who believe that to be pro-environment is to be anti-human activity. These are people who hate logging more than they hate dead forests. It strongly suggests that their agenda is driven mostly by an ongoing battle against the timber industry, and has little if anything to do with the health of our forests. Like so many of the "battles" that sustain today's environmental movement with membership checks and grant funds, it uses people's emotional attachment to their environment, but in the final analysis really does nothing to protect that environment. In fact, perhaps more with forest issues than any other, the environmental lobby's agenda is devastating the very environment it claims to champion.

Think about the alarming impact of large-scale forest decline on the climate, one of the favorite issues of environmental organizations. Trees are nature's most important storehouse of carbon dioxide. The death of billions of trees that normally *capture* carbon dioxide causes instead the *release* of carbon dioxide. Canadian Forest Service scientist Werner Kurz has estimated the beetle's devastation will release almost a billion megatons of greenhouse gases into the atmosphere by 2020, the equivalent of five years of emissions from all the trains, planes and automobiles in Canada. A study published in *Nature Geoscience* in 2010 showed that the great American "carbon sink"—Alaska—has now become a carbon emitter because of dead forests and large wildfires. Aside from the release of carbon dioxide, which is invisible, dying forests when they burn cause significant air pollution that is easy to see. The catastrophic wildfires in Colorado during one season alone (2002) produced more particulate pollution than all the fossil fuels burned in the city of Denver during the 20th Century.

On a more personal level, the impact is everywhere. Consider what people must do whose livelihoods depend upon healthy forests. For instance, the ski industry throughout the West attracts its customers by selling a world-class recreational experience in beautiful forested mountains. If the trees die the area is no longer beautiful, and it can even be dangerous. In Colorado and Wyoming, federal officials have closed 38 campgrounds over the past few years for fear of dead trees falling on campers. After clearing the trees they can re-open the campgrounds, though that often takes several years of budget competition—about half of those campgrounds remain closed today. At the Vail ski area, the ski company itself paid workers to remove dead trees throughout the resort (all on federal property) to avoid falling trees, and planted thousands of new trees at private expense. The resulting healthy stands of trees are a drop in the bucket, though, compared to the millions of acres in desperate need of similar restoration.

On extremely large landscapes, when the entire forest dies,

managers have little choice but to clear cut the trees, just as many communities are being forced to clear-cut large stands of forest to create "defensible space" for firefighters in case a catastrophic wildfire threatens the town. Such clear-cutting is, of course, exactly the kind of forest management we have always wanted to avoid. It is exactly the approach Roosevelt and Pinchot worked so hard to stop! The far better alternative would have been careful and judicious thinning when the forest was still healthy, to maintain strong trees that would be resistant to the beetles. Even after a beetle infestation begins and many trees start to die, removing the infected trees is still the best solution to save the remaining healthy trees (and the dead trees still have commercial value). However, that requires a chain saw—and it faces just as much opposition as cutting perfectly healthy trees. There is no difference to many of today's environmental leaders. John Muir once wrote, "God has cared for these trees, saved them from drought, disease, avalanches, and a thousand tempests and floods. But he cannot save them from fools."

Let Nature Take its Course

In almost every debate on restoring health to our national forests, opponents argue that we should do nothing. It has become conventional wisdom to the environmental lobby that mankind caused this problem by suppressing fires over the past century, and therefore returning fire to the landscape is the answer. These advocates argue that man is the evil cause of the bark beetle infestation because we caused global warming, and that fire is the perfectly natural response to that. Thus, their argument goes, people should stay out of the way and "let nature take its course." Nature, they say, will restore these lands if we let her. There is one major problem with that seemingly reasonable view—these catastrophic fires are *not* natural at all.

In a natural healthy forest, a natural fire will occur every ten or twenty years, started by lightning strikes. We know this because tree rings from centuries-old trees clearly show the minor damage left behind by these semi-regular fires. These fires burn the smaller material but generally leave the larger trees mostly undamaged. Such fires are low level, not very intense, and they have a restorative effect on the forest. They accomplish two essential purposes: they thin out the underbrush, weeds, grasses, small saplings and other plants that compete with trees for water; and the heat from these fires is necessary to germinate the seeds contained in pine cones. Thus, they also result in a few new trees every few decades to replace the few old ones that die and fall down, resulting in a forest that is not very dense (almost park-like), and that has trees of varying ages.

Katrina of the West

This natural condition is in stark contrast with the condition of most of our national forests today. When there is no thinning action—either natural or manmade—over long periods of time, there is nothing to check the otherwise rapid growth of the underbrush. This brush competes with the trees for precious water, weakening the trees and making them more vulnerable to beetle-kill, as we have seen. Even worse, it adds to the "fuel load" in these forests and creates what firefighters call a "fire ladder" that allows small natural fires to climb all the way up to the tree canopy and quickly become total disasters. These are sometimes called "crown fires" because they burn the tops of trees, not just the ground beneath them. The small natural fires in healthy forests burn roughly 10-20% of the material in a forest, but these giant crown fires create firestorms with heat so intense that they destroy everything in their path—often more than 90% of all trees and virtually all wildlife. They frequently send embers through the air that start new fires, sometimes leaping more than a mile away, which makes stopping them nearly impossible because they do not respect fire lines or natural barriers like rivers.

The Hayman Fire (Colo. 2002) was a catastrophic "crown fire"

The heat from these fires not only burns all the trees and wildlife, it even destroys microbes in the soil itself, and sometimes melts the soil into glass, making future growth of any new trees impossible for decades. If you have ever walked through the woods and felt the soft forest floor, almost spongy because of the thick layers of decaying leaves, needles and branches, you have an idea of how vital such soil is to the health of the trees it supports. It is a strange experience to walk through a completely dead landscape in the aftermath of these catastrophic forest fires and feel the ground literally shattering like glass under every step.

It is even worse to realize that this alarming condition is only the beginning of the terrible aftermath. These damaged soils not only cannot support new growth, they also cause mud slides and damage water supplies for years to come, sometimes on a disastrous scale. For example, the water supply of the city of Denver was in danger for several years after a massive 1996 fire that resulted in mudslides that filled most of Strontia Springs Reservoir. About 80% of the city's water supply passes through that reservoir, and the mudslide eliminated 3/5 of its water storage capacity. The Denver Water Department found that restoring the reservoir was a $20 million project involving over a decade of studies, reports, engineering and a complex question of what to do with enough mud to fill a large lake. That restoration project is finally underway, now at projected cost of $30 million.

90-percent fires like the one in Yellowstone National Park leave nothing still alive

These fires are not the exception in national forests today; they are the rule. Twenty years ago, any wildfire exceeding 100,000 acres was considered catastrophic and said to be proof of an unusually severe fire season. Today they are sadly routine. In 2002, Colorado braved its worst fire season in history (its four largest-ever fires all burning at the same time) and lost over 600,000 acres of priceless forests. Across the country the situation has become worse yet. In 2007 four of the ten largest wildfires of the decade burned within days of each other, each destroying over 250,000 acres. Altogether, the United States lost 9 million acres of forests to wildfires in 2012 alone—an area larger than Massachusetts, Connecticut, Rhode Island and Long Island combined. A similar 9 million acres had burned in 2007, 5 million in 2008, 6 million in 2009, 3 million in 2010, and over 8 million in 2011. And not a single home was built with all that wood.

If by now these comparisons between the size of the forests and the fires to the sizes of various eastern states may seem overdone, here is the point. Can you imagine the reaction of the heavily populated eastern states if a catastrophe of such proportions hit their own regions? Actually, you don't have to image it—we have seen it. Other catastrophes of similar proportions have occurred recently, with the entire world witnessing the reaction.

Consider how the nation responded when a major hurricane hit the gulf coast in 2005, devastating the city of New Orleans and much of the Mississippi coast. Hurricane Katrina was said to be the worst natural disaster in American history, costing over 1,800 lives and billions of dollars worth of property damage. Within two days disaster emergencies had been declared in two states; the National Guard was dispatched to the region and the president and numerous national leaders personally toured the damage (the president visited the area eleven times). Within four days Congress had appropriated over $10 billion in emergency money; another $52 billion was added two days later; eventually Congress would spend well over $100 billion. Within two weeks a top federal agency manager was fired; Congress held oversight hearings and created a special commission to investigate, and the president appointed a Katrina czar to oversee recovery efforts. Reports issued by the commission, Congress and the Administration were scathing in their criticisms of each other and their demands for reform to ensure such a thing could never happen again. For more than a year, Hollywood actors and Nashville musicians held fund-raisers and created new charities to help the victims, and the effort to rebuild continues to this day.

The reaction was similar in 2012 when New York and New Jersey suffered horrific damage from Hurricane Sandy, which killed at least 40 people and caused perhaps $60 billion in property damage and lost business. Freddie Mac and Fannie Mae almost immediately announced mortgage relief for homeowners in the area, just the beginning of an avalanche of government assistance that is still underway.

Interior Secretary Ken Salazar has several times called the death of national forests and the resulting wildfires the "Katrina of the West." There are, of course, important differences, but the comparison is apt in terms of scope. We can compare the California wildfires of 2007 to the size of the state of New Jersey, but if the entire state of New Jersey suddenly burned to the ground, the reaction would certainly be different—as it was even when a small part of that State was damaged by Hurricane Sandy.

Hurricanes hit all at once, while the death of the forests takes longer. But the resulting wildfires have killed more than 1,000 people and damaged billions of dollars worth of property—over a much larger geographic region and a longer period of time. The damage to these forests will require decades, perhaps even centuries, to recover. Yet Congress has not responded with massive emergency appropriations. A few million more dollars have been put into additional firefighting costs (compared to over $100 billion on Katrina relief), and even that has only happened because of the unrelenting efforts of a handful of Congressmen and Senators from affected States. There is certainly no rush by all the politicians to be helpful. There have been no highly-publicized hearings demanding to know who is responsible, and no calls for anyone's head on a platter. No agency chief has been fired, and no one has criticized any president as cold or uncaring because of it. The Hollywood elite may have noticed the destruction of a few of their own homes in the California wildfires, but actors and musicians have held no fund-raising concerts and established no new charities to aid the thousands of victims of our dead and dying forests. There have been no blue-ribbon commissions seeking to get to the bottom of this disaster, and the national media does not cover congressional hearings on the subject.

One type of natural disaster can garner a year of major headline news coverage and a massive national response. The other goes largely unnoticed. That is mostly because a hurricane happens one day, whereas the death of our national forests took a generation. It is nonetheless a disaster of similarly devastating proportion.

Cleaning up the Mess

Part of the problem with this large-scale death of trees across the landscape is that it presents such a significant clean-up problem. Of course, some still argue against doing anything at all, still trying to convince the public that the situation is natural, and that if left alone nature will eventually recover these forests. The trouble is that the dead forests present very real problems for today's generation of Americans. Consider the vast threat to watersheds and many city water supplies, and the unparalleled air pollution caused by catastrophic wildfires, as mentioned earlier. In addition, the dead forests cannot support the wildlife that historically relies upon this important habitat. As a result, we are seeing unnatural migration of many species—sometimes into lower elevation cities and towns—looking for food and water.

Paradoxically, many of the same groups that file lawsuits against the Forest Service to stop management activities also raise millions of dollars every year to "save" forest lands from development. They often cite the loss of habitat as a primary reason we must all contribute to save these important places from the ravages of mankind. Yet their own activities, to the extent they prevent forest managers from doing their jobs, actually lead to the massive loss of critical habitat. By creating the perfect storm, the deforestation their activities have caused is far worse than any ever caused by logging.

There are now hundreds of at-risk species whose forest habitat must be restored if we are to have any hope of saving them for future generations. The extremely rare Pawnee Montane Skipper, a yellow butterfly that lives only in a 23-mile by 5-mile stretch of river canyon woodlands, lost more than half its entire habitat in the 2002 "Hayman Fire." A decade later the butterfly's future remains uncertain. The fate of the Mexican Spotted Owl and dozens of other species is similarly imperiled by this habitat destruction.

The substantial cost to taxpayers is hard to accurately quantify. The costs of fighting catastrophic wildfires on national forests have more than tripled in the past decade, from just over $300 million a year in the late 1990s to over $1.5 billion today. Sometimes a single wildfire can bust the budget of a regional office of the Forest Service and its state and local partners. California's Zaca fire in 2007, for example, not only burned a quarter-million acres, it cost taxpayers over $100 million to put out. Congress has frequently had to add supplemental appropriations to the Forest Service budget to handle fires for which it did not—and could not—plan.

Dead trees also pose a huge risk to public facilities throughout the national forest system. The dead trees can become fuel for massive fires, but they can also blow down in windstorms, sometimes causing horrific damage. Dead trees will eventually fall over, but it is hard to know where. Thus, standing dead trees are a threat to hundreds of campgrounds and picnic areas, thousands of miles of roads and highways, power lines, trails and railroads. Keeping these facilities open and operational is a massive expense, and it is difficult to quantify because so much of it is paid by state and local governments, private companies and individuals. For example, state and local governments in some areas must clear a strip of 100 feet of dead trees along highways so falling trees do not close the road or, worse yet, land on passing cars. Utility companies and railroads have spent millions removing swaths of dead trees that threaten power lines, pipelines, and rail routes. Private homeowners must pay to remove trees to create "defensible space" in case catastrophic wildfires threaten to burn down their homes. Ski areas like Vail have been forced to finance the clearing of dead trees on slopes so steep that expensive helicopter logging is required.

Finally, we face a national dilemma about what to do with all the dead wood and brush. It can, of course, be seen as an asset because there are uses for some of it—just not on a scale even close to the trillions of dead trees spread across millions of acres in 15 states. Because we all but stopped logging on the national forests over the past 20 years, the number of sawmills has declined dramatically, so there are nowhere near enough mills to use the available timber. All over the country, entrepreneurs are working with government officials to find ways to use it. Several pellet plants have been built in various regions, which turn the trees into sawdust and then pack them into clean-burning pellets used in wood stoves. There is a growing market for the pellets, although the volume required cannot use but a small portion of the mass which must be removed from dead forests. Furthermore, investors have found it very difficult to make a profit on such wood "by-products" unless they also make at least some profit on lumber. And with new housing starts at historic lows since 2008, the price of lumber plummeted to the point where making 2x4 studs was no longer profitable in many areas, either.

Some byproducts are also being shredded for use in biomass boilers, which can generate electricity, steam and heat, so there is a promising future for some of the dead material in conversion to energy. This process is especially useful in reducing the fuel loads on national forests, because it can use not only large trees, but especially small-diameter trees, brush, bark, sawdust and other material that is otherwise mostly considered "waste." Still, biomass is not by itself a complete solution to the problem of miles of dead trees—including large ones.

Some creative carpenters have learned to make interesting furniture and other products from the beetle-killed pine, in spite of the blue stains the bugs cause. Companies make products from belt buckles to pens from such damaged wood. But however creative some of these "solutions" seem, they can never be more than a footnote in the forest health debate because of the volume. After all, a single large tree could produce enough belt buckles for an entire city. A few cities have begun encouraging building with dead, blue-stained wood. There are also some companies experimenting with such blue-stained wood to manufacture newsprint and other low-grade paper. They are finding, predictably, that the cost of extra bleaching makes the paper more expensive to make and therefore less competitive to sell.

All these problems leave very little doubt that the public must subsidize the restoration of the national forests. We are already doing so, of course, spending billions on fire suppression, fuel load removal, and other actions required by the death and decay of our forests. Would it not be far more efficient to treat the forests (thin the overload and restore healthy plants) than to put out fires and deal with the dead landscapes left in their wake? Top leaders in both parties have been saying so for several years, but Congress can only do so much against the well-funded environmental lobby. Agriculture Secretary Tom Vilsack, who oversees the Forest Service, toured the 2011 fires in New Mexico and Arizona—some of the 130 fires burning at the time—and told the press how important thinning these forests is:

I saw for myself the aftermath of the Wallow fire on a stand of trees that had been previously thinned in order to improve forest health. Where the Forest Service had worked to remove excess fuel, I saw healthy trees with burned underbrush. In the lands that were untouched by thinning practices, the fire left only scorched earth behind. It is clear that forest restoration work can make a significant impact on reducing the fuel for these fires. While it may not be possible to avoid wildfire, the best way to minimize impact of fire on communities is by managing vegetation and restoring the forests to healthier, fire-resistant landscapes.

Given that these forests are dead and dying across landscapes as large as entire states, the question is: if the leaders understand what needs to be done, why aren't they doing it?

One Size Fits All

Before the argument over what to do now can even get started, activists from all sides want to argue instead about what has gone wrong. How in the world did this happen? Whose fault was it? How could we have allowed the national forests to die, decay, fall down and burn up on such a grand scale? Why didn't we see this coming in time to stop it? Actually, some of us did.

Professional foresters have been warning Congress for years that there was a disaster in the making, and numerous organizations and communities throughout the West have been crying out for help. When I was president of Club 20 during the early 1990s, the group published a white paper called "Decline of the Aspens," which argued that Colorado's famous quaking aspen trees were disappearing from the landscape at an alarming rate. The report relied heavily on expert data from the State Forester's office, where officials were tracking the statewide death of the trees that give the Colorado Rockies their famous autumn colors. Club 20's members include Colorado's twenty counties and 75 towns west of the Continental

Divide, along with hundreds of businesses, chambers of commerce, non-profits and community leaders. Citing the lack of management by the federal government and the short life-span of aspen trees, the report showed how over a period of time the species was vanishing, replaced by stands of mixed conifers (spruce and pine species). It also pointed out the flawed reasoning of groups who opposed all logging, by explaining that aspen stands must be clear-cut in order to grow back. The report was immediately dismissed by environmental organizations as a biased argument from timber advocates, despite the fact that virtually all the research was from government experts, not timber interests. The press virtually ignored the debate, as the news media across the nation took little notice of similar reports being published elsewhere. Today there are entire books and treatises on what is now called "sudden aspen decline." There is, of course, nothing "sudden" about it, and these new books and white papers merely add credence and volume to the alarms sounded years ago by groups like Club 20 all across the West.

The environmental lobby and the news media have demonized the timber industry so thoroughly and effectively that when most people hear arguments about the need to cut trees they immediately react by visualizing the abuse of forests. David Brower led the charge against the lumber companies for two generations, first as the Sierra Club's first executive director (1952–1969), then as founder of Friends of the Earth and the Earth Island Institute, and finally as an active leader of the League of Conservation Voters and Earth First! (Clearly, one person can make a difference in this country.) Brower compared loggers to the Nazis during the holocaust: "Loggers losing their jobs because of Spotted Owl legislation is, in my eyes, no different than people being out of work after the furnaces of Dachau shut down." And he thought using resources from the mountains was the moral equivalent of sending troops to die in war: "While the death of young men in war is unfortunate, it is no more serious than the touching of mountains and wilderness areas by humankind."

A tool that has been especially useful to the environmental lobby is accusing the Forest Service of being "in the hip pocket of the timber industry." It is laughable to those who deal with the agency regularly, virtually all of whom say that the relationship has been more adversarial than not for at least 30 years. Yet facing this constant accusation, the agency feels the need to defend itself, and has typically responded to it by being especially careful not to rely on—or in some cases even consider—the opinions of those in the industry. Many of those industry people are among the World's most highly educated and trained forestry experts, whose opinions in fact ought to be considered seriously.

The public image of the timber industry went from benign to malignant fairly quickly during the 1980s and '90s. The public began viewing loggers as bulldozers, raping and pillaging the last of America's wilderness for quick profits. The shift in public opinion was aided by countless reports of environmental lawsuits and challenges, mostly portrayed as grassroots activists desperately trying to stop the mammoth corporations, sometimes at great apparent personal risk (think of people chaining themselves to trees, lying down in front of bulldozers, or sitting on platforms high up in old trees). These strategies very effectively portrayed timber companies as cold and uncaring, of both the forests and the people trying to "save" them.

There have been numerous abuses, though the worst examples have generally been on private lands, not in the national forests. Nevertheless, nothing helps environmental groups drum up support (along with membership checks and grants) better than a nasty enemy, and the timber industry became their favorite foe. Experience showed that certain logging practices could be painted as especially harmful, such as "clear-cutting" and logging in "old growth forests." Terminology like that is very effective, and most people are instinctively put off by such concepts. "Clear-cutting" just sounds wrong to most people, and of course in many areas, it is—some of the most abusive land management calamities in the past have been in that category. So the battle cries of the environmental lobby were "save the old growth" and "no more clear-cutting."

The result was that governments began to react to public pressure, as democratic governments are supposed to do. But the general public is not trained in the management of forests (most people are not scientists, and forestry is a science), and management based on political slogans is bad management. It assumes that one size fits all; that all trees grow the same way and all forests require the same decisions. That is pure nonsense, of course. Some forests are wet and some are arid; some are at high altitude and some at sea level; some are on rocky slopes and others on sandy plains. That means completely different species of trees grow in various forests, and managing them all the same way not only doesn't work—it is a death sentence for some, as we have seen.

Here is the problem with these simplistic slogans in the context of forest management. Some trees have a life-span of only 50 years; others can live to be 1,000. Thus, chanting "save the old growth" in a forest of aspen trees makes no sense, as there is no such thing as "old growth" aspen. With respect to clear-cutting, some trees will *not* grow back if they are clear-cut; others will grow back *only* if they are clear-cut. Thus, ending the practice of clear-cutting will help some forests, but doom others.

Aspens live only about 100 years, unless disturbed by fire, logging or some other phenomenon that destroys the entire stand all at once. The reason for that is not complex, but it is not understood by very many people. Put simply, an entire forest or stand of aspen trees, sometimes larger than 100 acres, is actually a single living plant—connected by a vast network of roots. Aspens come up from roots, not seeds, and when the entire stand is cut or burned or blown down by windstorms, it all grows back at once from roots, newly healthy and ready for another century. But if just a few trees are cut the roots do not respond in the same way, so no regeneration takes place. Thus, leaving these trees alone is the worst option of all, since in old age they give way to conifers and other stronger trees. Without active management, aspen trees will disappear from the landscape.

Other species of trees common to the national forests are completely different. For example, ponderosa pine trees grow from seeds enclosed in pine cones, not from roots, and each tree is a separate plant. Pine cones can lay on the forest floor for years, finally opening and depositing seeds when burned by small fires. But even the various species of pine and spruce trees are different in other respects. Some pine species will grow only in the shade, so clear-cutting makes regeneration impossible in such species. Others require direct sunlight, so selective cutting that leaves the largest "old growth" trees prevents new growth in those species. In other words, "old growth" is vitally important in some forest types, but not all.

One can study forestry for years before fully understanding all these details. The point is that forestry is complex, and requires careful management by trained professionals. That was the tradition of the U.S. Forest Service from the days of its founder, Gifford Pinchot. Pinchot was America's first highly-educated and classically trained forester. He created an agency where professionals trained in the field rose to the top based on merit, and where the forests were managed with a very long-term perspective. There is an old saying that it takes a great deal of character for a person to plant an oak tree, knowing that he will never enjoy it personally. It was one of Pinchot's favorite sayings, and the national forest legacy he left behind was based on that kind of future-thinking management. Sadly, Congress no longer permits the agency to manage our national forests from that long-term, science-based perspective. Responding to pressure from the environmental groups, reacting to the aftermath of catastrophic wildfires and juggling pressures from competing parts of the country, today's Congress (with considerable help from federal judges) has micromanaged the Forest Service budget to the point that science is completely eclipsed by politics.

Political meddling is among the greatest threats to the environment. It is, therefore, one of the favorite accusations of the environmental organizations when battling almost any government policy. Managers are almost routinely accused of trying to superimpose their political judgment on scientists, but in fact, that is precisely what the environmental lobby—and its friends in Congress, the media and the judiciary—has done. That is why the Forest Service cannot even come close to funding its timber management program, fuel reduction program, safety efforts or recreation programs. Congress has forced the agency to spend vast portions of its annual budgets on fire suppression, dictated where in the nation (in whose districts or states) it must spend its limited timber funds, and required enormous resources to be spent on reporting to Congress and defending lawsuits, rather than actual forest management. Indeed, the resource allocation within the agency does not come close to aligning expertise with need, because it is managed by political pressure and lawsuits, not science. And it is unquestionably the environmental lobby—not the timber industry—that dominates that process.

Now what?

If you have ever tried to put together a jigsaw puzzle without the picture on the box top, you know what it is like to argue about the tools of forest management without any concept of what the forest should look like. That is precisely what is wrong with the current debate about forest management. Slogans and sound bites still abound: "save the old growth," "no more clear-cutting," "below-cost timber sales," "in the hip pocket of the timber industry," and others. My personal favorites are "sustainable" and "appropriately sized." Many environmental leaders now say we should make sure forests are managed by an "appropriately sized" industry—meaning, of course, no big companies (as if a chain saw cuts the tree differently if held by a small businessman). And they support biomass energy facilities because those will help create a "sustainable" forest products industry. In other words, cutting trees to produce energy is "sustainable," but cutting trees to make lumber is not. That hidden agenda is not very well hidden. Forest management is more or less "sustainable" based on the level of clearing needed to manage the forest forever, not on what the final product of the trees will be, nor on whether anyone makes money from the timber.

The timber companies make a compelling argument about their importance to forest management, pointing out that clearing overgrown jungles requires both a timber industry and a market for the cleared material. They point out the dramatic loss of much of that infrastructure over the past few years (267 sawmills closed since 2000, causing 189,000 layoffs), and the historically low prices of forest products because the recession put the skids on new home construction. These factors combine, they argue, to make the timber industry largely unprofitable, and if the government wants to manage the forests into the future it must find ways to maintain a healthy industry.

On the other side, environmental groups continue to oppose any logging as a part of any solution, and push for other "newer" approaches to the problem. In most cases, they attempt to argue that the massive decay of the forests is natural, and we should let nature take its course (it is *not* natural, as we have seen). Faced with the political disaster caused by large wildfires destroying homes, and not wanting to be blamed for such a disaster, environmentalists frequently concede that forests should be thinned, but only in the "wildland urban interface" (WUI), sometimes called the "red zone." Those terms describe forests that are no different than any others, except that people have built homes in them. So in populous states like Colorado and California, the environmental lobby wants all the emphasis—and thus the funding—targeted to specific areas where there are many homes at risk, places where the city has encroached into the forest.

Both arguments miss the point by a mile. If we truly care about the environment, the issue is not the health of the timber industry, or the safety of homes. The issue is the health of the forest.

The point so many people seem to miss is that all trees and all plants continue to grow as long as they live, and eventually they die. A forest cannot be preserved in its current condition forever—no matter what managers do. So the reality is a very clear and simple choice that is never presented to the public, much less to elected officials. Forests must be thinned, or allowed to die, fall down or burn. Do we want logging, or do we want catastrophic forest fires?

Most people readily understand the need to prune rose bushes, mow grass and cut back encroaching vines and other plants to create a healthy landscape in their yards. The only difference in a forest is that the landscape is much larger, and trees are bigger than rose bushes, but the principle is the same. Like a lawn, a forest must be "pruned," and that can be done by logging or by fire, but if ignored, it will die. A "natural" forest condition can be maintained over time with responsible and active management. That includes thinning of small-diameter brush, logging of some trees, replanting in some cases, low-level prescribed fires in some areas, and an expert management that knows when and where to use which. But that cannot be done without careful use of all those tools, including logging. Viewed properly, logging is merely a management tool (like a gardener's hoe), not worthy of the emotion and vitriol it invokes.

The crocodile tears shed by some environmental leaders over the "loss" of a logged forest are disingenuous, at best. Ironically, they respond to the destruction of forests by wildfires by re-assuring everyone that this is natural, and the forest will recover naturally. Yet if a tree is cut, they pretend outrage, claiming the tree is lost forever and the forest will never recover. Of course, the truth is that careful thinning preserves a green forest much better, and no "deforestation" by any forest manager or timber company has ever come close to the devastation of a giant catastrophic fire. That is why the discussion cannot be just about logging or fire—it must be about the healthy condition of the whole forest.

The right approach to this discussion must begin with an understanding of, and an agreement on, what the forest should look like at the end of the process, like the picture on a puzzle box. Once people agree on the desired condition, then policy-makers and stakeholders can work backward on how best to get from here to there. On the other hand, if they continue to argue first about which tools to use and where to use them, they will never get to the discussion about the picture on the box.

Returning such a forest to that natural condition must begin with an agreement that this is what it should look like when the project is finished. Then, an agreement would soon follow about how much brush and how many trees should be removed, and which ones should be left alone. That would probably include trees of varying ages, in order to guarantee long-term sustainability. If the argument is about logging versus not logging, it becomes very emotional. But if the discussion is about how many live trees, of what ages and conditions, and in what spacing, should be left, the decision is less emotional and easier. Again, if we begin with a clear understanding of a healthy forest, and not political issues, we may just end up with a healthy forest. Why is that so complicated and difficult?

Analysis Paralysis

When F. Dale Robertson served as Chief of the Forest Service (1987–1993), he had high hopes for tackling the problem head-on. He worked hard to put professional foresters back in charge, and to implement forest health restoration projects across the nation.

He found the same frustrations other foresters find, and began to sound the warning that the national forests suffered from a dramatic "outbreak of trees." In numerous speeches he talked about what he called "analysis paralysis," a process so thoroughly dominated by interest groups, lawsuits, court orders, congressional hearings, budget earmarks and other hindrances to good management, that decision-making had become almost impossible. Every agency chief since then has attempted to solve the same problems, and all of them have run into the same buzz saw—a system that puts process ahead of results. It is the reason the agency has almost stopped trying. One recent chief tried to lower the bar, saying "We want to under-promise, then over-produce." Predictably, under his leadership the agency under-promised, then under-produced—when you set low expectations, you get low performance.

A generation of Americans should have seen these recent wildfires coming, but the truth is that too few people understand the science of forests. Most of us are not biologists, or horticulturists, or silviculturists, or scientists of any other sort. Yet many Americans take great pride in having very strong opinions about forest management, much to the detriment of the forests.

This process-obsessed system has caused good management to grind to a halt in two ways. First, it slows decision-making to a near standstill because of challenges and appeals. Second, it dramatically raises the cost of operating the Forest Service. One of the most ironic aspects of this dilemma is that the Forest Service cannot *afford* to remove the overgrowth of trees, a bizarre paradox because those trees have tremendous commercial value. For decades the agency made its own budget by selling the trees it needed to have removed from overgrown forests, regenerating sustainable forests while making money.

In recent years the overblown process with which we have saddled forest managers has added so much to the cost of management that the sale of trees no longer pays for management of the forests, even if the environmental groups all agreed to stop challenging timber sales. Today's leaders should give serious thought to the alternatives—if there are no sawmills left to harvest trees, or the cost of doing so becomes prohibitive, the government will have no choice but to *pay* for the removal of this overgrowth, rather than *being paid* to allow it. We are dangerously close to that outcome—timber sales are on a competitive bid basis, but today the average timber sale in the U.S. receives barely 2 bids and dozens of sales are offered that receive no bids at all. How will the government manage forests if there is no customer left? That is the dilemma created by the high costs of this process.

As we will see, these high costs were created on purpose by a well organized and funded "environmental industry" determined to stop logging by altering the economics. The success of that strategy prompted Congress to begin demanding an end to "below-cost timber sales" in the 1980s. Forest managers were told they should not use the traditional timber sale process to clear overgrowth if it cost more to offer a sale than it produced in revenue. Since nearly all timber sales were in that category, the tactic has nearly driven the last nail into the coffin for healthy forests. Today, the average cost of timber sales attributed by government accountants includes only 40% for preparation of the sale (marking trees in the field, creating the required documentation in the office), 10% for administrative oversight, but 50% for compliance with required environmental processes. In other words, half the cost of timber sales is attributed to these imposed costs that have nothing to do with trees.

Even with such processes in place, environmental organizations are rarely satisfied that timber sales can proceed in a responsible manner to restore forests. They continually argue against cutting "old growth" or "destroying critical habitat," even though the agency can and does structure timber sales to protect those very values. For instance, in recent years western timber sales more often proposed selective cutting of smaller-diameter material, while saving the right mix of larger and older trees. Still, the challenges and appeals continue. In some parts of the country, virtually every single timber sale offered by the agency is challenged by environmental groups, despite the managers' best efforts to comply with all the required rules. A Google search for "timber sale appeals" produces over 95,000 hits; a search for "timber sale challenged" produces over 25,000 hits; "timber sale stopped" finds another 42,000 hits.

A few representative headlines from recent newspapers illustrate the non-stop battle waged against forest managers across the country, trying to do their jobs:

- Forest Service Drops Challenged Timber Sale (MT, 2-6-09)
- Officials Cancel Logging Project Near White Sulphur Springs (MT, 2-6-09)
- Conservation Group Files Lawsuit Over Timber Sale (AK, 3-5-09)
- Appeal Challenges Timber Sale North of Grand Canyon... (AZ, 4-1-09)
- Timber Sale Challenged Over Owl Habitat (MT, 4-17-09)
- Timber Sale Challenged (MT 10-23-08)
- Salvage Sale Stopped, at Least for Now (OR, 6-30-07)
- Judge Blocks Timber Sale in Mt. Hood Forest (OR, 3-7-07)
- Injunction Halts Two East Oregon Timber Sales (OR, 12-9-08)
- Rio Grande National Forest Timber Project Appealed (CO, 6-2-09)
- Timber Sale Appealed in New Mexico National Forest (NM, 9-7-11)
- DU Law Students Block SW Colorado Logging Permit (CO, 2-10-12)
- Federal Judge Explains Decision to Block Seeley-Swan Timber Sale (MT, 7-12-12)
- BLM Timber Sales Targeted by Lawsuits (OR, 9-1-12)
- Giant Sequoia Timber Sale Blocked (WA, 11-15-05)
- Logging Protesters Continue to Block Reedsport Timber Sale Site (OR, 7-7-09)
- National Forest Timber Sale Challenged (OR, 5-7-12)
- Groups Challenge Timber Sale Near Lake Keokee (VA, 6-27-12)
- Pair of Owls Used to Challenge Oregon Timber Sales (OR, 10-15-10)
- Conservation Groups File Legal Challenge Against Timber Sale (OR-1027-10)

Keep in mind that every one of these sales, and the hundreds more that were challenged, appealed or blocked in recent years, were subject to rigorous environmental regulations and went through a long and tedious process before being offered for sale. Further, once offered, such timber sales are made on a competitive-bid basis, and carefully overseen by agency managers throughout the process. Nevertheless, Forest Service Regional Offices annually report huge volumes of timber sales that cannot be cleared because they remain under appeal. In 2008, the largest region (based in Montana) said more than 1/5 of all its offered volume was under appeal and on hold.

After the 1991 "Red Star Fire" burned over 10,000 acres west of Lake Tahoe, the Forest Service tried to sell some of the dead trees to stimulate re-growth (requiring helicopters, not new logging roads). Yet challenges and appeals by the Sierra Club and five other organizations delayed the project so long (a federal judge finally ruled against the Forest Service after 13 years, in 2004) that the trees had rotted away and become worthless for timber anyway. The government spent millions of tax dollars on the litigation, but in the end, did not sell a stick of wood.

If the process is so badly flawed that timber sales cannot be used to help clear the overgrowth killing our national forests, then clearly we ought to fix the process. It now slows timber sales and other management practices to such a snail's pace that the agency cannot begin to keep up with the progress of bark beetles and other factors that destroy the forests faster than managers can restore them. It is impossible to escape the conclusion that these groups have some agenda other than restoring healthy forests.

Save the Dead Trees!

Congress has tried more than once to authorize the Forest Service at least to restore lands already burned by catastrophic wildfires or already dead from bark beetles. Reasonable leaders can certainly see the wisdom in clearing these giant tinderboxes before they ignite and burn. Once they have burned, it is easy to justify the need to restore the devastated watersheds and wildlife habitat.

Unfortunately, the obstructionism continues unabated, even in such seemingly "no-brainer" circumstances.

Forest managers know that in the aftermath of fires, blow-downs, and beetle outbreaks, the dead trees still have value. Bark beetles leave the dead wood horribly stained a blue-gray color. That makes the wood unsuitable for some purposes, but it does not generally weaken it structurally, so timber companies can still make joists, studs and other building products from it. Similarly, trees killed by forest fires can still be very valuable. Although black and dead, they often still have a core of solid wood with undiminished structural value that can be salvaged. Timber companies still bid on such sales, called "salvage sales," and the Forest Service can still make money on them, even though the price is somewhat lower. That is, unless legal challenges add so much to the time and cost that the sales become unprofitable. Sadly, that is often the case.

In an especially poignant article published in the *Sacramento Bee* (July 12, 2008), a professional forester named William Wade Keye wrote about the aftermath of the Angora fire in South Lake Tahoe:

> ... *The dead trees, debris and rubble are cleared from the devastated neighborhoods. New homes are sprouting from the earth to the tune of contractors' blaring rock music, hammers and nail guns. Lumber to sustain the rhythm is being transported from Canada, Oregon and Washington. Dozens of structures are rising in a cacophony of recovery and new life. It's all taking place within the afternoon shadows cast by the thousands of dead trees that remain standing on adjacent national forest lands. Although seared and killed by high heat, inside their charred bark is unburned wood, light and bright. Yet despite this volume of usable fiber, these cellulose skeletons will never be tapped to help build a single structure. Rather, the trees killed by the fire will be left to rot, under assault by insects and fungi, as the U.S. Forest Service plans and plans, and then plans some more, about what to do in the aftermath of last year's disaster. It doesn't want to get sued, having lost the will to fight against environmental activists and their attorneys. Dead trees maintain value for several years while still standing, until eventually they fall and rot away. During those few years,*

though, the government can sell the trees, recover or plant stands of new trees, and accomplish restoration of a healthy forest—if it can move quickly enough. Congress has authorized the Forest Service to do so.

Healthy Forest Restoration Act

Because of the national concern about dying forests, and partly because of George W. Bush's personal interest in the issue, Congress passed the "Healthy Forest Restoration Act" in 2003. The goal was to streamline some of the legal processes that were delaying the government's ability to clear overgrown and dying forests. The Act contained several provisions to speed up hazardous-fuel reduction and forest-restoration projects on specific types of federal land that are at risk of wildfire or insect and disease epidemics. It was signed into law with great fanfare, signaling a new era for professional management of the national forests.

The new law declared a national goal to thin overgrown forests and clear away enough brush and trees to create shaded fuel breaks. It provided funding and guidance to reduce "hazardous fuels" in national forests, improve wildfire-fighting capability, and research new ways to halt the destructive progress of bark beetles. The new law also sought to protect at-risk neighborhoods by requiring that communities within the "wildland urban interface" create "wildfire protection plans," defining the defensible space that must be thinned or cleared to keep wildfires from burning directly into those areas.

The results of this new landmark legislation have been—almost nothing. The hotly debated bill was finally passed with bipartisan support, but it did not succeed in solving the environmental lobby's opposition to any role for private logging companies in thinning stands and clearing fire-breaks. Their agenda is more about the timber companies than the forests, so these groups not only continued their opposition, they stepped it up.

The new law created a way for the Forest Service to streamline its process by declaring a "categorical exclusion" for salvage and restoration projects, eliminating the need for a complex and time-consuming "environmental impact statement" to be written. However, as soon as the agency tried to use this new process, the Sierra Club, Natural Resources Defense Council, Wilderness Society and several other groups filed a major lawsuit. The suit stopped the process for three years, and predictably, the 9th Circuit Court of Appeals threw out the new procedure, calling the categorical exclusion "arbitrary and capricious" (despite the fact that Congress had debated it for a year, then explicitly and deliberately authorized it).

The forest restoration effort remains as deadlocked today as before the new law was passed. The result is that our forests continue to die, fall down and burn, and the agency we expect to do something about it has both hands tied behind its back. In one highly-publicized 2009 case, the Supreme Court actually ruled against the "standing" of environmental groups to file lawsuits against timber sales unless they could show specific harm to themselves from a specific sale. One environmental official involved in the suit, reacted by saying, "We're obviously disappointed that the court issued a ruling that allows many of these Forest Service decisions to go unchecked by the public." He and others have so often portrayed themselves as representatives of "the public" that they may actually have come to believe it. But in a democracy, the public gets to decide who represents the public. That means Congress and the president, not self-appointed activists elected by and accountable to no one, especially those who refuse to disclose their membership or funding sources, as we will discuss in Chapter 8.

In spite of this push-back from the Supreme Court, "environmental industry" opposition to forest management has been so thoroughly successful that in many cases the forest managers do not even attempt large-scale thinning operations, because experience has taught them to expect a lawsuit that they will probably lose. An article published by the National Center for Policy Analysis highlighted one such outcome in an area near Storrie, California. A wildfire struck there in 2000 and burned more than 55,000 acres, including 52,000 acres in two national forests (Plumas and Lassen) and about 3,000 acres on private land. It is a perfect case study of the problem of "analysis paralysis," because the same fire hit both private and national forest land. As the authors (Lani Cohen and H. Sterling Burnett) pointed out, the difference in the way the acres of burned trees were treated afterwards speaks volumes. In the Lassen National Forest, only 1,026 acres were cleared and 230 acres replanted. In the Plumas, only 181 burned acres were reforested.

By contrast, on the privately owned land, managers "reduced wildfire by removing 30,633 tons of dry material, enough to fuel 3,600 homes for a year. They harvested enough larger dead trees to build 4,300 homes, and they spent millions of dollars to reforest burned land and increase the number of different tree species. Virtually all of the privately-owned acres have been replanted or restored, while only 2.2% of the national forests have been treated at all. For five years the government pursued its case against Union Pacific Railroad for accidentally starting the fire, and settled for over $100 million in damages. The money was to be used for restoration projects in those two forests, although by that time most of the dead trees were no longer useful.

Even though Congress and the president have specifically authorized and directed the Forest Service to thin over-crowded or already burned lands to reduce fire risk, environmental appeals and lawsuits have delayed and limited the ability to carry out restoration plans, increasing wildfires and reducing the ability to fight them by limiting access.

Tool Time

If we want to save our great national forest legacy and pass it along to the next generation "increased and not impaired in value," as Theodore Roosevelt admonished, we need to get busy. We must put professional foresters back in charge and give them the tools they need to restore health to the forests. And we must hurry—we may not run out of time, but the forests will.

First, the long-running emotional war against the lumberjacks may motivate some people to write checks and join organizations, but it does nothing to help the forests. Reducing the overgrown jungle of brush and unhealthy trees clogging our forests requires two things: a market for the resulting products, and people who know how, and are willing to do the work. There is no need to worry about the former, unless you foresee a time when nobody needs wood or paper. But the latter is a very real concern. It will become virtually impossible to thin and restore forests if there is no one left with the equipment, plant, distribution network and infrastructure to do so. That does not mean forest management decisions should be made for the purpose of maintaining the industry. Rather, it emphasizes the need to start with a clear puzzle-box picture of the end result, and working backward from that, to contract with the industry to get the job done. We do not maintain an Air Force for the purpose of keeping airplane manufacturers in business, but we could scarcely have an Air Force without those companies. In the same way, logging is not the mission of the Forest Service, but it cannot fulfill its mission without loggers.

Second, a Forest Service budget problem desperately needs fixing. The problem is not so much the *amount* of the budget, but the way it is structured and funded. There is no other federal agency expected to handle unforeseen natural disasters within existing budgets, yet the Forest Service must pay for fire suppression every year within its existing funding—even though there is no way to anticipate the number of fires, their location or their severity. Over half the agency's budget is now spent fighting fires. Imagine if the Federal Emergency Management Agency (FEMA) had been expected to handle the aftermath of Hurricane Katrina within its existing administrative budget. FEMA cannot anticipate hurricanes during its budget process a year earlier, so Congress was quite willing to add a "supplemental" $100 billion in that case. But the Forest Service rarely gets "supplemental" funding at all, and when it does the amounts are small. So instead, the agency must address catastrophic fires by pulling money from its existing budgets for restoration, timber management, fuels reduction, recreation and other line items routinely funded. In 2008, for example, the fire fighting budget was $1.2 billion, but when the fires were worse than expected, the agency had to transfer over $400 million from other programs (Congress later restored some of that 2008 funding, but in most years it has not done so). Some members of Congress have tried for several years to separate fire funding permanently into a separate budget from the regular Forest Service budget. At best, those efforts have been only partially and temporarily successful.

There is another, perhaps even more insidious, problem with the Forest Service budget process. In the National Park Service, Congress funds a budget broken down by parks, but in the Forest Service the budget is allocated by program. In other words, in the Park Service's budget a member of Congress can look at the annual charts, see how much money is allocated to Yellowstone or Grand Canyon or Yosemite. Within those parks, there is further delineation for capital improvements, ongoing maintenance, new trails or campgrounds and other specific programs. By contrast, in the Forest Service budget Congress is not shown how much money is requested for the Gunnison, Medicine Bow or Bitterroot National Forests. That agency's budget allocates funds for specific programs—capital improvements, maintenance, trails or campgrounds, fuels reduction, fire suppression or timber sales—not by individual forests. Thus, no member of Congress can really tell (without major research) whether forests in their states are getting adequately funded. One result is that when a massive outbreak of bark beetles is centered in the southern Rockies, Congressmen and Senators cannot readily check to make sure the agency is appropriately targeting funds to that region.

Unfortunately, that process is an invitation to back-room lobbying by communities or organizations with a special geographic interest. As a result, during the eight years of the Bush Administration the forest plans for the northwest region (WA, OR) were fully funded, while forest plans in the Rocky Mountain Region were never fully funded. It is the reason there have been almost no timber sales over the past decade on some forests, while others have met all their "targets" or goals for timber sales. Clearly, if individual members of Congress could see whether their districts were faring adequately, the distribution of funds would be overseen by a more public and accountable process.

Third, the Forest Service should be run by professional foresters, not political appointees, judges or special interest groups. Science should be the basis for decision-making and whenever we substitute the judgment of federal courts or interest groups, the forests suffer. In addition to these external influences, the agency has also been populated with employees with varying agendas. Management by—and promotion of—trained foresters was a long-standing tradition in the agency until recent years, but today its employees are much more varied in their training and education: biologists, engineers, teachers, statisticians and others. Every Chief of the Forest Service has held forestry degrees, usually graduate degrees, except Max Peterson (appointed by President Carter) and Mike Dombeck (appointed by President Clinton). But it is an almost-universal concern among long-time professionals in the agency that new hires and promotions continue to go to people not trained in forestry. An agency whose mission is so specific should give specific weight in the personnel process to those trained in the discipline. Just as all agencies must give special consideration to veterans, the Forest Service should also give special consideration to applicants with forestry degrees from credible forestry programs. Politicians and their appointees should set the policy parameters and appropriate the funds, but foresters should implement them on the ground. Finally, Congress should rein in the ability of federal courts to make decisions on the management of forests, decisions for which federal judges are most certainly not trained.

Lastly, leaders should continue their current focus on developing new products and markets for the material that badly needs to be removed from the forests. Energy produced from "biomass" shows especially promising potential, and there are many products being developed to use wood chips, sawdust and other byproducts. Especially during tough economic times when the market for wood products and building materials is soft, such other markets could mean the difference between success and failure in the effort to restore health to our national forests.

One tool for reducing the political difficulty of such efforts is a growing use of the term "certified," which simply gives consumers a way to know that forest products they use were produced in a sustainable way, using standards designed to restore forests, not destroy them. There are "certified" building materials available in many markets, and there are a growing number of "certified forests" from which such products are taken. It is a very appealing strategy, and could be used more extensively, as a way to re-assure the public of a pro-active agenda based on healthy forests. If many national forests were certified in that manner, the volume could be turned way down on some of the most contentious forestry decisions, and this would provide the public with a way to support healthy forests directly with their consumer dollars, rather than giving to environmental groups whose agendas are less transparent.

The tool is so effective that there is now a raging controversy about who gets to decide what forests will be certified. A number of groups that combine conservationists, industry representatives, and governments are currently certifying forests as sustainable. Participation is voluntary, and the market for certified products creates strong incentives for better forest management. But one heavy-handed organization called the Forestry Stewardship Council (FSC, based in Germany) is trying to become the required standard—resorting to threats of boycotts and regulatory mandates to ensure that it gets all the money and power associated with being the keeper of the worldwide standard. The problem is that there is no common standard for determining what is sustainable and healthy in different climates and different forest types. A blatant attempt to establish a monopoly on certification, and to substitute mandates for voluntary compliance and consumer choice, illustrates perfectly how the environmental industry is actually hurting the environment. Certification requires payment of fees, and monopoly always leads to higher fees. Such money and power would be a boon to the FSC, but a significant disincentive to forestry companies already on the edge of economic viability.

America's national forest policy ought to be "green sustained-yield management" forever. Building a wall around our forests to keep out all people and all activity clearly does not work. That strategy has proven to be a death sentence for forests. But it cannot be replaced by the opposite strategy of cutting anything and everything from anywhere—the 19th Century proved that does not work either. If we get off the debate about process and quit arguing over which tools to use, though, we have a chance to refocus the entire debate on the condition of the forests—where it ought to be. Neither side today can claim success against that standard, but it is the way forward.

Is This How We Will Be Remembered?

An ancient philosopher once wrote that forests precede civilizations, and deserts follow. In ancient times, that was usually true because people needed the wood and simply cut everything they needed until it was all gone. But it does not have to be true in our generation. We know how to manage forests to sustain their yield and their beauty forever. We are failing miserably in that great task and we must get our act together while there are still great forests to be preserved and protected. Theodore Roosevelt wrote that "the nation behaves well if it treats the natural resources as assets which it must turn over to the next generation increased, and not impaired, in value." He and his contemporaries willed to our generation a great legacy of national parks and forests. But the forests we are turning over to the next generation are not increased in value; indeed, they are dead and dying. Our society in recent years has made a dreadful mistake in stopping all professional management, abdicating our responsibility to the future. Rather than assessing blame, we should fix the problem while there's still time.

CHAPTER 5

COOL, CLEAR WATER

"Water projects are the grease gun that lubricates the nation's legislative machinery. Congress without water projects would be like an engine without oil; it would simply seize up."
— *Marc Reisner, Cadillac Desert*

Congressman Wayne Aspinall once said that "In the West when you touch water, you touch everything." Today, it is the fitting inscription on a national memorial dedicated to the long-time Chairman of the House Interior Committee. He was not only right about the omnipresence of water politics, and the affect of water on everything else, but also about the uniqueness of water issues to the West.

The arid states of the American West developed, over the course of a century, a complex and distinctive system of laws to make scarce water available to human inhabitants, laws that seem peculiar to people in the green parts of the country where it rains often enough to negate the need for such laws.

To people whose communities are surrounded by rivers and oceans, the idea that a person might guard water rights as fiercely as the land itself may seem strange. Many even think it strange that a person would actually need to "own" water, or that the land itself may be worthless without "water rights."

Yet in the very Constitutions of nearly all the western states, a simple provision is found: if a person diverts water from a natural stream and puts it to beneficial use, he has acquired a property right, and may not be stopped. In most of those states, the only major exception is "unless someone else got there first." Because most western streams do not contain enough water for every need imaginable in the future, water courts "appropriate" the waters of the state to specific users, based on the "priority" of who was there first.

This "doctrine of prior appropriation" (first in time, first in right) is unique to the arid West, which simply could not have become home to millions of Americans without it.

Perhaps some people make too much of the differences between East and West on certain issues, but when it comes to water, we are almost like two separate countries, one brown and one green. In the East and South, water is regulated on a completely different set of principles than in the arid West, and the gulf of misunderstanding between the two is a metaphorical Grand Canyon. Many national leaders simply do not understand, and consequently do not support, the need—the absolute necessity—for water rights to be viewed as property that is owned by individuals or businesses.

To most people, the movement of water seems fairly simple. It falls from the clouds onto the land, flows to the sea, is evaporated into the clouds and falls again, creating an endless cycle that every school child learns. In current politics, the relationship of mankind to the water is mostly about water quality: we must use the water in ways that do not diminish its value to others, and in ways that do not endanger our health.

Maintaining the purity of our water supplies and eliminating pollution is important everywhere. But in much of the American West, issues of water *quality* are far less daunting than the nearly-insurmountable challenges of water *quantity*. An adequate and affordable water *supply* means the difference between life and death in the western half of the country, and owning older and more senior water rights literally conveys the power to control—even to wipe out—business, industries and even entire communities.

Leaders who seek to understand and succeed in the politics of the West must understand the politics and importance of water. A few harsh facts help explain why water is so dearly held and so controversial in the West:

- 90% of the water on Earth is too salty to be available for human use.

- Another 5% is locked in polar ice and glaciers.

- An additional 3% is in the form of clouds at any given time.

- That leaves barely 2% of the Earth's water available for use by all the plants, animals and humans in the world.

- Of that miniscule amount, more than 80% is found in the world's major river systems: the Nile, Amazon, Yangtze, Mississippi, Congo, Ob, Mekong, St. Lawrence, Volga, Zambezi, Rhein and a handful of others.

- Thus, the percentage of the Earth's water found in the arid states west of the Mississippi is not even statistically measurable.

For many parts of the West, the situation is even more complex. The water supply dilemma in Colorado helps illustrate the problem common to most of these western states:

- 80% of the state of Colorado's tiny annual water supply comes in the form of snow, mostly within a four-month period. Colorado is sometimes called the "rooftop state" because all of its water flows out of the state in eight small rivers—virtually none flows in from other states.

- Although there are almost five million people in the state, there are more than 100 million people in 14 other states that are at least partly dependent on water that originates in Colorado.

- Ten states even have legal claims that require Colorado to deliver portions of its water to them, further limiting its own ability to grow.

- Colorado does not have enough storage capacity, in all its combined reservoirs, in any of the eight river basins, to store the water to which it is entitled under these interstate agreements, so every year the state loses much of its own water because of the inability to capture and use it—even during severe droughts when water is rationed.

- Finally, as if those facts were not complicated enough for Colorado water providers, there is one more cruel reality: 80% of the state's water falls on the Western side of the Continental Divide, while 80% of the people live on the Eastern side.

For the people in the arid Western states, there will never be an end to the political battles over a much-too-small water supply. And those battles will never really be about the amount of snowfall, which we cannot control, but about storage and diversion, which we can. Western states must capture and store their limited water supply during the few months when the snow is melting and running toward the oceans, or there simply won't be any during most of the year. Put simply, westerners must store water during wet periods to live during dry periods. These arid regions cannot sustain life—much less prosperous businesses and fast-growing metropolitan cities—without water storage. This is, understandably, a difficult concept for national leaders who are not from the West. The five-mile stretch of the Potomac River in Washington, D.C. contains more water than the entire 7-state, thousand-mile length of the Colorado River and all its combined tributaries.

Since the late 1970s and President Jimmy Carter's infamous "hit list" of western "water projects," many people have viewed such projects as pure political pork, the bargaining chips of politicians in an obsolete era, perhaps even the historical precedent to today's scandalous "earmarks." Dams and reservoirs are now considered taxpayer-funded boondoggles that not only cost a fortune to build, but also cause significant damage to the environment. The latter is a debatable point, but it is beyond dispute that the West would not be inhabited like it is today without the reservoirs, tunnels and pipelines that bring water to its cities. Without water projects there could not be 5.1 million people in Colorado or 6.5 million in Arizona. There most certainly would not be over 38 million people in California without the Colorado River Aqueduct and a dozen other major water supply projects.

To be sure, many people, including me, wonder only partly in jest whether the West is improved by all these people. Like most natives of the region, I remember fondly the time when towns were smaller, life was slower and we had no traffic jams or long lines. As a fifth-generation native with deep roots in the mountains of Western Colorado, I do not think my home state has been improved by the mass migration of several million people who escaped the cities, only to create an equally-frustrating rat race in the mountains. Like most Coloradans, if I could go back in time and be involved in the political battles of the early 20th Century, I would probably oppose all the trans-mountain water diversions that allowed the extreme growth along the Front Range. Nor do I think there should be any similar giant water diversions in the future. I completely understand the common desire to stop the growth and keep these communities the way they are. But that describes a utopian world we are not privileged to inhabit.

The reality with which today's leaders must contend is that the arid Southwest is the fastest growing part of the United States—the huge desert region completely dependent upon the already-overused Colorado River. The fastest growing state in the nation in 2010 was Nevada. According to the Census Bureau in 2012, five of the ten fastest growing states in the nation are in the Colorado River Basin (Nevada, Arizona, Utah, Wyoming, and Colorado,). Americans continue to migrate from the large cities of the Northeast and Midwest toward the South and West. Of the 20 largest cities in 1950, all but four have actually lost population, some of them dramatically. Detroit, Buffalo, St. Louis, Cleveland and Pittsburg have all lost *more than half* their former populations, while America's fastest growing cities are places like Austin, San Jose, Phoenix, Dallas, Las Vegas, Denver, and Salt Lake City.

In short, Americans have developed a love affair with the Southwest, and in a free and mobile society there is precious little we can do to stop them from moving there. That enduring truth is the reason water has always been, and will always be, the principal political issue of the West. The challenge for real leaders is how to supply the water needed for prosperous communities in a manner that is environmentally responsible. The challenge is not new, but the magnitude of it is truly without precedent.

Making the Desert Bloom, or Not

Early conservationists believed it was their obligation to make uninhabitable places livable. They believed, as John F. Kennedy articulated in his inaugural address, "that here on Earth, God's work must truly be our own." They developed confidence in the American ability to build water projects on a scale massive enough to change the entire Great Plains, once called the "Great American Desert," into the "breadbasket of the world," and to alter the livable environment of the entire American Southwest. "Make the deserts bloom" became a sort-of national calling for conservationists, so that moving water from great distances to bring agriculture and civilization to arid lands was more than just one item on the agenda—it became synonymous with conservation.

Conservation leaders throughout America pursued water projects as a means for both restoring degraded environments and improving public health. For several generations of conservation pioneers, advances in agriculture went hand in hand with access to clean and plentiful water. One notable example was Cason J. Callaway, a Georgia textile magnate and friend of Franklin Roosevelt, who spent many productive retirement years improving agricultural sciences, preserving Blue Springs and other important watersheds, and founding the famous Callaway Gardens. His work in creating modern agribusiness programs was inextricably linked to restoration and improvement of water systems, and it was often said of Callaway (only half jokingly) that he tried to dam every stream in Georgia. It is beyond dispute that when he died in 1961, he left Georgia better than he found it, and like many of his contemporary conservationist colleagues, his legacy (still carried on faithfully by his family) will far outlast even his famous name in the fleeting memory of the public. The same is true of water leaders throughout the West, who struggled for years to create the giant water systems that make today's cities possible. History has already forgotten most of their names, but millions benefit from their work.

Sadly, today's water leaders spend far more time defending their existing facilities than envisioning creative and environmentally responsible ways to store more water. Reservoirs and water storage have been so vilified by the environmental lobby that they are not generally considered an option in addressing future water needs. In fact, when Bruce Babbitt said he wanted to be the first Interior Secretary "to tear down a really big dam," he was criticized by very few western leaders. On the contrary, he helped further popularize the perception of dams as ecological criminals, intentionally driving yet another nail into the coffin of future water storage projects.

He helped create today's conventional wisdom that human use of water is bad for the environment. Consider that this television ad is among the most effective draws for tourism in Michigan: "Water.

We take our showers with it; we make our coffee with it. But we rarely tap its true potential and just let it be itself, flowing freely into clean lakes, clear streams, and along more freshwater coastline than any other state......" Note the clear message that taking showers and making coffee is bad environmental policy.

Today, even across the arid western states, no more than a handful of new storage reservoirs are even planned. New reservoirs have become so unpopular that they are rarely proposed and when they are, the public instinctively reacts suspiciously. In the West water projects are, more often than not, viewed as a threat to the existing order. A 2003 plan to create a simple financial mechanism for funding new water projects became so thoroughly unpopular in Colorado that it was defeated on the ballot in every single county, and became a campaign issue against candidates (including me) in three consecutive election cycles. The measure did not authorize a single water project—it was merely a funding mechanism. Still, a century of history gave people in Colorado good reason to suspect the worst: that someone might eventually use it to build trans-mountain diversions to "steal" water from one basin and move it to another. So the proposal went down in flames at the ballot box and the result was, probably for another generation, no new water storage at all.

Similarly, in the race for alternative energy, hydro-electric power is rarely even mentioned, and not because it is un-renewable. Flowing water is more readily renewable than almost any energy source, and like the sun and wind, gravity is free. Nor is it because dams inevitably destroy fish migration routes; modern technology can solve the problem of fish passage around dams, and virtually all the other environmental issues associated with dams. It is simply because most Americans no longer view dams, reservoirs, tunnels, aqueducts and pipelines as necessary, much less as part of the future solution to growth problems.

If You Don't Build It, They Won't Come

Since the early 1970s environmental leaders have labored under the delusion of one very simple but remarkably powerful fallacy: if we refuse to provide the infrastructure needed for growing populations, we can stop the growth. "If you don't build it, they won't come," or so the theory goes. However, in a free and mobile society, that strategy has never worked, and it never will. Americans do not have—and do not want—any legal authority to tell people they are not allowed to move to desirable places. So like it or not, they move anyway, and then they require services like transportation, communications, food and water. Sooner or later, those services will be provided because this is a democracy and majorities eventually get what they demand.

To be clear, the arrogance of some people frustrates all of us, including people who build their home in the middle of the wilderness, then expect paved roads that are plowed in the winter, redundant fiber optic cable loops, police and fire protection, electric, water and sewer services. In such circumstances, taxpayers ought to say emphatically no. But to ignore the growth of major metropolitan cities and pretend it will go away if ignored long enough is foolhardy and futile, and therefore irresponsible.

In 1975, Colorado Governor Richard Lamm was so concerned about projected growth south of Denver that he led a campaign against building the city's beltway. He officially took a major segment out of the Interstate highway system and held a press conference to "drive a silver spike through the heart" of the project, saying it would foster urban sprawl. Of course, in the end, the sprawl occurred anyway, so a generation later three-fourths of the Denver beltway was completed (at exponentially higher cost). The last segment is still not built, and may never be, to the everlasting frustration of commuters frozen in the very gridlock Lamm sought to avert. Anti-growth activists all over America today can be counted on to oppose any public works project on the same theory, despite absolutely incontrovertible proof that lack of infrastructure does not keep people from moving where they want to move.

The reality is the same with water as with highways, power lines and communication systems. Delaying construction of the Central Arizona Project for more than 20 years after Congress authorized it did nothing to keep Phoenix from doubling in population during that period. Nor did the EPA's 1989 veto of the proposed "Two Forks Dam" keep another million people from moving to Denver since then. In fact, the entire "hit list" of water projects killed during the

Carter Administration did not cause even the slightest downward blip in the relentless migration of Americans to the South and West. Does that mean all these water projects were well-designed, responsible and visionary efforts that should have been built? Certainly not. But any discussion of water issues must at least begin with the underlying premise that water must be provided where people live—failing to provide the necessary infrastructure does not stop or control growth; it merely prolongs the inevitable, making solutions more difficult and more expensive. That is not leadership.

Conservation

Every discussion about water—in the East, West and everywhere—ought to begin with the essential foundation of conservation. Intelligent leadership on the issue presupposes that we use whatever water we have in the most efficient and responsible manner possible. The public should not be required to spend public funds on unnecessary water projects. Water should never be diverted from its natural stream in order for wasteful people to squander the precious resource. That principle seems obvious enough almost to go without saying. But it must be said, because water conservation is subjective, elusive and impossible to define.

From 2001–2004, several western states endured the worst drought in 500 years (we know that from tree ring analysis). Several major cities, including Denver and Cheyenne, implemented water rationing for a time, and the eastern plains saw wind and sand reminiscent of the 1930s dust bowl. The flow of the Colorado River was only about a third of its long-term natural flow, less than half of the flow during the 1930s. People in my home town were photographed walking across the river with their shoes on—unimaginable in prior generations. Worst of all, the drought of 2001—2004 resulted in all-time low water levels in many of the major reservoirs used to store water for such dry periods. Some of those reservoirs are still not filled to capacity again.

As Ben Franklin once wrote in Poor Richard's Almanac, "When the well's dry, we know the worth of water." Faced with a complete shut-off of the water to whole communities, and especially to hundreds of miles and thousands of acres of farms and ranches, water officials turned every stone and examined every means for saving limited water supplies. In Colorado we plowed entirely new ground in water conservation and established several principles that will benefit future generations.

For example, one quirk in western water law prohibits people from capturing and using rain water that falls on their roofs, because another water user downstream may own water rights that are "senior" to (older than) the upstream user who might otherwise save rainwater. Every individual homeowner could capture precipitation in that manner, but very few of them actually own water rights. So if an entire city of people did that, they could effectively "steal" a substantial amount of water owned by downstream farmers, and the law cannot permit that. During the drought, though, several of the large cities in the Denver area found they could capture wastewater for use and reuse, without harming downstream farmers by releasing other water the cities owned in upstream reservoirs, and letting it pass downstream to the farms. Such water "exchanges" allowed huge amounts of water to be conserved without the need for protracted legal procedures to buy, sell or trade water rights. Today, such water exchanges are commonly used all over the West as a more efficient means for moving water from one place to another without harming anyone.

To many people the idea of water conservation means low-flow toilets and shower heads, watering lawns a little less often, or even xeriscape landscaping. Such measures are second-nature to many conservation-minded Americans. That has not always been the case, and retrofitting entire cities with such modern technology is expensive and disruptive. It took Denver 20 years to accomplish it, and many cities are still in the process. Despite the difficulty and expense of such measures, they are a mere "drop in the bucket" in terms of saving water. Conservation on a larger scale—way beyond shower heads—is needed in much of the arid West. And getting people to live within their means is as difficult with water as with finances.

Weaning California

No conservation issue in my lifetime was more difficult—or more important—than the effort to wean California from its over-use of the Colorado River. It was an epic saga involving dozens of water leaders from 7 states and the federal Interior Department, debated for 10 years, which resulted in the most significant water conservation agreement since the original "Interstate Compact."

A brief background helps explain the difficult situation they faced. Within a few years of the settlement of the West in the mid-19th Century, it became obvious that the Colorado River and its tributaries could not support unlimited growth in all seven states that depended upon it. It took until 1922 for those states to reach an agreement—called the Interstate Compact—on how to divide the waters "fairly." The river was split into two halves, Upper Basin and Lower Basin, each entitled to half the annual flow of water. A later agreement divided the Upper Basin waters, half to Colorado and the other half to Utah, New Mexico and Wyoming. The Lower Basin States of Arizona, Nevada and California divided the water mostly according to population, meaning California got the lion's share, a much smaller portion went to Arizona, and almost none to Nevada (there were very few people in Nevada in 1922). But a complex part of that agreement that would come back to haunt everyone 80 years later, was the definition of California's entitled share. It included a specifically defined amount of water each year, *plus* any unused portion of Arizona and Nevada shares, *plus* any surplus water in the system during wet years.

"Surplus water" and "wet years" had never been officially defined, but it did not matter for many decades because there was always extra water from the Arizona and Nevada allotments. So California continued to grow unchecked, and it became dependent not only on its entitled share of the Colorado River, but another 25 percent—another million acre feet of the surplus water each year. But by the 1990s, when the Central Arizona Project completed a huge aqueduct to Phoenix, Arizona finally grew into its entire allotted share of the river. At the same time, the legendary growth of Las Vegas had resulted in Nevada using its entire share, and it was in dire need of more water itself. Neither state had any unused portion anymore. However, Colorado had never grown into its own entitled share and used about a million acre feet less than its entitlement. That meant California was using Colorado water (Lower Basin using Upper Basin water), a complete violation of the Interstate Compact—*unless* there was surplus water in the system because of exceptionally wet years.

That means every proposal to use any additional water in Colorado became a direct threat to existing uses in California, and for the first time in history, California badly needed a clear definition of the term "surplus." That was a legal hook the Upper Basin states had never had before, so they insisted on a water conservation plan to limit California's use of the river to its entitled share. But after so many years of already-existing uses, California simply could not reduce its use of the river without enormous expense and difficulty. So as a means of accomplishing the task, the Upper Basin states agreed to artificially declare "surpluses" while California ratcheted down its use of water, as long as certain measurable milestones were reached during a ten-year phase-in period. It was at times difficult, funny, sad, painful, nasty, statesmanlike, optimistic, pessimistic, futile, promising and rewarding—and in the end it worked.

It would be difficult to overestimate the difficulty of that effort for California water leaders. When the process began, southern California agriculture was almost entirely based on open-furrow irrigation, often in 120-degree desert summers. Almost the entire Imperial Valley had to be retro-fitted with gated pipe, concrete ditches, drip watering systems, and other expensive conservation measures. Even more difficult, they had to impose on a 100-year old system a legal means to quantify water rights. This was especially difficult for Upper Basin water leaders to understand, because in most of the West a water right can only be decreed after it is carefully shown how much water will be needed, for what exact purpose, in what exact location, and for exactly what duration. But several of the largest and oldest water rights in the California system belonged to large irrigation districts (not individual farmers), whose water rights decreed "such water as they in their judgment may require"—in other words, with no legal incentive whatsoever to conserve or use their water wisely. Forcing quantification on century-old systems was an enormous burden, requiring foresight, leadership and sometimes brutal political battles. Several times, California officials had to ask the other states for more time, but the others held firm, with rock-solid support from Interior Department officials in two Administrations. The final adoption of the California water conservation plan in 2003 was widely hailed as one of the great accomplishments in water conservation history. That requires, of course, that California continues to meet all the required milestones, and some Imperial Valley irrigators are already threatening to cancel the required water exchanges, which could re-open the entire deal again. That's proof that in the West water issues will never be fully resolved.

Changing the Incentives

The California experience underscored one of the central tenets of environmental policy. We can all come together and work on projects to increase the supply of water to growing populations, but that requires one prerequisite: people must use the water they already have as wisely as possible because the public can never be expected to pay for additional projects so water can be wasted. The incentives in quirky western water laws always had that intent, but not always that result.

In confronting the 2001–2004 drought, western states ran up against this cold reality in the form of an issue we called "conserved water rights." The plain language of the law provides that no one ever has the right to "waste" any water. That means when filing for water rights, the amount of the right is determined by how much can be put to beneficial use, and not one drop more. So if a farmer's water right provides enough water to irrigate 100 acres, that amount is predetermined. But if it can be shown that a farmer saved water by installing drip water systems, he is deemed to have been "wasting" any water that is saved. In other words, he has no incentive at all to upgrade water systems, because if he does he will lose some of his existing water right.

Especially in a drought cycle, western water rights have huge economic value, so if farmers could save water by upgrading their systems, others (especially growing cities) would happily pay for the cost of the upgrades—and purchase the saved water, sometimes at a very high price. But in the early stages of the drought, courts began to rule that farmers could not sell such "saved water," because they never legally owned it; they were "wasting" it, which no one has a right to do. Thus, our difficult political question was: how can we expect farmers to be more diligent and conserve more water at their own expense, especially if they can be cheated of the right to either use or sell the saved water? Why would they do that? Paradoxically, how could we eliminate that disincentive and allow such saved water to be sold, without repealing the vitally important prohibition against wasting water? This is not merely a philosophical exercise. Nearly 90% of all water in the arid West is used in agriculture, so even a little agricultural savings can provide a great deal of water for cities.

The solution was imperfect, but the legislatures in several states ultimately adopted provisions that allowed "saved water" to be sold, without it being considered "wasted" if it could be shown that the previous irrigation practices were common and accepted practice for the region. As a result, tens of thousands of farms across the West have been able to modernize their water systems and free up vast amounts of water for growing cities— without the worse alternative of cities simply buying out the farms and eliminating agriculture. Some states still have not updated these old laws, so there is still work to be done.

Another fascinating and creative tool Colorado developed was the use of conservation easements on water rights. Conservation easements are now in common use nationwide as a means to preserve land against future development. Landowners sell their "development rights" to a third party (a non-profit land trust or a government agency) and their deed is then restricted against the ability to subdivide, build houses or otherwise change the essential character of farms, ranches and natural areas. For the public, the advantage is in preservation of open space that we all value. For the landowner, this tool offers the ability to be compensated with the one thing it needs most—cash—by restricting his own land use without having to sell out to developers. There is no good reason the same tool cannot be used to preserve water rights on farms and ranches.

In many western regions, water rights are worth at least as much as land, and in many cases much more. It is hard to second-guess the wisdom of a farmer who sells his water rights to a thirsty and growing city for more money than he could ever hope to earn farming. It is a particularly difficult choice for farmers whose children have careers in the cities and no desire to take over the family farm. Yet in spite of the desperate need for water in many western cities, most residents think drying up farmland to gain the water is a long-term mistake. So Colorado reasoned, if society wants the farmers to hold out and refuse to sell their water rights to the cities, why shouldn't we pay them for that decision, just as we often pay them to decide against selling the land itself. Especially where the water is worth even more than the land, doing so would help the farmers stay in business better than anything else. In the case of land, a farmer can either sell a conservation easement for cash, or for tax credits, and because so many farms do not have a tax liability problem, legislatures have allowed such tax credits to be sold for cash.

All the same advantages should apply to water, if we really want to preserve agriculture and open space in the arid West. Thus, the Colorado legislature in 2003 explicitly authorized the use of conservation easements to save agricultural water rights, though several years later the idea is still considered experimental and few people have tried to buy or sell such an easement—yet. It is an idea whose time is surely coming, however, and should be considered wherever growing cities threaten to dry up agriculture.

There are other examples around the country where incentives can and should be changed to make sure the law is aligned with public goals for the 21st Century. Water conservation is essential to the future, and all efforts to facilitate "exchanges," system upgrades and efficiency should be encouraged. Old laws that discourage efficiency ought to be updated.

Water conservation ought to be the beginning of all water supply discussions in the West, but it can never be the end. Growing metropolitan areas simply need more water than can be supplied merely through conservation. It remains as crucial as ever that we store water during the wet years for use in dry years, and in most of the West, the current storage capacity is still considerably less than it could be. In Colorado, Western Slope residents will always feel threatened by any discussion of new water storage projects, because they know the population (and the money) is mostly centered across the mountains in Denver. But in fact, the Front Range also has the capacity to store much more of its own water, and use and reuse that water much more productively. There is a need for more water storage in every single river basin in the West, including all eight of the major basins in Colorado. And here is the blunt truth about east-west politics inside a state like Colorado: as long as the Front Range remains short of water, Western Slope water will always be threatened. The only long-term answer is to provide the population base with the water it needs, and that can be done without taking it away from anyone.

Federal Water Rights

If the most obvious threat to water in the rural West is trans-basin diversion to the big cities, the most insidious and perhaps more dangerous threat is the growing enforcement of a relatively new concept: federal water rights. It is a potential threat to water in both rural and urban areas, similarly onerous for both farms and growing cities.

The evolution of this issue is a good example of how initially well-meaning environmental protections have been twisted in recent years to suit the agenda of today's "environmental industry." When the public lands were first "reserved" by Congress to remain in public ownership forever, the intent was clear. These lands were to be preserved for the use and enjoyment of future generations, and managed in a way that allowed fair access to the resources for the current generation. The National Forest system, for instance, was created in 1897 "to improve and protect the forests" for two specific purposes: "to secure favorable conditions of water flows, and to furnish a continuous supply of timber."

It was well understood that if greedy people denuded the forests of all the trees, they would kill the ability to produce wood for future generations, *and* they would degrade the quality of water flowing from those forests. So the federal agencies were to manage the public lands to guarantee the availability of wood and water.

Early leaders in the West built reservoirs to store the spring runoff in the high country, which resulted in many reservoirs, ditches, pipelines and other water supply systems being built on federal land. They did so for two important reasons, as valid today as ever. First, at higher elevations closer to the original snowmelt the quality of water is higher, and the cost of water treatment is lower. The farther downstream water flows, the more minerals and pollutants it picks up, increasing treatment costs. Second, at high elevations considerably less water is lost to evaporation because it is colder. Thus, capturing and storing water is best accomplished high in the mountains, and that frequently means on federal property. That is one of the original purposes of the national forests, specifically discussed in the original legislation creating those forests. Yet today, municipalities and water districts across the West often find themselves at odds with federal land managers intent on regulating water for the benefit of the land, not the people—as if the two are mutually exclusive.

The "Ditch Bill": Enforcing Common Sense

For example, consider the continuing saga of the "Ditch Bill." It evolved from a series of disputes in which the Forest Service attempted to require permits for the owners of existing reservoirs and ditches on federal land to maintain or repair those water systems. In many cases, the government even tried to extort from the owners a portion of their private water rights in exchange for the permits. Owners argued that the reservoirs and ditches had been there for decades—many of them predate the existence of the national forests—and people have a right to maintain their property. And they were outraged by the agency's attempt to take part of their private property, a clever ploy the Forest Service called "bypass flows," meaning the water owners would be required to let part of their water "bypass" the ditch and remain behind in the stream—in exchange for a permit to maintain or repair a dam, head gate or ditch. In other words, the federal agency in effect says, "we'll allow you to repair and maintain your private property—if you give us part of it." To be clear, these are not cases where the government owns any water rights, just the land across which the ditches or pipes flow. The water rights and the ditches are private property. Since these water systems are vital to the survival of farms and ranches, since they fail to work unless properly cleaned and maintained, and since the Forest Service remained absolutely intransigent on the issue, Congress finally stepped in to resolve the matter.

The direction from Congress was clear—the Forest Service was to acknowledge existing ditches by issuing permanent easements, allowing maintenance and access as needed for operation, and the agency was given 10 years to work through the process once and for all. Specifically, the "Ditch Bill," passed in 1986, required the Forest Service to issue permanent easements for water conveyance systems that existed before 1976, if the owner requested the easement by 1996, as long as a valid water right exists under state law. It was intended to provide for continued agricultural irrigation in spite of other land management decisions, even wilderness designations. The latter became part of the congressional debate, and legislative language was included clarifying that maintenance on ditches that crossed wilderness areas must be "consistent with" *both* wilderness management *and* maintenance of the private easement. That simply meant that ranchers and forest managers should use common sense, and if possible try to maintain ditches without building roads or using motorized vehicles.

However, the environmental lobby, predictably, seized on that language as a means for slowing the process and declaring that simple dam repairs would be a "disaster" in wilderness areas. (Ironically, under the original Wilderness Act, areas should never be designated wilderness that contain dams, reservoirs, ditches or other structures built by people.) After all the debate, Congress determined that the farmers were right, and provided crystal clear direction.

Ranchers hailed the bill's passage as a victory for private property rights, expecting the years-long debate finally to end with an understanding that they had a right to keep and maintain their property. But in the world of environmental politics, nothing is ever simple. By the 1996 deadline, the Forest Service received 2500 requests for the easements, but a decade later had "processed" and issued only 300 of them. In 2004 the agency finally got around to issuing direction to its local managers on how to deal with the matter, though even today almost 40% of all the easements have still not been issued. That may be because although the law clearly exempts these easements from NEPA "analysis and review," the agency has mostly ignored that direction citing other laws, published lengthy analyses, and attached government-dictated operating and maintenance conditions to the easements.

This paralysis of federal land management agencies is not entirely their choice, and it is not an accident. It is a creation of the U.S. Congress. Congress alone can be blamed for creating the contradictory laws about who is in charge of water. In many instances Congress has made clear that water management is a function of state, not federal law. Yet it has also created federal reserved water rights, without a requirement that they be filed under state law, and in other instances Congress has plainly disclaimed the existence of such federal water rights. Congress passed a series of laws granting easements across federal lands for roads, rails and water systems. When those laws were repealed in 1976, Congress explicitly recognized the continued validity of all easements already granted under the previous laws. Yet Congress has also complicated that simple "grandfather" clause by acknowledging and tolerating administrative moratoria on the processing of old easements. Congress has passed some wilderness bills that included federal reserved water rights, and others specifically disclaiming such federal rights. It has taken action to release some claims, but held fast to others. Congress instructed the Forest Service to grant ditch easements, and gave it a deadline, but did not act when the deadline passed without a solution (and part of the delay was because of pressure from individual Members of Congress). Congress exempted those easements from NEPA, but not from the Endangered Species Act.

Congressional reaction to the mishmash of conflicting laws is all over the map, too. During angry hearings senators have alternately berated federal managers for asserting federal control over water, and for not doing so. Congress cannot have it both ways, and by trying to do so has created resentment and economic disruption across the West. We badly need a clearer understanding. One current senator has introduced legislation declaring all water in the United States to be federal property. It has not yet seen the light of day in any hearing room, but perhaps the outcome will eventually be the same, with Congress and federal agencies steadily chipping away at interstate agreements, state water laws and private water rights.

A Bigger Cistern

None of these issues would be nearly as difficult or contentious if there were an unlimited supply of water, of course. It is precisely because there is never enough that people must constantly wrangle over who is in control. In most of the U.S. there will never be enough water for an easy consensus, so much of the debate centers on how to better use the limited water we have, and how to get as much additional water as possible.

The wonders of the human mind and the advance of technology offer numerous ways to increase and improve the water supply. The arid West badly needs more water storage, as we have seen. But that does not necessarily always mean more new dams and reservoirs. There are several other approaches to new storage.

In California, some of the largest new reservoirs "built" in decades are actually not stored behind a dam on any stream, but underground. Students of geology know there are many underground rock formations that create "bowls" where water can be stored, places where an underlying rock layer is impermeable but topped by a layer of porous rock like sandstone, where water can be pumped underground and will stay in place until needed. That requires a bowl-shaped formation with no cracks, so water will not flow anywhere, and believe it or not there are lots of places like that (small and large) all over the country. Today's leaders should be investigating that possibility, using resources like the U.S. Geological Survey and its state counterparts to map not just the surface of our lands (most of which has been done), but its underlying structure. Manmade underground holes, especially abandoned mines, can also be used for water storage and several states have begun to do that. Water stored underground does not require dams, does not interrupt stream flow or fish habitat, and is not lost to evaporation.

Thousands of existing reservoirs can store more water than they do, including nearly *every single one* in the arid west. In many cases reservoirs no longer hold their original capacity because they fill with silt over time. In other cases their water level must be lowered or restricted because the dam is in need of repair. In Colorado alone, 176 dams are restricted from their full capacity because of dam safety issues. Nationally, more than 4,000 dams are considered structurally deficient. The Association of State Dam Safety Officials estimates that it would cost over $36 billion to rehabilitate all of those. However, when you consider the additional water storage that is possible without the need for new reservoirs, repairing existing dams may be considerably cheaper than building new ones. And in the case of existing dams, the political fights have already been waged and settled, so repairing and rebuilding is much easier than starting over in a different place.

Existing reservoirs can not only be filled to capacity, but in many cases can be enlarged considerably cheaper than the cost of new construction. One method for enlargement is adding height to the dam and in many cases it is feasible to do that. In far more cases, the structure can be enlarged by dredging the bottom deeper. In thousands of existing reservoirs, merely removing silt that has been deposited since the original dam construction can return a far greater storage capacity than what is left today. In many other instances, even the original floor of the reservoir can be deepened significantly, depending upon the geology. Leaders should also be carefully studying these options, to ensure that we are using all the storage capacity we have already paid for, conserving water to the maximum extent possible without new construction.

Pulling at the Roots of Demand

Before adding more capacity for storing the limited water in our rivers, we should explore ways to increase the amount of water flowing there. At the top of the list throughout the West is an invasive, non-native plant species variously known as tamarisk, tamarix or salt cedar. The plants were imported into the West by well-meaning settlers who liked the attractive color of their wispy spring blooms, and their rapid growth that helps inhibit erosion. However, no one anticipated how effectively they would spread across virtually every river system in half the United States, nor was there any understanding of how much water they consume. These trees grow more like dense shrubs, more than 20 feet tall, and form a dense thicket that chokes out virtually all other plant life, and they also poison the ground with salt that kills other plants. Tamarisk spreads both by roots and by seeds, which are borne on both wind and water. Worst of all, they are a "smart plant," with abilities to

Tamarisk lines the banks of the Colorado River near Grand Junction

protect and sustain themselves that few other species possess. Those who seek to control its spread, or eliminate it, are thwarted at every turn. Tamarisk sheds so many leaves and needles that it increases the frequency and intensity of wildfires that kill other plants, while tamarisk growth is actually stimulated by fire. Property owners today have learned that when a tamarisk tree is cut, it must also be sprayed with deadly herbicide within 5 minutes, because it can seal the wound almost immediately to protect its roots, which will sprout again very quickly. Thus, it has become one of the most difficult of all non-native species to control, and that is the beginning of one of the nation's most insidious and least known water problems.

Tamarisk is among the planet's thirstiest plants. Its tap roots extend down to 100 feet and can lower water tables and dry up entire springs, wetlands and riparian areas. A single tamarisk tree can drink more than 200 gallons of water per day (more than double what most people use), and they often grow in stands of over 3,000 trees per acre. Put another way, every acre of tamarisk can consume more than 330 Olympic-sized swimming pools every year. That is as much water as if an acre was flooded 4.5 feet deep every year—enough to supply a town of 1,500 people. And tamarisk now covers nearly 2 million acres of river and stream banks.

There are numerous efforts underway to control, and even try to eliminate, tamarisk from the rivers of the West. The Tamarisk Coalition was founded by Tim Carlson in 2002 and now includes representation from 17 states, 2 Canadian provinces, Mexico and several tribes. The group has raised national awareness of the magnitude of the problem, and made great progress in organizing the eradication effort, as well as adding to the body of scientific knowledge of the species. Its efforts ought to be better funded as a national priority, if only from a water perspective.

Simple math shows that if tamarisk could be completely eradicated from American rivers, the effort would actually be the largest water project in history. Consider the raw numbers. If there are 3,000 tamarisk trees per acre, covering almost 2 million acres of river banks, that is 6 billion tamarisk trees. If they consume 200 gallons of water per day each, that is 1.2 trillion gallons of water every day. If replaced by the native cottonwood and willow vegetation (which in their natural density consume less than a fourth as much water), roughly 75% of that water would remain in the rivers—nearly a trillion gallons *per day*. That is twice as much water as the entire United States uses domestically each day—clearly enough to supply the needs of thirsty cities *and* the environment.

The all-too-predictable response of national leaders to the discovery of the magnitude of the tamarisk problem has been to study it more. Legislation passed by Congress in 2003 was typical of the Washington mindset; it provided millions of federal dollars to universities with researchers, instead of companies with chain saws. Leaders actually should view the removal of tamarisk, Russian olives and other non-native plants in the context of a giant water project, one that could be quickly funded and successfully implemented without the political battles that accompany new dams and reservoirs. Most environmental organizations actually support removal of non-native species, so there is not a great deal of controversy about it. What generates controversy is funding, and turf. No agency thinks it is its job.

Congress ought to decide whose job it is, and provide the funding, along with clear direction. The Bureau of Reclamation was created for the purpose of building dams, power plants and canals to bring water to cities and farms. Congress no longer funds such major water projects, making the Bureau an agency badly in need of a mission. Today it is a major water management agency and a power provider, but not the largest in either case, nor is the federal government uniquely needed for either. Congress should charge the Bureau with the eradication of non-native plants that directly threaten water supplies, a productive and badly needed water project that is certainly consistent with the agency's original mission. The Bureau's annual budget today exceeds $1 billion, more than the combined costs of the Hoover and Grand Cooley Dams, and certainly more than enough to accomplish the task.

Evapotranspiration

Plants that grow along streams and rivers and soak up water are called "phreatophytes." Tamarisk and willows are examples of such plants, but they are not the only plants that keep large amounts of water from our rivers and lakes. In fact, culprits far larger than those are the overgrown forests that clog watersheds throughout the nation. Water leaders today find themselves debating all too often the peculiar question of how much water is supposed to be in the rivers. The Interstate Compacts that regulate most western rivers were negotiated at a specific moment in time, and divided up the water based on the best available information about how much was normally available, and where it was most needed. The latter half of that equation has changed dramatically as population growth has occurred in unexpected places like Las Vegas. But the amount of water native to the Colorado River should not have changed that much over time. Yet it has.

Today many of the nation's rivers, including the Colorado, have considerably less water than was there when the compacts were negotiated. Modern-day water leaders often assert that their predecessors were simply wrong about the amount of water available, or that a series of wet years in the early 1900s skewed their figures. It is a very convenient argument for anyone opposed to new water projects, who can simply claim there is no more available water. It is convenient, but it is wrong. Leaders who negotiated the interstate water agreements (mostly between 1920 and 1950) had decades of river measurements on which to base their assumptions, not just a few unreliable years. The Colorado River and its tributaries had been measured regularly for more than 40 years when the first compact was negotiated, and some of the best engineers in the country worked on it. They were not mistaken about the average amount of water in the system. There simply isn't as much water there today, and there is one plain and simple explanation—trees.

Normally, water moves from the land to the atmosphere in two ways. The most commonly understood is evaporation. The second occurs when water moves upward through plants, from roots to leaves or needles, then as they dry that water moves into the atmosphere, replaced by more from the roots—that process is called transpiration. But there is also a third process, recognized by scientists but largely unknown to political leaders until the past decade. Snow falling on the leaves and branches of trees can simply evaporate directly into vapor without ever reaching the ground. In this process, trees interrupt the normal flow of water from clouds to streams, rivers, oceans and back to clouds. That interruption is called "evapotranspiration," and it has reached crisis levels in the mountain west, where overgrown forests are preventing vast quantities of water from ever reaching the rivers. To be clear, evapotranspiration is a natural process. But remember, what is not natural is the amount of trees in the national forests, as mentioned in the previous chapter. When those forests are choked with 300–900 trees per acre when there should naturally be 30–50, the rate of evapotranspiration is exponentially greater than it should be.

To fully understand why the issue of evapotranspiration is so important in the West, one must understand at least the basics of the Colorado River Interstate Compact mentioned earlier. Water measurement sometimes sounds more complicated than it is. Amounts of water are measured in "acre feet," which is simply the amount of water it takes to cover one acre with one foot of water. The Colorado River system should contain an annual average of about 15 million acre feet of water, and the Compact distributed that water among the seven states in the river basin. Half (7.5 million acre feet) is for the Lower Basin (CA, AZ, NV) and the other half for the Upper

Basin (CO, WY, NM, UT). The Upper Basin states further agreed on a distribution of their half: half of it (3.75 million acre feet) to the state of Colorado and the rest to Wyoming, Utah and New Mexico in varying portions. The Lower Basin agreements give California 4.4 million acre feet, Arizona 2.8 million and the remainder (300,000 acre feet) to Nevada. The numbers are not essential to this part of the discussion, but I mention them to illustrate the importance of every acre foot of water.

Six of the seven basin states use their full entitlements every year, but under the agreement, Colorado is still entitled to develop and use about 1 million acre feet more than it does now. That much additional water is simply not there, so you can well imagine that any attempt in Colorado to develop that extra water (and thus take it out of the river) is a serious potential threat to all the other states. Being at the top of the river, Colorado could simply divert and use that water—it has a perfect legal right to do so—but that would necessarily take water from existing users in other states downstream. That is, unless there really were an extra million acre feet of unused water in the system, as there should be. Thus it is vital to find out why that water is missing, and if possible, to get it back.

A growing number of activists claim the water is gone due to global warming. However, there is a problem with the science backing that theory. Current measurements can easily show that the river flows are diminished over time, but studies of the amount of precipitation do not show such drastic reductions in snowfall over that same time. In fact, 2008 saw the heaviest snowfall Colorado had received in over 30 years, and 2011 was even better. So there should have been immediately noticeable increases in the spring runoff both years, accompanied by the rapid rise in reservoir water levels, maybe even a public celebration that our rivers were back! But there wasn't.

In fact, runoff levels and reservoir levels did not see the highest levels in 30 years during either 2008 or 2011. In short, the snow is falling, but the water is disappearing in alarming quantities before it ever gets to the ground, because evapotranspiration is at an all-time unnatural high. And the amount of water that can be lost in this manner is astonishing. The Bureau of Reclamation estimates that the Lower Basin loses almost 4 million acre feet per year to evapotranspiration—nearly as much as California's entire allotment!

studies have actually skewed the definition between "transpiration" and "evapotranspiration," publishing statistics about losses from "agricultural evapotranspiration." In other words, blaming farmers is acceptable, but questioning government management of national forests is apparently off limits. Numerous studies also make much of the potential danger of global warming, pointing out that significantly higher temperatures would increase evapotranspiration. That is obvious enough without government studies, but where is the analysis of the phenomenon already occurring?

The federal agency responsible for keeping track of water in these rivers is, again, the Bureau of Reclamation, but that agency has all but completely removed this discussion from its studies. The Bureau does publish reports on "consumptive uses and losses" of water in the Upper Basin. The charts track (loosely) the evaporation from reservoirs in the Upper Basin, said to be between 183,000 and 469,000 acre feet per year during the past few years, but there is no analysis whatsoever of losses to evapotranspiration. Several good studies about the effect of forest thinning on water flows, such as those done in the Fraser Experimental Forest, are available, but it has become politically incorrect *even to discuss* what role national forest management *may have played* in reducing the flow of the Colorado River system by a million acre feet per year.

In 2003 the Colorado Department of Natural Resources began highlighting this problem and demonstrating that the management of national forests was at least partly responsible for the disappearance of large amounts of western water. The condition was especially noticeable—and measurable—during the significant drought that hit the entire western United States in 2002–2004, so Colorado began to call on the Forest Service to thin the forests back to their normal condition. If that could be done on a landscape scale, the missing water would miraculously re-appear in the streams and rivers where it used to be, and ought to be still. Environmental leaders went ballistic over the idea, and—ever quick with clever slogans— branded the strategy as "logging for water," because they knew that while finding more water might be popular with the public, logging is not. So if they could make the argument about logging rather than water, the public would be suspicious of the effort. Thus, "logging went ballistic over the idea, and—ever quick with clever slogans— branded the strategy as "logging for water," because they knew that while finding more water might be popular with the public, logging is not. So if they could make the argument about logging rather than water, the public would be suspicious of the effort. Thus, "logging for water" became a negative battle cry in the press, providing the environmental groups with another crisis to rally around—and yet another fund-raising bonanza.

Actually the idea of making the Forest Service responsible for adequate water flow is not radical or new. It is the heart of the agency's original mission. As mentioned earlier, the "Organic Act of 1897," which created the national forest system, made clear its two-fold mission: "to improve and protect the forest within the reservation, *for securing favorable conditions of water flows, and to furnish a continuous supply of timber for the use and necessities of citizens of the United States*" (emphasis mine). In other words, leaders 100 years ago understood clearly that management of forests was directly connected to the amount and quality of water flows, and it was the first priority—supplying timber was the second.

Today some Forest Service officials simply reinterpret this mission statement, which is still the law, including in their new interpretation what they now call "intangible" resources—ones that are harder to define than water and timber, and of course, ones that have not been authorized by Congress. A good example of the new thinking was written by a University of Arizona professor (with federal grant money) and published under the title, "Sustaining Flows of Crucial Watershed Resources." Notice the subtle difference between "crucial watersheds" and "crucial watershed resources." The reason that last word appears, of course, is because the author, Professor J.E. de Steiguer, thinks the mission of watershed managers should include things other than water. This is how he described it in the paper:

> *When sustaining the flows of crucial watershed resources, watershed managers must recognize that the "crucial resources" involve not only those tangible, commodity resources such as clean water, timber, recreation and the like. Crucial resources*

also include intangibles such as amenity, option, bequest, existence and stewardship values. These latter values have increasingly been recognized as having significant economic value to society.

In other words, values such as "bequest" and "existence" are said to be as important economically as water and wood products. In fact, if a resource is that important economically, it cannot really be "intangible." Yet that has become the new mission of the national forests—preserving resources for future generations at the expense of people living today. The problem, as we have seen, is that it is also at the expense of both the forests and the water.

Clear Water

Not surprisingly, land management has a direct effect not only on water supply, but also on water quality. Remembering the massive mudslide that followed the Buffalo Creek fire and filled Strontia Springs Reservoir with mud in 1996, consider the even worse possibility should such a fire destroy the West's largest watershed—the headwaters of the Colorado River. Remember, the Colorado River supplies most of the water to over 50 million people in seven states, including California. The River originates on the west side of Rocky Mountain National Park at a beautiful place called Grand Lake. A series of reservoirs in Grand County now stores the most pristine quality water during spring runoff, for use on both sides of the Continental Divide and by all the downstream states throughout the year. Those reservoirs are completely surrounded by mountains on every side now covered entirely by dead trees waiting for the lightning strike that will set off an unprecedented conflagration.

Grand Lake, headwaters of the Colorado River, now surrounded by dead trees in Rocky Mountain National Park—a water quality disaster waiting to happen

At a congressional hearing in July, 2009, experts from the Forest Service and concerned water district officials testified that in Grand County 90% of all trees more than 5 inches diameter are now dead. They told Congress that if a wildfire should break out in these dead forests (considered probable by nearly every witness), it would likely be followed by massive erosion during the next rainstorm or the next spring runoff. And that, they testified, could create a water quality disaster like nothing the West has seen. They showed the Committee this map to help illustrate the magnitude of the problem—not from a forestry perspective, but speaking of the implications for water supplies and water quality:

Northern Colo. Water Conservancy District

On this map, the green areas show live forests, and the pink areas show forests killed by bark beetles. The dead forests surround *every* important water supply facility in the Colorado River headwaters region: Grand Lake and Lake Granby, as well as Windy Gap, Willow Creek and Shadow Mountain Reservoirs. Witnesses at the hearing warned that if a catastrophic fire and subsequent erosion were to fill these lakes with mud (as happened at Strontia Springs in 1996), it would be virtually impossible to supply the water required from Denver to Fort Collins, to administer the Interstate Compact with the downstream states, or to supply irrigation water upon which much of the West's agriculture depends. These dire warnings have been sounded by water leaders throughout the West, and if that happens, members of Congress will not be able to point fingers elsewhere and indignantly demand to know why they were not briefed.

Pollution, by Any Other Name

In the traditional view of most policy-makers, water quality is all about pollution. But as recent events are teaching us, traditional pollution—factories dumping waste into the river—is only one way water quality is degraded. That kind of pollution is much easier to regulate, even to stop. Thirty-seven years after the Clean Water Act became law, there are very few examples of the kind of blatant water pollution that caused the Cuyahoga River to catch fire in 1969. Toxic sludge cannot simply be dumped into rivers anymore, and our waterways are much cleaner as a result. Technology has improved our ability to test water for less visible pollution, too. After the law was passed in 1972 the EPA began measuring chemicals and elements like lead and mercury in the water supply. Initially able to measure "parts per thousand," the agency could later monitor for "parts per million" and today's scientists can detect some pollutants in "parts per trillion." That presents a dilemma all its own, because we can now measure to such a minute degree that cleaning the water beyond that level is nearly impossible. Nevertheless, we ought to view the cleaning of America's rivers as one of the great environmental successes in history, and we ought to be proud of it. Instead, the EPA has become one of the nation's most feared and distrusted regulatory agencies, whose over-reach is legendary.

The Washington Legal Foundation spent several years assisting the case of James Knott of Massachusetts, a Harvard alumnus and recipient of a Governor's Award for developing pollution control technology. His company, Riverdale Mills, which produces plastic-coated wire mesh for erosion control, fencing and aquaculture, always did its best to comply with a complex myriad of EPA regulations for meticulous record-keeping, but in 1997 a harmless mistake–not in clean water compliance, but in record keeping–led to an enforcement nightmare for Mr. Knott and his employees. The EPA accused the company of discharging over-acidic rinse water into a local river (one time), because an incorrect PH number had been entered in a record book–though the alleged discharge never actually happened. A no-knock raid by a federal SWAT team of 21 heavily-armed federal agents stormed the plant, terrifying the employees, who were photographed, videotaped, and interrogated–some in their homes in front of their families. Knott himself was indicted on felony charges carrying a penalty of six years in prison and $1.5 million in fines.

After a two-year legal battle, the charges were finally dropped because EPA officials were found to have altered the evidence. Mr. Knott then sued the EPA to recover his legal expenses, and a trial judge agreed. But the government appealed and after several years and two unsuccessful trips to the U.S. Supreme Court, Knott ended up with nothing. The saga had cost the company more than a million dollars, though it was never proven that its bookkeeping error had *any effect whatsoever on the environment*. One federal judge excoriated the EPA for its heavy-handed treatment, including a finding that the raid itself had been unconstitutional, yet refused to order the agency to reimburse Knott's expenses. In the end, an appeals court ruled that the government's conduct was "insufficiently egregious" to warrant reimbursement. The lesson for many Americans is that paperwork and process are more important to regulators than the environment itself. But government officials whose job is to stop pollution have to look for new ways to justify their existence, because the pollution battles of the past have been mostly won.

The fact that Americans have all but eliminated industrial pollution from our waterways is all the more satisfying if we remember the difficulty of the battle. When Rachael Carson published *Silent Spring* in 1962, the firestorm of controversy it aroused belies the hero status she now enjoys in the conservation movement. Some experts challenged her findings (some of which are now known to be wrong), and some businesses tried to suppress the book. When CBS News planned an hour-long special on what the book called "rivers of death," two of the network's major corporate sponsors cancelled their advertising. All the controversy just helped sell books, and *Silent Spring* remained on the bestseller list for months. The publisher has now exceeded its 40th edition in hardback, in addition to dozens of Book-of-the-Month-Club printings and paperback editions still being printed today.

"Only within the moment of time represented by the present century has one species—man—acquired significant power to alter the nature of his world," Carson wrote. With respect to water quality,

Americans have certainly done that, coming close to destroying the very ability of water in some places to sustain life, and also in many areas improving the quality of water beyond what any generation of people anywhere in the world have ever dreamed possible.

Today's challenges are more complicated, partly because we know so much more about the elements that can diminish water quality than was known in Carson's time, and partly because there are so many more ways for "pollution" to be defined and so many more places for it to originate. In dealing with degraded water quality, if the source of pollution can be traced to a single location, regulators can stop it. That is referred to as "point source" pollution. But what if the pollution seems to occur throughout a river system and a single source cannot be pinned down? That is referred to as "non point source" pollution, and it is much harder to regulate—who do we regulate if no single person or company is to blame?

The Water Quality Blame Game

Water quality can be impaired seriously by the presence of completely natural substances if they are in higher concentrations than normal. For example, salt in its various forms (salinity, selenium and others) is dissolved into the water by agricultural irrigation in many parts of the country. The salt is a natural component of the dirt, and very small amounts are in most rivers, but when the water is filtered through the soil on farms, then drained back into a river, the amount of salt in the river increases. Even though salt is a natural substance, the amount can be increased to the point of killing fish and vegetation in some cases. Yet no specific farmer can be blamed for something that happens over a massive region of the country, and putting an end to farming is obviously not a solution. Instead, the government has partnered with private landowners in spending billions to upgrade farms and ranches with more water-saving irrigation systems (gated pipe, concrete ditches, and drip water systems). These techniques have reduced salinity pollution in the nation's waters, but not eliminated it. Keep in mind, adding to the salt and mineral concentrations in America's rivers is illegal today. But who is going to tell all the nation's farmers to quit farming?

Adding to this indirect form of water pollution is another phenomenon even more difficult for today's conservation leaders: the cumulative effect of diversions over a long period of time. This is among the most difficult of all water quality issues, because there is no one responsible for it, and no specific place where it can be stopped. In most states the water laws do not even acknowledge the existence of this problem. It begins with the very simple fact that water is cleanest at the highest altitude. When the snow first melts, water is pristine, and everywhere it flows from then on, it picks up more and more dirt, sand, minerals, chemicals and other "pollutants." The closer water gets to the ocean, the dirtier it gets. Thus, water diversions upstream invariably take "cleaner" water out of the stream, leaving "dirtier" water downstream. There used to be a common expression, "dilution is the solution to pollution." It is considered discredited and obsolete today because it was used as an excuse to forgive polluters. But the reverse still holds true today: if you take out the cleaner water, you are left with the dirtier water.

Here is the oversight in historic water laws: in western states where water rights are property rights, no user is allowed to degrade the quality of water *so much that it is not useable* by downstream owners. In other words, you are not allowed to degrade water to the extent that it prevents someone else from using his water. But that is a very high standard, virtually impossible to prove. What if you degrade water, *but not that much?* If one user hundreds of miles upstream takes a very small amount of water out of the stream, it is difficult to show that the water far downstream is degraded *to the point of uselessness.* However, when hundreds of upstream water users divert the cleanest water for more than a century, it clearly has a significant impact on the quality of water downstream.

In the case of the main stream of the Colorado River, fully half of Colorado's share of the water is diverted across the Continental Divide to the Front Range cities—half of all the high-altitude cleanest water in the system. Virtually all of those diversions are at the highest altitude possible, near the Continental Divide (where it is much cheaper to divert the water a shorter distance). That means all of the water left in the river for all downstream users—including millions of people in Western Colorado, Utah, Arizona, New Mexico, Nevada and California—is of lower quality than it would otherwise be. That makes water treatment more expensive for western cities, it degrades fisheries for a thousand miles, and it has an impact on irrigated agriculture in six states. But what can regulators do about that? No specific water diversion can be blamed, and clearly no one is going to shut down multiple water systems that people have depended upon for generations. Still, for the legal system to pretend these diversions have no effect on downstream water quality is unrealistic and outdated.

A handful of states have just begun to understand the cumulative impact on water quality of numerous upstream water projects, and a few have tried to adjust the laws. In Colorado, for example, water judges issuing decrees for new water rights have always been prohibited from even considering the effect on downstream water *quality*—as long as water *quantity* was protected, and as long as the proposed project did not harm water quality *so severely that another user could not use his water*. It has become a serious political issue in recent years as the city of Aurora began buying agricultural water rights from the lower Arkansas River Valley, drying up farms to supply the growing city. Aside from the long-term bad policy that represents, the less obvious problem was that all the proposed new diversions to the city were far upstream from the agricultural rights being purchased. As a result, water quality would be significantly degraded for those farmers and communities that chose not to sell their water rights. Colorado wildlife officials and others asked the legislature to authorize water courts to consider the cumulative impact of all the existing diversions on water quality before issuing more decrees for more upstream diversion rights. Ultimately, they placed limits on the new policy, and it may seem like a small change, but it was long overdue.

What issues like this boil down to is that there are more than just environmental and health costs of polluted water; there is also an economic cost. It is relatively simple for legislators and regulators to put a stop to "point source" pollution. If someone washes toxic chemicals directly into the river, he can be fined or imprisoned. So we set standards for various elements and make laws that punish anyone adding those elements in greater concentrations than allowed. Simple enough.

In more recent years, we have focused more on "non point source" pollution, partly because we have been so successful at stopping the more direct offenses, and largely because these cumulative impacts are so much more difficult. They are not, however, impossible. Efforts should focus on three areas:

- Stop pollutants from entering the system, to the extent possible,
- Add as much clear water to the system as possible,
- Use new methods to treat and clean the water at every opportunity.

First, we cannot stop all minerals and chemicals from ever entering the water supply; some occur naturally, and others result from activity vital to our survival, such as agriculture. But to the extent possible, we should continually upgrade irrigation systems, modernize industrial facilities, improve domestic water treatment plants, and find other ways to prevent degradation of water quality. These processes will never be perfect, especially since the ability to detect minute amounts continues to improve, but we should always keep trying.

Second, remembering the old adage about dilution, any cleaner and purer water we can add to the river systems will help. And as we have seen, the conventional wisdom that man cannot change the amount of water in the river is plainly untrue. Efforts to properly manage public lands, programs to eradicate non-native species like tamarisk, and the addition of more water storage can dramatically increase the amount of clean water flowing in our rivers. Those activities ought to be top priority for water leaders.

Third, we can improve water treatment, including through a closer examination (and duplication) of nature's own processes. Many states, cities and companies have constructed wetlands to mimic nature's cleansing processes—with great success. Frequently, this approach turns out to be less expensive and more effective than traditional water treatment plants. Colorado also used it instead of punitive fines against polluters (which may be satisfying to those seeking revenge, but do nothing for the environment). One particularly damaging spill into an important stream resulted in the death of thousands of fish in 2002. Rather than levy fines, Colorado reached an agreement with the responsible company, whereby the firm paid for a constructed wetlands treatment facility that is a great success today. It treats all the effluent from the plant itself and from the nearby town, it provides a great educational experience for hundreds of students and classes that visit each year, and it was cheaper than building a new wastewater treatment plant. Wetlands are the most nearly perfect water filter ever discovered and we ought to make much greater use of their potential to further clean the nation's waters.

Our Legacy

Like so many other environmental issues, clean water presents stark choices for today's leaders. We can take the punitive route and simply try to stop everything we think is harmful. There is a place for that, and we should not let down our guard on the impressive improvements already achieved. But our legacy to the next generation could be so much more if we also take the proactive approach. We have the ability to leave our nation's water cleaner and healthier than ever, and we should do that in all the ways discussed. We also have the ability not only to preserve, but to improve our environment and our standard of living by ensuring greater supplies of water. We should do that, too.

Communities cannot thrive and prosper without enough water to supply the growing needs of a growing population and a growing economy. Adding more water storage does not have to be a threat to the environment. On the contrary, it is one of the few ways we can actually improve our surroundings, add more habitat for more species, help the land become more productive, and make our corner of the world a better place to live, work and raise families. The stigma attached to water projects is outdated, especially as we have learned new and creative ways to store water: underground, off-stream, in existing reservoirs, and occasionally in new ones built to modern standards. Some environmental groups continue to demonize virtually any use of water for any purpose other than watching it flow to the ocean. But once again, stopping human activity is not a solution to anything, it does not result in a healthier environment, and it is not leadership. Leadership requires doing things right, not stopping all activity and leaving no good choices for future generations.

With respect to water, doing absolutely nothing is a poor option. Maybe the sky will not fall on us, but the future will bring significant droughts again—those cycles are a part of nature. If we do nothing at all to improve our water supply, then our grandchildren will blame us for a lack of foresight, and they will be right to do so. Infrastructure will certainly cost more in the future than it does now. Do we really want future generations to wonder why we lacked the political will to protect our environment and provide for the needs of our descendants? True conservation leaders must begin to talk about water projects again, not in an apologetic manner, but aggressively promoting storage and utilization as a positive way to provide for inevitable growth, and especially as a way to improve our environment.

If we do not act, future generations will remain short of precious water, catastrophic wildfires will continue, watersheds will fill with silt and debris, and we will have done nothing to mitigate the disasters that will result. Do we really want to spend our lives entangled in these petty arguments about a false agenda, or do we want to leave behind a more honorable legacy?

However much more complex today's legal and political climate may be, we cannot escape the reality that the management—or lack of management—of our national forests has led to a drastic reduction in the availability of water in the arid west. So as we discuss ways to use our water more efficiently, we should begin with an understanding that water conservation begins long before the water reaches our faucet. It begins with responsible public land management.

CHAPTER 6

THIS LAND IS MY LAND

"To put the bounty and the health of our land, our only commonwealth, into the hands of people who do not live on it and share its fate will always be an error. For whatever determines the fortune of the land determines also the fortunes of the people. If history... teaches anything, it teaches that."

——Wendell Berry

Several years ago I had a fairly spirited conversation with a congressional staffer from Rhode Island, whose boss was pushing legislation to designate wilderness areas in Colorado. I had failed miserably to convince him that Rhode Island congressmen should leave Colorado land management decisions to Coloradans. These lands belong to all the people, he rightly pointed out. I had also failed to persuade him that most of the people who live there had a decidedly different viewpoint. He maintained that the people who live there are a minority, which is also true. I said the people who lived there knew more about the land and the issues involving it, but that offended him. He said he worked for constituents in Rhode Island and it was not his job to care what the people living in the West thought. As a last resort, I tried to explain the importance of some of the current activities in one of the chosen areas, activities upon which businesses and communities were dependent and which the proposed wilderness legislation would effectively ban. He countered with a glowing description of the area as one of the last great places in America, so I asked the question many Westerners often wonder, "Have you ever been there?" He had not, but I will always remember his response: "We don't have to visit the place to care about it. For many of us," he said, "it's enough just to know it's there."

For millions of people who live in the American West, it is *not* enough just to know these beautiful places are there. It is a requirement of life that we use the water and other resources of these lands, because throughout most of the West, the federal government owns the resources upon which life depends. The fact that our back yards are also some of the world's most beautiful places is a happy coincidence to us. It is at once a great blessing, and our everlasting curse. We are blessed to live in an area so spectacular and special that the rest of the nation cares, sometimes passionately, about how we take care of it.

The United States government paid just over $55 million for the entire Western United States. That's less than the annual budget of Dubuque, Iowa. In five separate treaties, the U.S. acquired the whole country from the Mississippi River to the Pacific Ocean, including Alaska. In order to encourage settlement of the West, the government then gave away or sold this land to homesteaders, railroads and new states. Ironically, today we pay more than that original purchase price every year for the U.S. to buy back parts of the same lands it once gave away.

How the West Was Won (Purchased)

The Treaty of Paris extended the original boundaries of the U.S. to the Mississippi River in 1783, and Spain ceded Florida to the U.S. in 1819. This USGS map illustrates the process by which the rest of the continental United States was acquired.

With the Louisiana Purchase in 1803, President Jefferson bought essentially all the land between the Mississippi River and the Continental Divide. We paid the French government $23.2 million for the 828,000 square miles, or roughly 2.9 cents per acre.

In 1818 a treaty with England resolving fishing rights disputes also clarified the U.S. northern boundary, thus acquiring for the U.S. the northern plains of Minnesota and North Dakota.

In 1846 President Polk managed to resolve a 30-year dispute with England over the joint occupation of the "Oregon Country." The resulting "Buchanan-Pakenham Treaty" gave the U.S. complete ownership of what is now Washington, Oregon, Idaho and Western

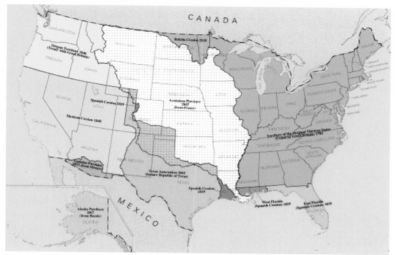

Territorial Acquisitions of the United States, USGS

Montana, an area of 285,580 square miles. The U.S. did not pay a cent for it, but simply asserted U.S. ownership and Great Britain backed down.

Texas was annexed in 1845, touching off the Mexican War. It was ended by the Treaty of Guadalupe Hidalgo in 1848, in which the U.S. acquired from Mexico the land that is now Arizona, New Mexico, California, Nevada, Utah and Western Colorado. We paid Mexico $15 million for the 525,000 square miles, the equivalent of 4.5 cents per acre.

Five years after the Mexican War, plans for a railroad to California required the land south of the Gila River. We purchased it from Mexico for $10 million. The 29,670 square miles of land totaled about 53 cents per acre (the most expensive western land purchase, but still less than half the price the U.S. paid for the Virgin Islands 65 years later).

Finally, the West was complete when Secretary of State William Seward bought Alaska from Russia for $7.2 million. That is 1.9 cents per acre for Alaska's 586,412 square miles. Contemporaries who thought it a waste of money called it "Seward's Folly," and "Seward's Ice Box." One Senator in voting against the treaty called it "Andrew Johnson's Polar Bear Garden"—and was derided by his colleagues for using the word "garden."

In all, the U.S., especially under President Polk, had fulfilled what was popularly called its "manifest destiny," making the Pacific Ocean its Western border. Still, occupying so much of the North American continent was a different matter than owning it, so putting all this land to use and persuading people to move west was essential public policy from the start.

Free Land

After acquiring the Western United States, the government's purpose for the rest of the 19th Century was to convince Americans to settle this land, own and occupy it, and turn it into productive and prosperous new states. It was viewed as crucial to the future prosperity of America, hence the famed Horace Greeley admonition, "Go West, young man."

Remember, in the 19th Century and before, governments could own land, but they really could not control—and hope to keep—the land except by occupation. And free people could not necessarily be counted upon to join armies and go to war to defend land they did not care about. Thus for the United States, adding the entire continent to its borders would be of no value unless it could persuade its people to occupy the land, make it their home, and think of it as part of the country they were willing to fight and die to protect. Perhaps even more important, the new land in the West was already known to contain vast stores of natural resources, including some that were unavailable in the existing states. But getting the land occupied was no small task at a time when the total U.S. population (1860) was less than a tenth what it is today. So both government and business did what was logical, and offered very strong incentives for Americans to move and settle the West.

The government privatized vast tracts of this new land for farming and settlement. The effort began with the Pre-emption Act of 1841, which offered up to 160 acres of land to homesteaders for $1.25 an acre. A large portion of the lands acquired in the Louisiana Purchase were settled under this arrangement. In 1850 Congress passed a different law for the new "Oregon Country," offering the 160 acre tracts free of charge to people already there, and for $1.25

an acre to anyone else who could get there within 4 years. Finally in 1862 President Lincoln signed the Homestead Act, offering 160 acres of land free to settlers who would move west, stake their claims, occupy the new lands, build a home, plow the land, plant a crop and file for title.

These land privatization laws proved to be very powerful incentives. Settlers in the Midwest and West could buy larger tracts of land than were available in the already populated East. Even more important, Western lands would appreciate much faster, so money could be made not only on crops, but also on land. Considering that in 1850 the average value of land in the Northeast was $17.00 per acre, no wonder thousands of people moved west for cheap—or free—land. In 1850, nearly 50% of all settlers in the Midwest owned real estate, but by 1860 that number was nearly 75%.

For the rest of the 19th Century, as the various Indian treaties were made and new tracts of land opened for settlement, the Homestead Act remained the primary mechanism for privatizing and settling previously vacant federal lands.

By the 1970s Americans' environmental consciousness made the very idea of giving away federal lands unpopular, especially in light of the pollution and corporate abuses so frequently in the news during that era. In 1976, Congress finally repealed the privatization laws, ended homesteading, and "reserved" all remaining lands into permanent federal ownership. An exception was made only for Alaska, where homesteading remained legal until 1986.

The first homesteader was Daniel Freeman, who filed his claim in Brownville, Nebraska 10 minutes after the new law went into effect in 1863. The site of his claim is now the Homestead National Monument of America, which honors the lives and accomplishments of the pioneers. The last claim under the Homestead Act was filed in 1979 by a Vietnam veteran named Kenneth Deardorff for 80 acres on the Stony River in Alaska. In the 123 years between Freeman and Deardorff, more than 1.6 million homesteads were granted, and the law successfully privatized 270 million acres in the West—still only 10% of all the land in the United States. Today much of the West remains primarily in federal ownership simply because there were not enough Americans to homestead and occupy it all.

In addition to farming, the Homestead Act was sometimes used to gain ownership of timber and oil-producing land, since the government charged royalties for extraction of such resources from public lands. Also, some speculators ruthlessly claimed lands near waterholes and rivers that they had no intention of farming, in order to block access for others and thereby monopolize tracts much larger than 160 acres. That had the long-term effect of preventing the privatization of large segments of land.

On the other hand, homesteading was generally not used for land containing what the government called "locatable minerals," such as coal, gold and silver. Those lands could be obtained through mining claims on which the government did not charge royalties. The 1872 Mining Law—as we will see—has been the source of considerable controversy in recent years, but in the 19th Century it was yet another way for the government to encourage people to settle the West and put its resources to beneficial use in building a prosperous and growing nation.

You Can't Get There From Here

The greatest challenge the nation faced in settling these lands was the complete lack of any transportation system. Aside from the Oregon Trail, the Santa Fe Trail, and the Old Spanish Trail, there were no roads to begin with. Since people needed roads to get to these lands and resources, land was given away for that, too. For railroads in particular, the government offered huge rights-of-way, along with the mineral rights and water rights associated with the land. Railroads could then sell or lease those other assets to finance construction of new routes, many of which were enormously expensive because of rough mountain terrain. They were also given the right to locate stations, water tanks, switches and other facilities just about anywhere they wanted. Congress readily subsidized the needed surveys and expeditions to find the best routes. National leaders offered whatever incentives it took to get roads built so people could settle the West, and get their goods to market.

In addition to railroads, people needed regular roads so they could get to and from their communities and their farms, however remote. This turned out to be a very significant problem, since such access roads would have to cross lands that had not yet been privatized. So if a rancher wanted to access his farm and it was located many miles from the nearest town, would he have to homestead or otherwise buy all the land in between, just so he could build a road? The Homestead Act did not accommodate this problem, because it required a farmer to "prove up on" the land (meaning live on it and produce a crop several years in a row) in order to own it. But these new settlers did not need all the land in between their new farms and the nearest town, and certainly could not grow crops on every inch of it if all they needed was an access road. Within 5 years of the Homestead Act's passage it became clear that a law authorizing roads across remaining public lands was badly needed. The lack of such a law had already become a major hindrance to the government's goal of encouraging settlement of the West.

Congress solved the problem by passing a very simple authorization, granting anyone and everyone the right to build roads to access anything and everything. Known as Revised Statute 2477 (RS-2477), we now know the law was too simple to survive the challenges of today's environmental lawyers and their friendly activist judges. It said, plainly enough:

The right-of-way for the construction of highways over public lands, not reserved for public uses, is hereby granted.

The statute was "self enacting." That is, rights of way were by definition established by the very act of "construction" of a "highway" on unreserved public lands, without any form of acknowledgement or action by any official of the federal government. Further, the right was granted to anyone—individuals, companies, local governments, and states—anyone who needed to build a road. The law remained in force until repealed in 1976, when Congress "reserved" all remaining federal lands for public purposes, with a clause grandfathering all existing roads built under the old right-of-way law. Unfortunately, as we will see, the definitions of "construction" and "highway" changed dramatically during the intervening century, leading federal bureaucrats to ignore the grandfather clause and close thousands of roads Congress had granted under the law.

The Checkerboard

The patchwork of complex land ownership in the West was more than a century in the making. In addition to the incentives offered for people to go west and settle, creating a never-ending string of private farms surrounded by public lands, Congress also encouraged the creation of new states. The government even helped finance the new states—especially the costs of schools—with grants of land, from which states could produce revenue. States were given a portion of each land "section" for the purpose of raising money for public schools and these "state school lands" formed a bizarre checkerboard pattern in nearly all the western states.

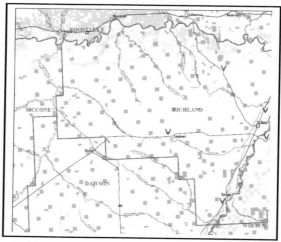

Richland County, Montana - state school trust lands in blue
Source: Montana Natural Resource Information System, MT State Library

Today, 23 states manage 146 million acres of such lands. They also own and manage another 220 million acres of mineral rights, mostly resulting from the original federal grant of state school trust lands. By comparison, the U.S. government owns nearly 650 million acres (almost a third of the country), nearly all of it in the West. State and federal governments in the South and East do not own land on a scale even a fraction of that. The U.S. government owns less than 1% of the land in Rhode Island, Connecticut, and New York, and less than 2% of the land in Maine, Kansas, Nebraska, Alabama, Ohio, or Illinois.

An even bigger contributor to this checkerboard land ownership pattern was the federal policy of land grants to railroads. In addition to the railroad right-of-way, the government also granted the railroads half of the parcels of land along each side, often in a swath as wide as 40 miles or more. For Congress, that was a means of financing railroad construction without direct appropriations. But to ensure that there would also be room for farms and towns, the government split the land into checkerboards, giving the railroads every other square mile and leaving the rest for homesteading. As with so much of the western lands, some of these parcels were claimed and settled, and many were not. In those cases, the railroad parcels remained private, and the other remained federal.

The result is that in nearly every Western state, much of that original checkerboard of land ownership still exists today. A number of those railroad right-of-way checkerboards were in areas later designated as national forests, and the railroads often financed construction by selling these lands to timber companies (as Congress intended). Thus, in many western forests there remain today these strange checkerboards of private and public forests, frequently with very different logging histories that make cohesive management of an entire watershed almost impossible.

A classic example of the policy was Congress's 1864 Northern Pacific Railroad land grant. To encourage the company to build and operate a railroad from Lake Superior to the Pacific Ocean—and especially to help finance it—the grant created a swath of checkerboard lands nearly 2,000 miles long and up to 120 miles wide along the entire route. For every mile of track built, Congress gave the Northern Pacific Railroad 40 square miles of public lands, including the mineral rights. The Act also allowed the company to select lands it wanted in special "indemnity belts" located at the outer reaches of the checkerboard. These "belts" were 20 miles wide, and frequently included lands considered the most potentially profitable—those with timber or minerals.

These land grant policies, however strange they may seem today, helped settle the American West and create numerous states and prosperous communities, a result that could not have been achieved without the mobility provided by railroads. The same policies also created these checkerboard ownership patterns—a management nightmare with which modern generations still struggle more than a century later. Many of the public lands that were not claimed and homesteaded became national parks and forests, and the rest was left to the Bureau of Land Management (BLM). Thus, today large portions of the West are made up of a bizarre checkerboard of lands intermittently private, state-owned and federal (managed by numerous agencies with varying management plans and rules).

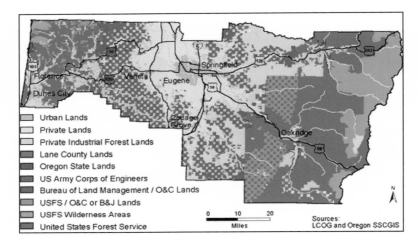

This modern map of Lane County, Oregon shows how that history results in most of the West's private land and its towns, surrounded by federal lands which hold many of the natural resources necessary for these communities to exist. And because the rest of the nation cares so much about federal land management policies, Westerners must forever deal with what they see as the "interference" of outsiders in "local" decisions.

Notice especially on the Lane County map how much of the original checkerboard is brown—BLM land. By the end of the homestead era, some of the land had been privatized and settled, but much of it never was. People settled land that was viewed at the time as more potentially productive, easier to farm, easier to access, nearer to lakes and rivers, covered with timber or underlain with valuable minerals. They left unsettled the lands with steep slopes, difficult terrain, no access, no water, no gold or silver—all the places deemed less desirable. They settled the valleys and left the mountains; they built towns along the rivers and left the deserts alone. Those high mountains and vast deserts are today considered some of the most beautiful places on Earth, the crown jewels of America. But during an era when families had to raise their own food to survive, these vast open spaces seemed daunting, inaccessible and worthless. This land remained in federal ownership for one and only one reason— no one else wanted it. Congress wanted to give it away and no one would take it.

In later years when the conservation movement began and the value of these beautiful places was realized, the government began to "reserve" them for public use, taking them off the homestead and mining claims market forever. Those "reserved" lands became national forests, parks and wildlife refuges. All the rest was given to the BLM for leasing to ranchers, miners, oil and gas companies, or anyone who might be able to use it, and to continue privatizing whenever possible. The remaining BLM land was finally "reserved" by Congress in 1976 (when the Homestead Act and the road right-of-way law were repealed) and will, for the most part, remain public land for the foreseeable future.

This history of western lands results in two vitally important realities today, and public lands issues can only be understood in light of these two central facts. First, the vast majority of public lands are in the West, creating issues unique to the region, issues which do not exist in the East. Second, government policies left in their wake a convoluted and complex checkerboard of land ownership that dominates the West, surrounding nearly every community with federal lands and the U.S. government as the largest landowner. It eliminates most of the tax base of western states, makes federal land managers very influential players in local communities, and fuels disputes about how to manage those lands (and who gets to decide), disputes that in some cases may never be fully resolved.

Federal Lands in the United States, USGS

A Tale of Two Cities

Notice on the map how nearly all land owned by the U.S. government is in the West. Some Midwestern and Eastern states have virtually no federal land at all, while some Western states are almost entirely federal property. In Colorado there is a town called Lake City. It is the county seat of Hinsdale County; in fact it is the only town in Hinsdale County because the government owns all the rest. Hinsdale County is almost as big as the state of Rhode Island, but aside from a tourism economy, that is about the only similarity between the two.

At almost 9,000 feet above sea level and inhabited by 843 hardy and hearty souls, Lake City is the poster child for this unique Western land management problem. Hinsdale County is 95.3% federal land, and fully half of that federal land—more than 500 square miles—is in designated wilderness areas. Put simply, in Lake City you do business on public lands, or you are out of business. Thus, its economy was built on mining, logging and grazing on these public lands. In the modern era, with the political incorrectness of mining, logging and grazing, Lake City has survived because of the absolutely unparalleled beauty of the place—thanks to hunting, fishing, hiking, camping, guest ranches and other recreational uses of the same public lands. But make no mistake; every single decision made about the management of those public lands is a make-or-break decision for the people of Lake City. Simple access and management decisions affect the very survival of communities like Lake City.

Because state and local governments cannot tax the federal government, Hinsdale County has virtually no tax base; it receives a total of $1 million from property taxes and takes in less than $250,000 from sales taxes. By contrast, Rhode Island—almost the same size—has over 1 million people living in 39 towns and 5 counties, and enjoys an annual budget of $8 billion. Rhode Island's population is 1,400 times larger than Hinsdale County's, but its budget is 1,700 times larger.

Hinsdale County will never enjoy the robust economy of Rhode Island for a number of reasons. It can never hold over a million people because we don't allow houses in the national forests so there isn't room. It can never have any more towns, or much more of anything else for that matter, because the federal government owns all the land. It would be difficult for people in Rhode Island ever to fully understand the constant dilemma this represents for the

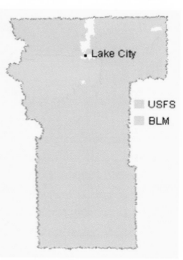

Federal Lands - Hinsdale County

people of Hinsdale County. Although small and limited in its own resources, Rhode Island is virtually all private land and precisely because it is limited, that land is worth billions, and is always for sale if the price is high enough. The federal government is an insignificant landlord and most residents don't even know the names of the federal land managers in their state, nor can many recall the names of the four national wildlife refuges or the name of the agency that manages them. Changes in the management of those very small wildlife refuges do not significantly affect the lives of the people or the economy of the state. The people in Hinsdale County not only know the names of the national forests, but also the ranger districts within them, the BLM districts, all the managers of each parcel and their families, and what all of them are doing every week. They know all about every decision of those federal agencies and the process leading to those decisions. They must follow these decisions closely—even participate in all the meetings—because their livelihood depends upon it.

Federal Lands - Rhode Island

Nothing about this difference is unique to Hinsdale County, or to Rhode Island. I use them as examples because of their similar size, and possibly because I still harbor some resentment about that Rhode Island congressional staffer who didn't care about the opinions of the people who live in the West. He really didn't care, but not because he is a bad person. He didn't care because he is not supposed to. To be clear, people like him not only don't care about the opinions of the locals or how dependent they are on the public lands, they *don't think they should* care.

Control Issues

It has become an important part of the culture of the modern environmental movement that people and their economy should not be a consideration in making environmental decisions, and that it is actually immoral to take such factors into consideration. This is an important distinction. I believe the resource ought to come first, that the conservation ethic requires us to consider what is right for the environment as the *first* priority. But the pervasive view of many environmental organizations is that the environment should be the *only* consideration.

In the long run, that unrealistic and impractical view is harmful to the environment itself. It fuels the "us-against-them" mindset because in the end, people will do what needs to be done to protect their way of life and their ability to put food on the table. Remember, starving people cannot worry about an endangered species. People will spend resources on environmental protection only when they think they can afford to do so. Affluent countries like the United States spend a fortune on environmental protection and improvement; poor countries like Rwanda do not. If backed against a wall, their very survival threatened, people will fight back, making environmental protection and those who advocate it "the enemy."

Nothing about that dynamic is good for the environment, but it is the dynamic at work in public lands counties all over the West. It continually fuels the East-West split in national politics, because hundreds of counties in the West are predominantly federally owned, and no Eastern county faces those same problems. Even huge states like New York contain almost no federal lands, whereas the even-larger state of Nevada is nearly all federal land. So when people in the West become convinced that people in the East don't care about them, they inevitably become resentful.

The Jimmy Carter "hit list" of water projects did untold damage to the conservation movement in driving a wedge between the West and the rest of the country. Since the West is generally arid and the East is generally not, a huge majority of the American population has never lived where lack of water is a constant problem. In addition to the climate, the difference in federal land ownership widens the gulf of understanding between West and East. So once that trust was broken, it has proven impossible—so far—to repair. Nearly every federal environmental policy decision is inherently "unfair" to one region or another, and it is a sad fact that many policies are not enforced the same throughout the country. How can they be? Eastern locations with few federal lands will never attract the most zealous federal land managers hoping to enhance their careers by managing the nation's crown jewels. Why would one want to manage a 10-acre wildlife refuge if one could run a wilderness area bigger than most counties? The east-west distinction is inherently unequal—and unfair. Decisions to limit the use of public lands simply cannot affect New York or Rhode Island the same way they affect Colorado or Nevada.

Limiting the use of public lands is precisely what the environmental industry and the federal government have been doing for more than a generation now. It is no coincidence that virtually every action taken in the last 30 years by either the Administration or Congress that changed the management of public lands has further restricted public use. No federal lands in the past generation have been opened for multiple uses that were previously wilderness areas. No motorized access is now allowed where it was once legally denied. No areas are now available for energy or timber production that used to be off-limits. On the contrary, millions of acres of public land are now wilderness areas that once hosted significant public activity; thousands of square miles of rich energy deposits have been placed off limits to Americans; thousands of miles of roads once used by generations of hunters and anglers no longer exist. And the push to further restrict public access to public lands continues unabated. Does managing public lands require barring the public?

Do As I Say, Not As I Do

There was a time when the rules of congressional courtesy practically forbid a congressman from introducing a bill affecting another congressman's district without a very specific agreement between the two. The standard was simple: "you take care of your district and I'll take care of mine." As recently as 25 years ago, no member from Massachusetts would have dreamed of introducing a bill changing the management of public lands in Utah. In fact, even a congressman from Denver would never have introduced legislation designating wilderness areas in another part of Colorado. Today it is routine. The common courtesies of a civil government have disappeared almost across the board in Washington, but especially with respect to environmental issues.

The deference shown to congressmen from the area involved in any particular decision was more than just old-fashioned and outdated senatorial courtesy. Public land policies were largely based on a cooperative model that presumed state and local governments knew more about the situation than federal officials. People who lived in the area were considered knowledgeable about what would and would not work in their areas, and it was assumed that they had the public's best interests at heart. It was not sentimentality; it was public policy. In fact, Congress included language in many of the environmental laws providing deference to state or local government recommendations, and in some cases even for actual delegation of federal enforcement powers to state governments. The Clean Water Act is an example of that cooperative approach, where many states handle the enforcement of federal rules.

This view began to change quickly in the aftermath of James Watt's appointment as Interior Secretary in 1981 (he was so closely identified with the West) and the dramatic growth of the "environmental industry" that followed. National environmental organizations began to portray local people, and even their state and local governments, as a major part of the problem. They began to demonize local people as yokels who would sell their grandmother for a buck, and who did not care at all about preserving the environment. However offensive that is to most westerners (not caring about their own back yard?), it has become the conventional wisdom in Washington, D.C.—even though few federal managers would admit it. Local and state governments are rarely trusted to make the right recommendations, and most land management agencies give states' views no more weight than the views of private citizens in other states. A few laws still require federal agencies to defer to state judgment, but if there is a disagreement, deference virtually disappears—along with any actual delegation of decisions, implementation or enforcement.

Once Bitten, Twice Shy

One clear example of this evolution and the mistrust of states is the RS-2477 road right-of-way issue mentioned earlier. Since most of that debate today hinges on whether particular roads were actually in existence before 1976, it is a clear area for such deference to state and local governments. Interest groups in Washington, D.C. can have very legitimate views on whether there *should be a road* across a particular section of public land. But surely it can be conceded that local people are more likely to know whether there actually *is a road* there. Yet despite the obvious, the Interior Department for more than a decade has refused to accept county or even state certifications as to whether specific roads predate 1976. And the government has continued to close existing roads as if there were no dispute underway.

Another example of this federal-state tension is the Black Canyon of the Gunnison water rights battle. The federal and state governments both represent the public, and they both have legal ability to preserve the flow of water in natural streams for the public benefit. Both have legal protections in place for endangered fish, both have strong enforcement abilities, and both care deeply about protecting such special places. Yet the federal government did not trust the state to protect stream flows in the Black Canyon, and the resulting legal battle lasted for more than 20 years, with the public paying the legal fees for both sides. That ironic and costly scenario is played out almost every day all across the country because the federal government no longer treats state and local governments as partners, but as potential abusers that must be regulated and controlled.

That growing mistrust has changed the nature of environmental politics in Congress and in state legislatures. Denver Congresswomen Pat Schroeder and Diana DeGette both introduced several wilderness bills designating lands in Western Colorado without incurring anything like the wrath they would have experienced from the affected region's own congressman 25 years earlier. If a congressman from Rhode Island doesn't think twice about trying to change federal land management in rural Colorado, why should members from elsewhere in Colorado? A congressman who tried to stop others from "meddling" in his district might look almost silly today because the practice is so routine. Thus, a 2010 Utah Wilderness bill was introduced by 19 senators from California, Connecticut, Indiana, Iowa, Maryland, Massachusetts, Michigan, New York, Ohio, Rhode Island, Vermont, Washington and Wisconsin—not by either senator from Utah. Environmental leaders and the media characterized the objection of Utah's own senators as partisan, parochial, small-minded and self-serving. If they don't support wilderness designations in their own state, they must not care about the environment; anyway these lands do not belong to people in Utah, but to the entire nation.

That latter argument is, of course, true. But senators from these other states certainly do not really understand the defining wilderness characteristics of specific portions of the Book Cliffs or Dead Horse Cliffs in Utah. Nor did they (or their staffs) participate in several years of public meetings on the issues, and they certainly were not involved in 20 years of studies of wilderness in the Rocky Mountain West or the next 20 years of similar studies of BLM lands. Many people in Utah stayed involved throughout that entire process, and both senators had been involved in the issue for most of their professional lives. That doesn't mean the local officials are always right, nor does it mean the rest of the nation is not entitled to its opinions. It merely means that due deference to the expertise of local and state officials and their congressional delegation is common sense.

I am not a pure states-rights advocate on environmental issues. Federal supremacists frequently point out how deference to state governments was used to hinder the civil rights struggles of the 1960s. They are right, and clearly some decisions must be made at the federal level, including decisions on managing federal lands. However, making those decisions without understanding the specific local circumstances defies logic, so to be credible the process must include the knowledge of—and concern about—the people who live there.

Good decisions must begin with an understanding of the facts. The federal government has a huge staff and can get those facts by sending its own employees to live in the area in question. Federal workers can stay in the local motel, eat in the local cafe, or even move to the area, buy a house and open an office. But they cannot replace the in-depth knowledge and institutional memory of people who have lived there for generations. The federal system brings a national perspective and an understanding of national goals. When combined with sound local knowledge of the facts on the ground, that can lead to informed decisions that the public will accept as based on sound reasoning. That is why the input of locals cannot just be superficial lip service; it must play an accepted role in the decision itself. Thus, state and local governments should be relied upon to supply the facts, and there should be a built-in presumption of the accuracy of such facts, so the resulting federal management decisions can be intelligent, believable and accepted by the public.

Clearly, federal land management decisions belong at the federal level—that is a cornerstone of the conservation movement. But increasingly, local people do not trust that such decisions are based on facts, especially when they see examples such as wilderness designations in areas they know perfectly well are not really wilderness. They understand that many of these congressional wilderness debates are not really about wilderness, but driven by environmental groups with another agenda. That's why environmental groups don't care what the facts are—this is not about facts. It is, as usual, about money, power and control.

It has become a bitter and partisan "gotcha" game designed to help win elections, embarrass certain politicians, stop particular business activities, and especially to raise money for environmental organizations. If it were really about protecting wilderness areas for the future, it would not be terribly difficult to get agreement on both sides of the aisle. As a matter of fact, nearly every western senator of the past 30 years (in both parties) has supported wilderness bills in his own state, including conservatives like Bill Armstrong, Hank Brown, Wayne Allard, Orrin Hatch, Jake Garn, Bob Bennett, Jim McClure, Steve Symms, Dirk Kempthorne, Larry Craig, Mike Crapo, Alan Simpson, Malcolm Wallop, Craig Thomas, Mike Enzi, Paul Laxalt, John Ensign, Pete Domenici, John McCain, Jon Kyl and even Barry Goldwater. In every case, these western states and their delegations in Congress have worked on wilderness designations, wildlife refuges, national parks and monuments, wild and scenic rivers and other forms of protection for the nation's public lands.

For the environmental lobby, as you may surmise, that is not enough. There will never be enough. If we stopped all uses of all public lands in America and built walls that barred all public access forever, it still would not be enough for some groups. Even that would not fulfill their objective, because if the "problems" were "solved" these groups would no longer be needed. People would stop writing checks and, of course, that would not do. So the battle to "protect" more public lands goes on endlessly. But from whom are we "protecting" these lands?

Give Me Land, Lots of Land

Protecting and preserving "open space" is a top priority for the environmental industry, and for the federal government. Most Americans share a concern about that, to, as suburban sprawl continues to eat away at farms, ranches, and other open lands. But there is a disturbing aspect of the process most often used to preserve open space–the view that it can only be saved by government ownership.

Governments own only about a third of the land in the United States, and the most valuable private land is usually in places subject to potential development. So it seems incredible that anyone would realistically think government could save all the remaining open space by buying all the remaining land. No government will ever have that much money. Yet that is precisely what many environmental leaders think.

The Colorado Department of Natural Resources in 2001 estimated that the value of the remaining ranchland in the Roaring Fork Valley alone (from Glenwood Springs to Aspen) was more than the entire state budget. The same was true of the scenic ranches in Gunnison County, but using conservation easements and wildlife management agreements, the State protected a huge portion of that entire area from future development, preserved habitat for the threatened sage grouse (which are now recovering nicely), and maintained one of Colorado's most famous and majestic mountain valleys. Had the focus been on fee title acquisition alone, which environmental organizations once advocated, the State would now own several unprofitable ranches with no clear mission, and thousands of acres of important habitat would now likely be covered with houses and condominiums.

The idea that government should preserve the open space and save wildlife habitat by owning the land is simply unrealistic. There are places, of course, where it makes sense, and there is little public sympathy for proposals to sell off public lands (as James Watt discovered in the 1980's). I have been involved in numerous efforts to arrange federal land exchanges, especially where boundary lines need straightening or where there are unworkable "in-holdings" (privately-owned parcels of land inside national parks and forests). However, the balance of public and private land is very delicate. Just as attempts to sell public lands are generally unpopular, efforts to buy considerably more government land are fraught with peril, too.

There are numerous reasons why government purchases of farm and ranch lands may be ill-advised. In particular, they run counter to our national desire to maintain agriculture. In every community, there is a "critical mass" in farming and ranching. That is to say, you cannot keep farming if you are the only one left. There must be a great enough mass to sustain the required services: the implement dealer, the hardware store, the coop, the fuel delivery business, the sale barn or grain elevator, and even the local café. So any government action that takes a farm or ranch out of production agriculture may be, in the long run, a mistake for that reason. Further, all those lands remain on local tax rolls as long as they remain private land. Once converted to public property, they are no longer subject to property taxes. Many communities simply have trouble surviving without that tax base, especially to support the local schools, fire departments, water and sewer systems and other important services. Earlier, we used the example of Hinsdale County, but there are thousands of others across the country.

Put simply, converting private land to public land on a mass scale would save the open space, but at an unacceptable cost to our economy, history, culture, and quality of life. More to the point, it is unnecessary because there are more efficient ways to preserve open space without destroying our economy. Since most wildlife habitat and open space are provided by private landowners, we must find ways to work closely with them to preserve these important values. And there are dozens of ways to do that.

Wildlife management agreements can be an especially useful tool to ensure that farms do not destroy important habitat or unnecessarily kill wildlife. Thousands of acres throughout the country are successfully managed to everyone's benefit under such agreements. They give wildlife professionals access to the otherwise closed private land, so they can monitor populations of threatened and endangered species, keep tabs on air and water quality, trap and tag wildlife for better tracking, inventory and study nests, and many other activities important to their duties. And for the landowner, these agreements provide assurances against policy changes and other "surprises." They are often called agreements "with assurances," meaning the landowner received "assurances" from the government that he will not be penalized for his normal management practices if future endangered species are found on the property, if he agrees to certain "best management practices" designed to protect habitat reasonably.

The most important advantage of working closely with landowners—instead of against them—is that it changes the culture over time. In the past, many landowners have been so worried about potential government control of their property that they dared not admit to finding an endangered species on their property. Many ranchers refer only half-jokingly to the old "triple-S strategy: shoot, shovel, and shut up." But management agreements with strong assurances are beginning to change that culture, as government managers learn that there are alternatives to regulation and punitive actions. This "cultural shift" is vitally important to both sides.

In *A Sand County Almanac*, Aldo Leopold wrote, "We abuse land because we regard it as a commodity belonging to us. When we see land as a community to which we belong, we may begin to use it with love and respect." That is the cultural shift we see when private landowners work with management agreements, conservation easements, and other programs to save both agriculture and wildlife. But an equally important cultural shift happens with the regulators. To paraphrase Leopold, we abuse landowners because we regard them as the enemy of the land, but when we see them as partners in conservation, we create love and respect for both the land *and* each other.

Nevertheless, faced with a choice between better partnerships with landowners and more federal land acquisition, the federal system still invariably chooses the latter. The environmental lobby simply cannot bring itself to trust people with good stewardship of their own land, and the federal system shares that distrust. Thus, we spend more tax dollars every year on buying more federal land than the entire country originally cost.

Remember, Congress spent just over $55 million buying the entire Western United States (most of the East was acquired without purchases). Today, land acquisition is a significant portion of the annual budget of all the federal land management agencies:

- The Bureau of Land Management's 2012 budget is $1.1 billion. It includes $50 million for land acquisition a $20 million increase over 2011.

- The U.S. Forest Service's 2012 budget is $5.1 billion, which includes $91 million for land acquisition–a $26 million increase over 2011.

- The National Park Service's 2012 budget is $2.9 billion, including $74 million for land acquisition.

- The U.S. Fish and Wildlife Service's 2012 budget is $1.7 billion, including $140 million for land acquisition–four times what it spent on acquisition in 2008.

That's over $350 million for land acquisition in those four agencies alone–excluding land bought by the Defense Department, Homeland Security, and others. In fact, almost every government agency has a land acquisition budget each year. Like most government programs, the amount we spend increases every year–though the amount of land in the country does not. And land acquisition has become more than a means for environmental protection; it is its own goal.

Consider the case of Tom and Nancy Kellenberger of Chillicothe, Ohio. They waged a battle for several years against the National Park Service and the Archeological Conservancy, to keep intact the 350 acre farm their family had occupied for 4 generations. The Park Service wanted 64 acres of their farm to add to its Hopewell Culture National Historic Park (NHP), a site that preserves ancient Indian burial mounds. That might have made sense, except that there were no such burial mounds on the Kellenberger property, just farmland and two family homes. Nevertheless, the government wanted that land (to which the public would have no access) and the Kellenbergers were vilified in the news media for not wanting to give it away. The neighboring burial mounds were preserved by creation of a national monument in 1923, but in 1992 Congress authorized land purchases to expand the park's boundaries, assuming all the nearby property owners would happily sell to the Park Service. The purpose of the park should still be historic preservation of important archeological sites, but the park literature says, "Since the 1992 legislation, a primary objective at Hopewell Culture NHP has been land acquisition… the process of building the park has been slow and blocked by many legal hurdles." Such hurdles have included the fact that some property owners actually want to keep their land, and have children who want to continue farming.

How much government land is enough? The answer is: it depends. It depends upon whether or not we think environmental values can be safeguarded *only* if government owns the land. If you believe that, then you must believe the environment will never be fully protected until government owns every square inch of land in the country. If that seems either financially unrealistic, or philosophically questionable, then better ways must be found for protecting public values on private land.

There is one more overwhelming argument against more government land grabs: government has trouble responsibly managing the 650 million acres it already owns. Remember that national forests have been allowed through complete mismanagement to die, fall down, and burn up across the country. Efforts to balance energy exploration and production with environmental protection on public lands have been met with an inability to make decisions, the "analysis paralysis" mentioned earlier. The public decision-making process is complex enough the way Congress designed it. But the actual implementation over the years has made it even worse, partly because of environmental organizations that sustain themselves by filing lawsuits and appeals, partly because federal judges with personal political agendas have frustrated the process almost beyond repair, and partly because some government officials themselves are more interested in preserving their status quo than the environment.

The federal government refers to the land it owns as "public land," on the theory that it belongs to the public—the government holds and manages it in trust for the public. Most people in the West, however, refer to it as "federal land," because they think the government agencies act more like distant landlords than public trustees.

After all, it doesn't seem like your land if you're not allowed to use it.

Similarly, the government agencies charged with managing these assets consider themselves to be "land managers" or "wildlife managers." In a larger sense, though, they do not really manage land or wildlife. They regulate, permit, tax and limit the relationship of people to these resources. They manage hunting seasons, game management areas, over-the-counter tags or drawing lotteries. What these government agencies really manage is people and their activities.

So when we put officials in charge of "managing" public lands, wildlife and other resources, and we define their roles in terms of regulating, permitting, taxing and limiting people and their activities, we inevitably create an antagonistic mindset. If I am a wildlife manager and you are a hunter, it is my job to "regulate" your activity. If I am a public land manager and you are a miner, it is my job to "permit" and "limit" your activity on "my" land. Even if you are a hiker who wants to camp out, it is my job to decide where you can camp and what trails you should use to hike. That dynamic rarely creates a positive partnership between the public and its appointed trustees. Rather, it creates an enforcement mentality that cannot but result in tense relationships between public land and resource managers and the communities in which they live and work. In many instances, that is an understatement.

The Roads Not Taken

The headlong rush to deny public access to public lands took a turn toward complete absurdity in the 1990s, when government agencies began closing roads by the thousands. Government agencies used Forest Management Plans and recreation plans to change old existing uses and close existing roads and trails. Individual national forests began to rewrite and adopt new "travel management plans" to regulate how and where people could travel on these lands. In many cases, these planning processes were thinly veiled excuses to close existing roads into areas where environmental groups and federal land managers wanted more pristine "wilderness" management. If Congress would not designate the desired areas as wilderness, these groups would simply use "travel management" as a tool to accomplish the same thing on the ground.

Western landowners, communities, counties and states, concerned about proposals to close existing roads, began to assert their existing rights-of-way under the old 1868 road law, RS-2477. Remember, Congress had granted permanent rights-of-way to anyone and everyone for the "construction of highways" across public lands. But now there emerged a nonsensical debate about what a "highway" is and what was meant by the term "construction." Bureaucrats did what they do best—spent months on interagency committees and tens of thousands of tax dollars writing rules about how to interpret those terms. They decided that no road right-of-way would be recognized unless it had been "constructed" in the modern sense of the word. That is, "mechanical equipment" had to have been used to build the road. Many westerners objected, pointing out that in the 19th Century most landowners did not own road construction equipment, and that in many areas, crossing flat deserts or rocky river bottoms did not require equipment.

The paved road on the left is clearly a "highway" and obviously was "constructed." The middle road is not a "highway" today, but it certainly was in 1880. Was it "constructed" with mechanical equipment, or just by ongoing use? No existing record shows its construction, or that of the trail on the right—but both were shown as existing "roads" on old government maps.

On-the-ground facts, however, did not prevail because they did not support the political agenda of the environmental groups seeking to lock up the public lands. Interior Secretary Bruce Babbitt ordered what he called a "moratorium on any consideration" of RS-2477 "claims." He instructed the BLM to simply stop "processing" or even studying any roads claimed as RS-2477 rights-of-way, by state governments or anyone else. Keep in mind, the original congressional grant did not require approval of the Interior Department, and no subsequent law has *ever* given the Interior Department any authority to grant or deny such claims.

The law said simply that anyone who built a road across public lands had acquired a permanent legal right-of-way. Since Congress repealed the old law in 1976, and in the process grandfathered all existing roads built under that law, the only decision affecting the legal status of such roads is whether or not they were built before 1976. If that can be established, no federal agency has any right to close or limit access to such a road. And believe it or not, it is not that difficult to prove whether a road is older than 1976, because by that time there were very good maps of the entire United States. Many westerners even offered to be bound by the government's own maps, since the USGS, BLM, Forest Service and other agencies have all printed road maps for over 100 years. Prior to Babbitt's tenure, the government's policy was that in the case of a dispute it would accept a state or county government's assurance that a road pre-dated 1976. Following the Babbitt moratorium, the federal government no longer trusts states or counties to know when their own local roads were built or used.

Babbitt's "moratorium on consideration" of RS-2477 claims had no legal authority, nor do federal courts particularly care whether the Interior Department "recognizes" such a right-of-way (they either exist or they don't under the law). But the policy had a huge impact on federal land management policy, because there was no corresponding "moratorium" on federal road *closures*. During Babbitt's tenure at Interior, and during much of the Bush and Obama Administrations that followed, the BLM and the Forest Service continued to close thousands of miles of roads with no consideration whatsoever to the legal status of those roads. In 2002 the Interior Department made a deal with the state of Utah to "resolve" the issue by accepting only a state government certification of roads, only if they met the federal description (mechanically constructed and used for a series of specified purposes), and only before an agreed-upon deadline. It was an attempt by the government to repeal valid existing rights while maintaining an appearance of working with state and local stakeholders.

The Utah deal did not last until the ink on it dried, partly because it had no legal basis, but mostly because no other states were consulted. No other western state was prepared to let Utah determine how their rights-of-way disputes would be resolved. In Colorado, many landowners and several local governments did not even trust their own state to represent their interests (many of these rights-of-way belong to private landowners and local governments, not to states). Further, numerous local governments had differing points of view. For instance, Moffat County in Colorado had mapped and documented miles of old roads to keep BLM from closing them, whereas San Miguel County actually supported federal efforts to close a number of such roads. Either way, the state could not represent both points of view. So Colorado, Nevada and several other states simply maintained that the rights-of-way belonged to whoever had acquired them, not to the Interior Department. In most places the issue remains unresolved today.

In the meantime, the government has continued to close and even physically obliterate numerous roads that had been used for public access to public lands. The theory that any road on federal land is a federal road subject to federal whims has all but completely replaced a legal right created *and still acknowledged* by Congress. The lands may belong to the public, but to the federal government that does not mean the public has any right to visit them.

Rewriting History, Government-Style

The government's non-stop effort to close public access to public lands has been especially noticeable in the use of "travel management" over the past generation. Nearly all national forests and most BLM districts have gone through an elaborate process of adopting new "Travel Management Plans," designed to publish new maps showing where the public could and could not go—in vehicles, on horses, or on foot. Old Forest Service maps had to be updated, the agency said, to reflect modern times. The primary driving force behind the national effort was the growing controversy about "off-highway vehicles (OHVs)" such as 3- and 4-wheeled all-terrain vehicles (ATVs) and snowmobiles.

Throughout the 1970s and '80s, these personal-sized vehicles had grown in popularity to such an extent that many land managers worried about the destruction of natural resources by the unchecked carving of new trails across vast areas of the landscape. In many places, such as national parks, the government attempted an outright ban on ATVs and snowmobiles. However, the fierce opposition of well-organized off-road vehicle user groups made such bans very difficult to implement, much less enforce. Coalitions of off-road enthusiasts sprang up across the country to fight all attempts to ban the vehicles, or to close miles of roads and trails. Such groups were seldom well-financed, but often boasted hundreds of active members in local communities. These members were highly-motivated, willing to show up at public hearings in mass numbers, and ready to vote and to campaign against politicians who supported OHV bans.

Opposite that grass-roots activity stood the vast "environmental industry," spending a fortune pushing for "wilderness management" of as much public land as possible. They pressured Congress and federal land managers to ban OHVs, close roads and trails, ban construction of any new routes, impose noise and dust regulations, and generally any approach that would make the use of OHVs more difficult on public lands. The growing use of OHVs became a ready excuse to close thousands of miles of roads, not just OHV trails, but regular vehicle roads used by generations to access public lands.

This is a perfect example of a "bait and switch" tactic that has become common in today's environmental lobby. Its leaders know that they can make OHVs unpopular with the public, because very few people actually own one. So if they can get people upset about the abuses of OHVs there will be general support for their proposed solution—closing the roads used by these OHVs. So they use the most egregious examples of tire tracks in the mud crossing wetlands and meadows, or deep gashes in steep slopes resulting in erosion, to demonstrate the ongoing abuses (already illegal) and call for immediate action to save the outdoors from such abuse. Immediate action always begins with the need to join the effort and write checks, couched in terms that make it seem that ordinary people at the grassroots level have to join to fight off the abuses of giant industries, though of course the reverse is the truth in this case. Nevertheless, the effort is effective because most people genuinely care about the environment and want to help stop abuses. So, people by the thousands join these efforts, helping create the giant "industry" the environmental movement itself has become. And that "industry" in turn has beefed up its effort to end the abuses of OHVs by demanding closure of thousands of miles of roads—not just roads inappropriately carved out by hell-raising OHVs but full-sized vehicle roads used by ordinary people to access public lands generations before OHVs were even invented. If the battle were really about OHVs, that response goes way beyond a necessary solution, like swatting flies with sledgehammers. That is a strong clue that the agenda was never really about OHVs, yet these small but tough vehicles have become the focus of a national "cause."

At a congressional hearing in March, 2012, Intermountain Regional Forester Harv Forsgren said public road closures are part of "an ongoing process" across the West. He acknowledged that the unpopular road closures "may force changes in the way people experience national forests." But he cited an explosion in the use of off-highway vehicles over the past 15 years, using data about the increase in OHV registrations in Utah (which he said more than tripled between 1998 and 2006). In other words, 15 years ago lots of people purchased OHV's in Utah, so the Forest Service thinks it ought to close roads throughout the region—without having to show whether those OHV's have even used, much less abused, the national forests in question.

The Forest Service and BLM have both helped feed the growing opposition to OHV's with a national effort, underway for about 20 years now, to rewrite all their "travel management plans." This involves a public process designed to reach compromise between the competing interest groups and publish new travel maps upon which everyone can agree. Such a collaborative process—touted by Administrations of both parties—can be highly successful everywhere (and has been in a few places), but only if all the participants approach the debate with honesty and openness, spelling out their goals up front and sticking to agreements that are made. Unfortunately, in environmental debates such honesty has been the exception rather than the rule.

Consider the process by which the U.S. Forest Service rewrote the travel management plan for the Grand Mesa National Forest, beginning in the late 1990s, and resulting in new travel maps in 2003, and again in 2008. Nothing about the procedure there was particularly unusual, and it is a representative example of the way this process plays out all too frequently. The Forest Service began with public announcements about the process, seeking "stakeholders" from all sides to serve on committees and attend the required public meetings. Predictably, hundreds of OHV enthusiasts, environmental leaders (both local and otherwise), elected officials, news media and other interest groups began packing the meetings. The Forest Service then began to establish "official" stakeholders, those who would be specifically invited to represent certain interests— and thus inevitably leaving hundreds of interested people out of the process, people who would feel no sense of ownership of the final agreement, and no obligation to accept it. Furthermore, as usual very few people were able to stick with a process that lasted well over a decade—the system simply wears down even strong leaders with a process that never seems to end.

Once the various interests were seated, the divisions became crystal clear from the beginning. Environmental groups wanted to close down virtually all existing roads and trails on the forest; the OHV groups wanted the right to go anywhere and everywhere whenever they chose. Neither side would publicly admit to those positions, but the battle lines were drawn.

I was there, too, serving as president and CEO of a giant coalition called Club 20, a 55-year-old organization of counties, communities, businesses, non-profits and individuals in the 20 counties west of the Continental Divide in Colorado. Its dues-paying members include all the elected officials in those counties, most of the major businesses and industries, and dozens of interest groups on both sides of these issues. Its policies are made by a vote of a democratically-elected board with voting representation from all 20 counties.

The united communities that make up Club 20 had decided on a moderate approach to travel management on national forests that would put the environment first, protect important existing business and agricultural interests, and make reasonable compromises on vehicle access issues. We began with the assumption that both of the extreme sides had their heels dug in too deeply, and that there was reasonable middle ground. We proposed that OHVs be limited to the use of existing roads and trails that are wide enough to accommodate them. We suggested preserving existing roads, banning construction of any new ones, and seasonal use restrictions where appropriate. Our members did not agree with OHV advocates who believed they should be allowed to go anywhere they wanted just because they could. It seemed clear to us that the technology had made these vehicles capable of going straight up and down steep slopes where erosion would result, and other places where their use seemed obviously damaging to the environment. It also seemed reasonable to impose some seasonal limits in crucial elk calving grounds, important wildlife migration routes, and delicate riparian zones (lakes, streams and wetlands). This seemed to most Western Slope residents like grounds for a reasonable compromise, and since nearly all elected officials endorsed this approach, we believed the Forest Service would ultimately produce a plan along those lines. We were even more confident of success when most of the local environmental leaders also endorsed such an approach.

Unfortunately, that is where the honesty in the process ended, supplanted by the hidden agendas of those who sought to close miles of existing roads. Although the entire debate had focused on OHVs, it turned out that for environmental leaders and Forest Service officials, the real agenda was also to close old roads and ban regular cars and jeeps—even though not one person had presented a shred of evidence that such family vehicles were creating problems. They were not guilty of carving out new roads, nor were their numbers said to have increased notably. Those accusations were made about ATVs and snowmobiles, but it turned out that much of the exercise was not really about managing the difficulties of this modern travel technology. It was about closing roads and ending all public access to vast tracts of public land. Thus, the Forest Service began by agreeing to "grandfather" most *existing* roads, but in the end the agency simply denied the *existence* of hundreds of miles of such roads. In this manner, officials could say they had protected existing roads and rights, while in fact limiting access to hunting grounds and fishing lakes used by generations of families. It is worth noting that the existing roads in question were not carved by hell-raisers on ATV's, but built under the Forest Service's supervision by irrigation companies and ranchers to access their reservoirs, by lumber companies to access timber sales, and by FDR's Civilian Conservation Corps to provide hunting, fishing and camping access.

When confronted with new maps that omitted old roads, the Forest Service claimed such roads were never "authorized" to begin with, and had been "illegally" carved into the landscape by renegades. Officials at first flatly denied many of these old roads had been there very long, or that the government had ever acknowledged them. But the Forest Service's own travel maps, published 40 years earlier, proved otherwise. We succeeded in showing that the Forest Service

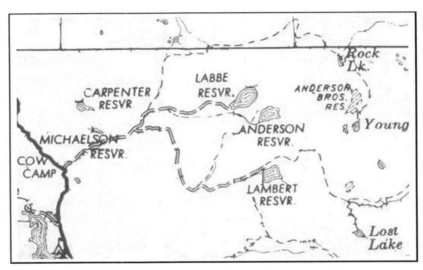

1959 Grand Mesa Travel Map, U.S. Forest Service (detail)
Single lines are foot trails; double lines are vehicle roads

had acknowledged and permitted numerous roads it now sought to close, and in a few places persuaded the agency to leave those roads alone. But in most cases we were shouted down or ignored and the result was obliteration of hundreds of miles of old roads and closing public access to future generations. People like my father (now in his 70s and no longer able to hike for miles) will never again see some of their favorite Grand Mesa lakes.

For example, on these pages you see a comparison from the two official Grand Mesa Travel Management Maps, both published by the U.S. Forest Service, one in 1959 and the other in 2008. They show a section of the forest just southeast of the town of Collbran.

Notice the road shown on the 1959 travel map (at left) going northeast from Michaelson Reservoir to Labbe Reservoir, and the more southern route to Lambert Reservoir. On the 2008 map (below) the Forest Service road follows the older trail route between Anderson and Lambert, but both the direct southern Lambert Road, and the northern route to Labbe Reservoir are gone—as if they never existed.

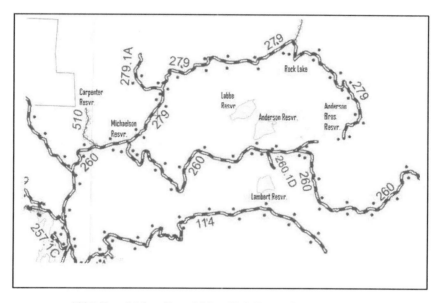

2008 Grand Mesa Travel Map, U.S. Forest Service (detail)

The 1959 official travel map shows numerous roads and trails that were closed in the 2003 and 2008 travel plan amendments. Some were obliterated, others simply closed to the public or turned into foot trails. Many of these old roads are still there, of course, you just can't drive over them anymore.

Travel plans like that for the Grand Mesa National Forest have been amended and rewritten throughout the national forest system over the past few years. The disappearance of roads to places like

Labbe Reservoir is not the slightest bit uncommon. Indeed, it is a story that has played out all across the country over the past few years and the details are familiar to community leaders wherever there are public lands. There are arguments about the cost of road maintenance, but the larger problem is simply an agency culture that opposes public access, especially motorized access. Today, many people are simply made to feel like they have committed some great atrocity by visiting the national forests for hunting, fishing, camping, hiking or just driving around to admire the scenery. Are the people really destroying our national forests by enjoying them? Are we loving the land to death, as some have put it?

On the contrary, the truth is that if people cannot enjoy public lands and beautiful places, they are likely to care less about those places. The generations of westerners who grew up fishing and hunting in these special places not only know them best, they love them most. If we care about raising generations of Americans who will continue the tradition of stewardship of these national treasures, then it is a grave mistake to ban the public from public lands. The future of these places depends on the extent to which we care, and like it or not, it is hard to care about a place you've never seen. Of course, there is the Rhode Island congressional staffer's view that "it is enough just to know it's there," and many share that legitimate view. But where have they been during the past few years of catastrophic fires that have burned millions of acres of forests? Where is their outrage about the Forest Service's budgets being decimated by "borrowing" for such emergencies? Where is their concern when whole towns have to be evacuated in the wake of these massive fires?

People who never visit public lands may "care" in an academic sense, but will never share the passion of people who visit regularly and use these places for their recreation, for their business, or just to recharge their batteries. Barring such people from the public lands over time has begun to alter the relationship between people and nature—to the disadvantage of nature. Perhaps it is understandable, or even predictable, that most Americans seem unaware of the extremely unhealthy condition of our national forests, because most people have never seen them. That is precisely why the access and involvement of local people is important; it creates a "constituency," a dedicated core of advocates, for each individual forest. Absent that, even local people who inhabit nearby towns have become largely oblivious to the miles and miles of dead and dying trees all around their communities, and the fire danger that poses to their own homes. Should we really be surprised that so many people are unaware of what is happening in the forests if they have never been there? In the long run, barring the public from public lands is a death sentence for the national forests, which will quite simply have no local constituency.

Without roads people will not have access to nature and the very activities for which the "public" lands were set aside. What it means to be an American will be different. This redrawing of the maps locks the public out of its own birthright. We shake our heads and do what we're told because we have been led to believe these government actions are all in the name of environmental protection. But these "road erasures" are not about the environment and are no accident. What some locals who are denied access to their favorite fishing holes or camping spots can't see is that each road erasure is not just a single act, but another brick in the wall of the true environmental industry agenda, because it helps create "roadless areas."

Roadless Areas

Clearly, some public lands should not be opened for certain uses, and some ought to be preserved forever in a pristine condition, but deciding which areas those should be has generated tremendous controversy. Congress passed the Wilderness Act of 1964, legislating that some lands should be set aside for different treatment than all the other federal lands "reserved" by Congress in the past. Wilderness areas would be kept in their original pristine condition, not available for leasing for any purpose (grazing, logging, mining, oil and gas) and unavailable for off-road recreation, or any public access except by hiking and horseback riding. All motorized or mechanical access (including bicycles) was prohibited. These unique and special places would be kept forever in a condition defined almost poetically in the law as "......*an area where the earth and its community of life are untrammeled by man, where man himself is a visitor who does not remain.*"

Because access is so severely restricted, wilderness areas can only be designated by an Act of Congress, the same as national parks. The law is crystal clear about that. But Congress planned to rely heavily on two factors in determining what should be designated wilderness: support of the state and local communities involved, and a recommendation by the Forest Service after finding that the area was in fact roadless (untrammeled) and contained no previous development. As it turns out, "previous development," "roadless," and even "local support," are in the mind of the beholder.

Throughout the 1980s the U.S. Forest Service struggled with a congressional mandate to study all its lands to determine what areas were roadless. Called the "Roadless Area Review and Evaluation," the effort saw two consecutive reports over a ten-year period (RARE and RARE II). The Forest Service made recommendations and with support of the congressional delegations of the various western states, Congress significantly expanded the nation's wilderness acreage. In the original 1964 law Congress had designated 9 million acres, but that was always seen as a starting point. Today, the wilderness system comprises over 100 million acres, now administered by the Forest Service, Park Service, BLM and Fish and Wildlife Service.

In spite of these accomplishments, the environmental lobby has always seen the Wilderness Act as a great tool for stopping potential future development, and has never ceased pressuring Congress to designate more and more wilderness. Whether or not an area is actually an untrammeled wilderness is of no importance to that effort; in fact these environmental groups frequently push to have areas designated that they know perfectly well contain roads (roads they want to close), power lines, mining claims, oil and gas leases, and sometimes even private homes. Because it has proven difficult for these groups to convince even a friendly Congress to ignore the pleas of people whose property values would be destroyed by wilderness designation, environmental organizations have developed tools for creating de-facto wilderness areas without Congress.

One example is Interior Secretary Ken Salazar's attempt to designate "Wild Lands" that the BLM would manage as wilderness, without an Act of Congress. Although Congress temporarily blocked implementation with an appropriations amendment, the Department continues to identify areas that it thinks warrant wilderness designation, and the Obama Administration continues to look for ways to shut down multiple uses of public lands, especially for oil and gas, timber and grazing.

During the second Bush Administration, the environmental lobby dusted off the old concept of "roadless" areas. The theory was that administrative directives and management plans (without legislation) could be adopted to protect roadless areas from development before it happened. All that was required was a good inventory of what areas are in fact roadless. Sound familiar? It is, of course, yet another roadless evaluation just like those done in the 1970s and '80s. In the 21st Century, there are no federal lands that have not been studied, inventoried, mapped, catalogued, categorized and studied again. The only difference was that all those earlier reports did not produce the result the environmental groups wanted; they didn't designate enough wilderness areas. So the environmentalists persuaded Congress and the Administration to go through the same exercise yet again.

The table was set by an eleventh-hour Clinton executive order (announced two weeks before his successor's election) forcing a re-review of 43 million acres of National Forests already determined not suitable for wilderness designation for one reason or another. Clinton proposed to create administrative rules prohibiting most uses on any lands found to be roadless. State governments throughout the West, along with landowners and affected communities cried foul and beseeched the Bush Administration to put the process on hold while Congress debated the merits of this new approach. The new Administration was divided on the issue, however, and in 2001 a final rule was adopted extending roadless protection to more than 58 million acres identified by environmental activists and federal bureaucrats as roadless (15 million acres more than Clinton had proposed). The Bush Administration waited until after its 2004 re-election, and then reversed the rule, touching off a series of lawsuits that are still mostly unsettled. And predictably, the Obama Administration has taken up the other side's torch, attempting not only to reinstate the Clinton rule, but to go even further with a new version that would voluntarily surrender hard-won Forest Service authority back to environmental groups and the courts.

During the Bush Administration, officials had tried to split the baby and create a clever solution to a major controversy instead of simply doing the right thing. Rather than undertaking a more thorough and detailed analysis of forest lands that were actually roadless, the Bush rules empowered state governors to petition for roadless designation after their own analysis and inventory. As expected, governors of different political parties were all over the map on the issue, creating completely different approaches to the same problem. Even those supporting this state approach (including me) complained that the federal government had reserved the final say on the matter, so it could accept, reject or modify these recommendations from governors. Communities, landowners and other "stakeholders" had to go through months of interminable committee meetings yet again studying the same lands they had been through at least twice before, and again having to rehash the same silly argument about what constitutes a road. Proponents of additional wilderness protection, where roads were undeniable, simply "cherry-stemmed" those roads out of their proposed new "roadless area" maps.

"Cherry-stem" is a euphemistic description for a road carved out of a wilderness area, so that the rest of the area can be considered "roadless" even though a road might go right through the middle. The idea is that all the surrounding area—except the roadway itself—can be called wilderness, and the resulting boundary line sticks into the middle of the wilderness like a cherry stem. This graphic from a group called the Re-Wilding Institute shows how the process works. The diagram on the right shows, of course, their first choice, but if existing roads cannot be closed outright, at least the land around them can be wilderness, as in the first two examples:

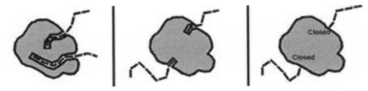

In theory, the practice may provide a compromise for keeping some historic roads open while still affording "protection" to beautiful areas. In practice, however, it has been used so extensively that many areas have been declared roadless, and managed as wilderness, that are not even close to any reasonable definition of "roadless" or "wilderness."

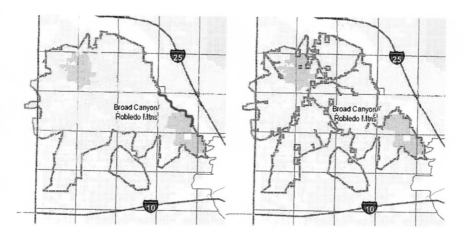

The map on the left shows an area in New Mexico that wilderness advocates pushed hard to declare roadless, as part of a larger effort to stop all future uses and close existing roads. Following a public process in which all the existing roads were identified, the compromises to grandfather existing uses by "cherry-stemming" these roads resulted in the wilderness proposal on the right. The dark blue lines, representing the boundaries of the proposed wilderness, show how many roads exist throughout the area.

Two other details about these maps are worth noting. First, the light blue color represents state trust lands, and the checkerboard common to Western states with such lands is apparent throughout the proposed wilderness area. Second, the two dark yellow parcels show the original wilderness study areas—places BLM's on-the-ground experts said were worthy of analysis because they had wilderness characteristics. It does not take a detailed analysis or years of committee meetings to see that the rest of this area is, quite simply, not a wilderness. It has been used for generations and is clearly not "untrammeled by man." It is checkered with land the federal government does not own, and crisscrossed by roads throughout. It would never pass wilderness muster in Congress, so the Clinton Roadless Rule process was used instead to gain wilderness management of these BLM lands *without an Act of Congress.*

A year after the Bush Administration repealed the Clinton Rule and empowered state governors to make their recommendations, five states (New Mexico, California, Virginia, North Carolina and South Carolina) did so, filing petitions requesting full protection of all the acres covered in the original Clinton Rule. However, later the same year, Idaho submitted a petition identifying some roadless acres, but fewer than those the Clinton rule had ordered protected. Environmental groups immediately criticized Idaho as "the first state to request less than 100% protection" of its roadless areas. The legal challenges in Idaho may go on for years. Ironically, the recommendations of the governors of five states seemed acceptable, but those of the governor of Idaho were not. Governors, it seemed, could be trusted only if they agreed with the environmental groups.

Several of these groups had already filed suit by the time Idaho's recommendations were received in Washington, D.C. Predictably, the first suit was not filed in Idaho, or any other state where the controversy was ongoing, but in a "friendly" federal court in California. As expected, Judge Elizabeth Laporte (U.S. District Court for the Northern District of California) ruled that the Bush Administration had violated several laws when it repealed the Clinton Rule. Clinton was not required to follow the prescribed complex procedures in issuing the rule, but Bush could not repeal it without doing so, she ruled. The court reinstated the Clinton Roadless Rule and enjoined the Forest Service from undertaking any activity (she specifically cited "road building or logging") inconsistent with it. After several more years of legal appeals, the Clinton Rule was finally left standing by the U.S. Supreme Court.

As if to make sure we all understood that the ruling was based on politics, not law, the judge's order exempted 9 million acres of the Tongass National Forest in Alaska because of a separate lawsuit that involved that state and its congressional delegation (too hot to handle). But the court specifically barred all road building in connection with more than 300 oil and gas leases already sold after the Clinton Rule was issued, along with a specific project in Idaho. Oil and gas leases are, of course, worthless if access is denied. When looking for hidden agendas, a good clue is who will be hurt in the end. The lawsuit and Judge Laporte's ruling were not about protecting truly "untrammeled" wilderness areas—they were about stopping oil and gas exploration and logging.

Both timber and energy production on public lands are legitimate disagreements and should be debated on their merits. But those disagreements are not about preserving wilderness, especially in places that are not wilderness by any reasonable standard. Using the Wilderness Act, the Endangered Species Act and other environmental laws as tools to stop energy production is not only dishonest, it often hurts the environment such laws were designed to protect. This is especially true when it turns people against these important laws for reasons that, again, have nothing to do with the environment. Pretending roads do not exist, and denying people access where they have traditionally enjoyed it, is more than wrong. It has caused inestimable damage to property values in the West and turned thousands of citizens who love their environment against the groups and systems established to protect it. Worst of all, it leaves nature itself vulnerable to angry reaction instead of deserved protection. It leaves our public lands, absent a strong local constituency, subject to the control of a massive "environmental industry" that seeks to control public lands, even by circumventing Congress, for reasons that have nothing to do with the environment.

Environmental Justice

All of these efforts to limit public access to public lands are based on a strange theory that mankind's presence is always bad for the environment. People are not part of the environment in this theory. They are an intrusion that should be stopped whenever and wherever possible. This idea has developed fairly recently, and it completely ignores one of the most important themes of the original conservation movement: justice.

The early writings of Theodore Roosevelt, Gifford Pinchot, and many other conservation pioneers contained three essential concepts. First, resources must be used wisely to supply the needs of mankind. Second, resources must be renewed and preserved so they will still be available for future generations. The conflict between those two concepts forms the basis for nearly all environmental arguments to this day. But there was also a third essential concept—nearly lost in the modern debate—that resources must be available equally to all people, not held as the province of an elite few. Pinchot often captured all three ideas in his simple slogan for national forest management: "the greatest good for the greatest number over the greatest time."

Consider the vital importance of the interconnection of all three ideas. Forests could provide *the greatest good* for the current generation by being cut all at once and thus providing cheap timber and paper—and lots of water in all the rivers. But that would provide nothing over time (in fact, it would be a disaster in the future). Conversely, forests could be entirely saved for future generations, guaranteeing they would last for *the greatest time*, (though the lack of any wood and paper products would be an economic disaster today). Finally, providing unlimited timber and paper to a small handful of corporate titans who controlled all the timber companies would not be providing the resources for *the greatest number* (remember, freeing the rest of society from the control of Gilded Age "robber barons" was central to Roosevelt's progressive movement).

The wisdom of this equation has not changed in the decades since Roosevelt's death. We still should not over-utilize natural resources for the sole benefit of today's generation, with no thought about the future. Nor should we fail to use these lands to provide vital resources needed in today's economy. Neither should we allow an elite few to be sole beneficiary of these resources that belong to all the people.

In Roosevelt's 1907 State of the Union Message, he outlined the recommendations of a public lands commission he had appointed to update the nation's management laws. Note the joint threats he outlined:

*Their examination specifically showed the existence of great fraud upon the public domain, and their recommendations for changes in the law were made with the design of conserving the natural resources of every part of the public lands by putting it to its best use. Especial attention was called to the prevention of settlement by the passage of great areas of public land **into the hands of a few men**, and to the enormous waste caused by **unrestricted grazing** upon the open range. The recommendations of the Public-Lands Commission are sound, for they are especially in the interest of the actual home-maker; and where the small home-maker cannot at* *present utilize the land they provide that the government shall keep control of it so that it may not be **monopolized by a few men**. [Emphasis added]*

In other words, Roosevelt thought the two great threats to future conservation of public resources were overuse and elitist control. One important detail has changed since the turn of the 20th Century. We now view forests and other public lands in a much broader framework than before. They still provide water, timber, paper, oil, gas, coal, silver, fur, fish and venison, just as they did in Roosevelt's time. But today these lands also provide recreation for which people in 1900 had little time. Today we value not only the minerals and trees, but also on a much larger scale than ever before the fun, exercise, photography, art, scenic beauty, solitude, quiet and inner peace many people get from simply visiting and viewing these places. But other than a longer list of resources we now know these lands hold, what else has changed? Can we now provide all this bounty for today's generation, with no thought about the future? Of course not. Can we now save it all for the future, with no thought about the needs of today's people? Again, of course not. So why would anyone think we can now provide all this bounty—*the greatest good over the greatest time*—but only for the benefit of an elite few?

Those who seek to lock up the public lands and exclude huge segments of the public are scarcely better than those who once sought to own and control the entire nation's timber supply, or to graze the public lands until every blade of grass was gone. Are these latter day elitists any different than the robber barons of history in pushing land policies that benefit only one segment? Our ancestors fought a revolution against the concept that all resources belonged to the crown and peasants could be executed for killing the king's deer. Yet today's environmental elites push the notion that public lands should only be used by a few people for permitted purposes, and some federal land managers treat these resources as their own, believing they must protect them *from the public*.

Roosevelt would never have embraced the idea that a few people can determine when and where the rest of the public can visit public lands, much less a view that hiking and horseback riding are OK but logging and bicycling are not. He believed very strongly in responsible use, preservation and justice as the three legs of conservation—what Pinchot described as managing resources for the greatest good of the greatest number over the greatest time.

The concept of justice has, unfortunately, been forgotten by many of today's environmental leaders, a modern-day aristocracy whose elitism and arrogance threatens that ideal. The resources belong to all of us, not just those who want to hike and be alone. The solitude of a national forest and the thrill of hooking a wild rainbow trout belong equally to people confined to wheelchairs, or elderly people no longer able to hike two miles to their favorite lake. Those who seek to stop the cutting of all trees drive up the cost of lumber, and are at least partly responsible for the higher cost of homes for all Americans. Their use of environmental laws to lock up America's oil and gas reserves are at least partly responsible for higher gas prices, which hurt the poorest among us most of all. Tillamook County (Oregon) Commissioner Charles Hurliman, in an eloquent letter to the *Daily Astorian*, called it the "tyranny of the minority" for which "the rest of us are paying the price."

Today's environmental leaders talk a great deal about what they call "environmental justice." Yet they completely ignore the actual meaning of the phrase. To them it means the forests do not belong only to timber interests, and that the Naval Oil Shale Reserve belongs to hikers as much as to oil and gas companies. They are right about that, of course, but they use the concept to build figurative walls around vast tracts of public spaces that will no longer be available to millions of Americans—for any purpose. They are the self-appointed arbiters of which land uses are permitted and what areas must be locked up. They represent the opposite of environmental justice. They are today's aristocracy, their elevated positions based not on personal wealth but on their perception of moral superiority. They are the Gilded Age robber barons of our time, seeking to use immense sums of money, and the political power it buys, to control the nation's natural resources for their own exclusive benefit. *The greatest good over the greatest time, for the people who share their political views.*

If much of this elitist agenda seems dishonest, that's because it is. Many environmental zealots have no problem with that. They have come to believe they serve a higher God in some way—that lying about their real agenda, or moving the line after an agreement has been reached, or filing lawsuits they promised not to file, are acceptable if done in the pursuit of an environmental goal. Many writers have gone so far as to compare modern environmentalism to a new religion. I know many environmental leaders well enough to know that is not quite an accurate portrayal. Environmentalism is not a religion in any traditional sense, of course, but it is often based on what its adherents see as the truth, which must be forced on everyone for their own good. They consider their standards high, but their standards certainly differ from mine. In the West where I was raised, a handshake is a contract and a man's word is his bond. We admire people whose agreement you can "take to the bank." Real leaders—in natural resources as in all other fields—always share that view. Some of these activists seem so "radical" precisely because they have a different view, a belief that all is fair in the pursuit of environmental victories. In other words, the ends justify the means.

A frequently-cited spokesman for that perspective is the famous activist, Tre Arrow. A federal judge in Oregon recently sent Arrow to prison for 6 ½ years for torching logging trucks as a protest against a timber sale. He has been a well-known figure in the Pacific Northwest environmental movement for many years. A one-time congressional candidate, he spent 11 days sitting on a narrow window ledge at a U.S. Forest Service office in 2000. When given his chance to express remorse for the vandalism that earned his prison sentence, he said, "My heart and my passion lie in being the person I feel is true to a higher power. I will continue to be that person through music and peaceful actions."

Perhaps Tre Arrow and others think burning other people's property is a "peaceful action." But more likely, they really believe they serve a "higher power" and have a moral obligation to do everything they can to stop uses of the public lands with which they disagree. It is a false morality. It ignores our *dual* obligation: to protect resources for the future, and to use those resources to provide a better life today. And the obvious problem is that the resources don't belong to Tre Arrow anymore than they belong to the CEO of the logging company. That is the essence of environmental justice that people like Arrow may never understand.

The year after leaving the White House, Theodore Roosevelt again explained his philosophy to an audience in Kansas. He recognized the right, he said, even the "duty" of his generation to use the nation's natural resources and public lands to create a prosperous America. "But I do not recognize the right to waste them," he added, "or to rob, by wasteful use, the generations that come after us." Today's environmental leaders often cite that speech, emphasizing the future (preservation) and claiming that Roosevelt made that the more important point by saving it for last, after mentioning the need for resources by the current generation. But he did not use the word "duty" by accident; it was at the core of his philosophy, and the balance between use and preservation is the essence of environmental justice.

These resources belong to all the people who will come after us, but also to the people alive today. And these resources belong to ALL the people, *not just* the loggers and drillers—and *not just* the environmentalists.

CHAPTER 7

AT THE RISK OF BEING CRUDE

"I wanted to be at my parents' house when the electricity came. It was in 1940. I remember my mother smiling. When the lights came on full, tears started to run down her cheeks…From there I went to my grandmother's house. It was a day of celebration. They had all kinds of parties-mountain people getting light for the first time."
—Clyde Ellis, Rural Electrification Administration

Things we take for granted today, like the lights in our homes, require the use of natural resources on a scale our grandparents could never have imagined. Every American born today will require 504,000 pounds of coal, 6,290,000 cubic feet of natural gas, and 72,000 gallons of oil to live the same lifestyle we now live. And that is just the beginning of the "non-renewable" natural resources we all use in our day-to-day lives.

The Mineral Information Institute (MII) keeps track of minerals Americans use, by averaging consumption statistics from the US Geological Survey and the Energy Information Administration with annual population estimates from the Census Bureau. The annual MII statistics are staggering. If you are an average American, you will need in your lifetime about:

- 969 pounds of copper,
- 12,000 pounds of clay,
- 1,090,000 pounds of stone, sand and gravel,
- 831 pounds of lead,
- 512 pounds of zinc,
- 1.53 troy ounces of gold,

- 40,053 pounds of cement,
- 26,591 pounds of iron,
- 6,063 pounds of aluminum,
- 31,577 pounds of salt,
- 31,049 pounds of various other minerals and metals.

Altogether, that means you will need in your lifetime about 3 million pounds of minerals, metals and fuels. Where in the world will you get all that?

Like so many other environmental discussions, the initial facts seem almost insurmountable and they present major challenges for policy makers, but like other environmental discussions, they also require context.

The truth is that we will never run out of natural resources and we will never run out of energy—not in your lifetime or in the lifetimes of your great grandchildren.

That is true for two reasons. First, most of the natural resources needed for our happiness and prosperity are "used," but not "consumed." Second, there is no limit to mankind's ability to discover, produce, create, invent and perfect new sources of energy. Ralph Waldo Emerson once wrote that *"Nothing is rich but the inexhaustible wealth of nature. She shows us only surfaces, but she is a million fathoms deep."* Even though he wrote that before the invention of the internal combustion engine, at a time when he could not imagine the levels of energy we use today, he is nonetheless continually proven right.

The Earth is a gigantic ball of fossil fuels, minerals, and energy. It supports an unimaginable growth of plants, is host to more kinds of life than we have yet been able to count, and is covered 70 percent with water. Some pessimists will say that water is mostly unusable because of its salt and minerals, but others may see it as yet another almost unlimited source of minerals—and energy. People whose glass is always half empty are constantly sounding the alarm that we are quickly running out of energy and minerals, but the next Century will prove them wrong—we will never run out.

Ultimately, the source of all energy on Earth is the sun. Traveling 186,000 miles per second, light from the sun takes about 8 minutes to reach the Earth. Those light rays are amazingly powerful in spite of the distance. Just the tiny fraction of the Sun's energy that hits the Earth (about one hundredth of one millionth of one percent) is enough to meet all the power needs of all the people on Earth many times over. In fact, every minute, enough energy arrives at the Earth to meet the entire planet's demands for a year—if it could be successfully put to use. That is our generation's great challenge and we are making remarkable progress. Vast advances have been made in using the sun's energy directly, especially with photovoltaic cells that generate electricity directly from the sun's rays. However, that is only one of the many ways we use the sun's energy. After all, the sun also warms the air, causes wind, melts snow, makes rivers, and moves oceans. And remember, the sun also creates fossil fuels, a process that is just as continuous.

Indeed, the concept of "renewable" and "non-renewable" resources is a bit misleading—all natural resources are renewed; some just take longer than others. A tree can grow in one human lifetime or less, where coal and oil take a few thousand years. Typical of our human arrogance, we view resources as renewable only if we can see them renewed in our own time, or if we can "use" without "consuming" them. The greatest of the "renewable" resources in that sense are air, sunlight and water. When we generate energy by taking advantage of the wind, the wind still blows afterwards. When we use sunlight to generate energy, the sun is still shining afterwards. We generate energy from the movement of water; we "impound" it by building dams; we divert it to other locations where it is needed; and we "consume" some of it, though only momentarily. Just as with wind and sun, we do not really stop the inevitable flow of water to the oceans, or its evaporation and precipitation back onto land. Because we can see those processes in our time, we consider that energy "renewable."

On the other hand, when we extract coal, oil and gas from the ground and burn them to generate energy, to us they appear gone forever. But of course, they are not. The carbon they emit helps grow plants and animals. Plants and animals are still dying, decaying, sinking into the ground, decomposing into compost, being heated and pressurized by a new overburden, and eventually turning into more coal, oil and gas. Because that takes longer than we can see, we consider those resources "non-renewable."

The question with these "non-renewable" resources is whether or not we can use them faster than they are being created. At worst, the answer is only maybe, because the technology for finding and extracting minerals more than keeps pace with demand. We really don't know how much usable energy lies beneath the Earth's surface, because technology keeps finding more, and also expanding our understanding of what is usable.

Today's geologists regularly find massive reserves of oil, gas and other minerals previously unknown. The known reserves of natural gas in the U.S., for example, have increased 5-fold in the last 5 years, especially with recent development of the Marcellus shale formation in the northeast and the Bakken formation in the Dakotas. Engineers regularly develop means for drilling in places unimaginable a few years ago, from extremely deep oceans to rugged mountainsides. Experts continually discover ways to use—and reuse—resources previously thought to be worthless, from garbage to weeds to mine waste. And manufacturers are getting better every year at generating electricity from the sun and wind, and storing it in ever smaller and more efficient batteries.

Pessimistic predictions about running out of energy must give way to a more realistic view that new sources will be developed as they are needed, as the market demands. That is the way our world works, and the law of supply and demand is the one law no government can ever repeal. Considering that it is possible to make electricity out of air, water and dirt, there is no chance of ever running out of electricity. The uncertainty and pessimism is really about politics and economics, not technology. And politics and economics change as rapidly as demand requires.

Minerals Require Mining

Although recycling now supplies a significant portion of the minerals our society needs, the rest must be mined from the

Earth. That is a simple truth that many environmental organizations choose to ignore or even deny, often loudly. They use pejorative terms like "extractive industries" to describe companies that mine or drill for resources. Americans have embraced a conventional wisdom that mining is generally a bad thing, harmful to the environment, dangerous to the workers, and mostly unnecessary.

There are numerous examples of mining gone wrong and abuses of the environment in the name of profit, many of them catastrophic and some of them deadly. But there are also plenty of examples of world-class technology and responsible leadership using the right processes not only to provide needed minerals, but also to improve our environment and our communities. Throughout the Rockies, there are numerous scars on the mountains left behind by mining, mostly 100 or more years ago. There are also many places all across the country where modern mines are invisible to observers, and several places where the environment is dramatically improved as a result of community-minded leadership in the mining industry. This is especially true in areas where modern reclamation techniques leave the land better than it had been, often leading to recovery of wildlife (including endangered species) populations. However debatable mining's affect on the environment may be, though, it cannot credibly be called unnecessary.

Clearly, there are good and bad aspects of any business, good and bad players in every profession. Those debates miss the point by a country mile. The point is that a healthy and prosperous modern society requires minerals to thrive. Someone has to supply those minerals, so that can either be done responsibly or irresponsibly–but healthy and prosperous people will get it done one way or the other.

Without mining and drilling, there would be no houses or offices, no cars, no electric lights, no air conditioners or furnaces, no hospitals or medicines, no computers or phones, no radio or TV, not even a book to read. No one seems to want a gravel pit anywhere, but without sand, gravel and aggregate there would be no highways, sidewalks or home foundations. Hypothetically, we could live without electricity, but most of us do not want to live in caves and huts, or to go back to growing all of our own food. Indeed, the computers that we can no longer live without, that save billions of trees' worth of paper and fossil fuels by allowing us to carry our work with us, require gold and other mining products.

The "environmental industry" is constantly challenging the existence, operation, and especially expansion, of mines. Yet despite so many controversies about mines and gravel pits, the real question is never really about *whether* mining should occur. The question is *how and where* it should occur. To the extent that we oppose mining ventures in our own country, we will simply import the minerals we need from around the world (as we do with oil). If we really care about mining responsibly and in ways that protect the environment, that should give us pause, because we can only control the process if we allow the mining here.

Permitting a new or expanded mine in the United States is a bureaucratic maze, almost unfathomable even to the people who get paid large sums of money to obtain those permits. The regulatory hurdles, authorizations and approvals are now beyond the reach of all but very sophisticated companies with substantial bank accounts and significant governmental affairs programs. Local permits are required from a host of local government entities, approval by numerous state agencies is required, and the National Environmental Policy Act (NEPA) process involves a number of federal agencies, too. Literally dozens of different permits and documents are needed, each of which requires significant amounts of information and substantial fees. And every single step of the process is subject to the appeals, lawsuits and delay tactics of environmental organizations. Any company in the business would testify to the millions of dollars in costs and delays imposed by the permitting process for mining in the modern era—and to the resulting higher cost of consumer goods for everyone.

Still, despite this almost endless matrix of permits, regulations and taxes, Americans often believe mining companies have an advantage in public subsidies beyond any enjoyed by other industries. That belief stems from 25 years of unrelenting press coverage about an old mining law that made public lands available for mining at cheap prices. The law made necessary minerals available from federal lands because that's where so many minerals are located, but today it is seen almost universally as a complete giveaway to the mining industry.

The Mother Lode of Mining Laws

As part of the massive effort to settle the American West and utilize its resources to build a more prosperous nation, Congress passed one of its landmark public land laws, which has come to be known simply as the 1872 Mining Law. It ushered in the industrial age and spawned a series of mining booms (and busts) that would last 75 years or more. The controversies it left behind linger today with astonishing intensity, and efforts by modern political leaders to reform the old law are among their most frustrating initiatives.

A quick historic footnote helps explain why it was once thought to be important to practically give away mineral rights on public lands. The Treaty of Guadalupe Hidalgo gave California to the United States in 1848, but before the federal government had established any presence there, gold was discovered at Sutter's Mill and touched off the first major gold rush in the West. Miners had to locate minerals and establish mines, towns, and a legal system before there was any legal jurisdiction established by the federal government. So they adopted—out of necessity—the only legal system most of them knew, based on the Mexican mining laws. Miners could stake their claims and the law would protect their ownership, as long as they continued to work the claim. The same system was used in the Nevada silver boom of 1858 and the Colorado gold rush of 1859, and became part of the informal "Code of the West" in the absence of any federal law. Congress was busy dealing with the Civil War and other higher priorities. So when they finally got around to addressing the matter during the Grant Administration, the only practical approach was to codify the system already in place and well understood. After all, substantial fortunes had already been made by that time, and millions of dollars worth of property was already owned. An entirely new structure could hardly be imposed.

Under the 1872 Mining Law, any U.S. citizen 18 or older has the right to locate a lode (hard rock) or placer (gravel) mining claim on federal lands. These claims may be filed as soon as a mineral discovery is made. The law now applies only to hard-rock minerals, because Congress later passed different laws to govern coal, oil and gas. The law also standardized the maximum size of mining claims, and granted "extra-lateral rights" to lode claims. That means the owner of an ore vein can follow that vein wherever it may lead, even *under* someone else's property (that provision has led to some spectacular court battles over the years).

In order to perfect a mining claim, the owner must discover a valuable mineral deposit on eligible federal lands (not in National Parks), post a notice on the property, mark its boundaries, and record the claim and location with local and federal authorities. That establishes a "non-patented" mining claim, a legal right to work the land and produce minerals. If the claimant can also demonstrate that he spent more than $500 on improvements or labor, he can get a "patent" or deed to the land for $5 per acre. That is the long and short of the old mining law, still very much on the books and in active use. Amid a flurry of contention, Congress finally placed a moratorium on new patents in 1994, but the government continues to process a backlog of prior claims, and Obama Administration attempts to repeal or reform the law have failed.

Although the law resulted in supplying a growing nation with immense quantities of platinum, gold, silver, copper, lead, zinc, uranium, molybdenum, tungsten, "and other valuable deposits," it has also become intensely controversial in recent years for several reasons:

- These valuable minerals helped create immense wealth and giant corporations (now considered evil by millions of modern Americans).

- The $5 per acre price was never indexed to inflation, nor was the requirement for improvements totaling $500. If they had been, the price per acre today would be $85 and the value of improvements would have to be $8,500. In many places today, the fair market value of the land is more than that, sometimes much more.

- The law was intended to provide minerals, but was also used simply to acquire land—sometimes spectacularly beautiful and valuable land—where little or no mining was ever really planned.

- Patented mining claims have become "in-holdings" (privately-owned parcels inside national forests and even wilderness areas), giving owners the right to build houses where they would otherwise be prohibited.

- Mining claims are senior property rights that trump other land uses, including some the public now considers more important.

Because of these controversies, and because the law does not seem to make as much sense in the modern era, Congress has struggled with various attempts to modernize or even repeal it. But those efforts have also met with difficulty because of the property interests involved. Consider the equally strong arguments of the miners about why the law still makes sense:

- The offer of land title in exchange for exploration and discovery was made in good faith by the Congress, and once accepted it became a contract.

- Failing to deliver patents (deeds) that have been duly earned under the law represents a taking of private property for public purposes without just compensation, a clear violation of the 5th Amendment to the Constitution.

- Mining claims have always required risky investment and substantial labor, and those who willingly put up their money and sweat are entitled to the resulting profit.

- Without a continued policy making American resources available to Americans, we will become as dependent on foreign countries for all minerals as we already are for oil.

As with so many other environmental issues, the discussion has become clouded with hidden agendas and false issues. The clear solution is easy to see if the hidden agendas can be set aside. A series of simple compromises could address most of the remaining controversies.

Mining Our Business

First, it is important to separate the discussion of mining from that about reclamation. The national need for minerals is a different matter than what to do about old mining claims left behind where no mining remains viable. Those are two completely different issues, but well organized and funded opponents of mining confuse them on purpose. They use an emotional argument about "public land giveaways" to poison public opinion against mining. Most Americans do not think public lands should be given away, or sold at less than market value, so the ploy is effective. The issues need to be separated.

If the land is still being mined, or remains rich with minerals for which there is a national need, then there is a legitimate debate about the need to update or modernize the old law. In particular, the fees and royalties ought to be set at a level that makes sense in the 21st Century. Reasonable leaders should settle on an amount that would not unnecessarily hamper the production of minerals, nor short-change the public. Whatever the amount is, it is clearly not the same as in 1872, so at least some inflation adjustment might make sense. But many of the most vocal opponents of mining cannot reach that debate because they are too busy yelling about what a "giveaway" and "fire sale" the mining law represents. That forces people on the other side to dig in their heels, too, to defend against a complete ban on mining, and the battle lines are drawn. As is becoming predictable, some groups are flatly opposed to any mining under any circumstances. However, unless they can propose a means for maintaining our economy without minerals, their view is not realistic, and cannot govern the discussion about mining laws. If the country needs the minerals, and the public already owns them, then they should be made available for production at fair prices. The alternative–imported minerals and exported jobs–is not acceptable.

Old abandoned mining claims are a completely different, though equally important, issue. The "in-holdings" left behind by old mining claims make forest management more difficult. Once again, the solution, though contentious, is not terribly complicated. The West contains thousands of abandoned mines, many of which have no owner that can be identified, but some of which are owned by people who have built houses and cabins, and even whole subdivisions inside national forests where such construction was never intended by Congress in granting the mining rights. In numerous other places, owners have threatened to build houses, or to tear down historic mining structures, in order to push the government to buy back the land at high prices. It is private property, so they have that legal right, but it often feels like extortion to the public. Such in-holdings ought to be somehow turned back to public lands.

These lands were privatized for the sole purpose of producing minerals. In places where the mines either produced their bounty and played out, or were dry to begin with, that mining purpose is no longer valid. Where no owner can be identified, Congress ought to simply reclaim such lands for the public; where there are willing owners, their interests should be bought back at fair market value.

Some opponents argue that the patents were practically "given away" in the first place, so paying modern land prices is wrong. But it is a false argument. My great-grandfather only had to pay a $2 filing fee for the 160-acre farm he claimed during the Oklahoma land rush—that was the deal under the homestead laws at the time. Is that farm (and thousands like it) worthless today just because the government originally gave it away? If the argument is about whether profit is good or evil, then environmentalists will advocate "regulatory taking," preventing the legitimate uses of the property, or demanding the owner sell at a bargain price. But if the argument is really about the environment, the simple solution is to buy back those in-holdings, whatever their current value, and return them to public lands.

I have participated in numerous projects with the Trust for Public Lands and other organizations to buy those claims back, and return them to public ownership as part of the national forests. These projects involve private fund-raising, which helps leverage limited public funds, and once purchased the land is given back to the government, complete with deed restrictions that prevent future development. These land trusts perform great services to the public—and to the environment. Such programs should be encouraged at every turn, and the strategy should be standard policy.

In some places the value of such lands today is very high, even beyond the reach of available budgets. In such cases, the government also has the ability to make trades. Because of the checkerboard patterns of public land ownership in the West, the Forest Service and BLM both own many parcels outside the boundaries of their major tracts, sometimes even in-holdings surrounded by private land and not very useful to the public. In hundreds of such cases over the past few years, a simple land trade has eliminated in-holdings on both sides, and often returned old mining claims to public ownership, where development inside a national forest would have been counterproductive. In either case, returning these lands to public ownership—through purchase or trade, not taking—is often the best solution to age-old controversies.

Finally, to put this issue to bed once and for all, Congress should eliminate the backlog and permit land patents to be issued where they have been legally earned. In places where private property should be returned to the public, private interests should be purchased at fair market value. But the government's "moratorium" on processing valid mining claims is a taking of private property, inconsistent with our Constitutional principles. And it is worth noting that in cases where such a "taking" creates bad feelings and a lack of cooperation, it may be bad for the environment, too.

The basis of a reasonable compromise can be distilled into one sentence: *Issuing those patents (or buying them back) should be part of a compromise package that also includes updating the old law with more current land and royalty prices, modern mining and environmental standards, and clear guidelines adopted for where mining is and is not allowed.* If the basics can be that straightforward, you might think Congress could eventually get there, too. Instead, stymied by the powerful effect of disingenuous arguments, hidden agendas and political posturing, Congress remains deadlocked. And in this case, no decision *is* a decision, with unwanted ramifications. As citizens are forced to choose between their private property rights and a vague environmental policy agenda, they often end up taking what seems like an "anti-environmental" stance, even if they are conservationists at heart. That does no good for anyone involved, or for the environment.

The same is true in the Appalachians, where the primary environmental issues are not about public land law, but about the environmental impact of mountaintop mining, or as some environmentalists call it, "mountaintop removal." The opponents of any and all mining use many of the same tactics we have seen in the Rocky Mountain West, confusing the issues so that environmental concerns can be used to stop mining altogether, rather than make sure it is done correctly. It is difficult to argue that America doesn't need the coal, since more than half the nation's electricity comes from coal, and without it many Americans simply could not afford their electric bills. So, opponents instead focus on the impacts of such mining on streams, mountain views, noise, dust, and other entirely fixable problems. There are serious debates in the legislatures of several states about updating their mitigation and reclamation requirements, and the coal companies will follow whatever procedures are required. But that debate should be about how to mitigate environmental impacts, and how to restore and improve landscapes, not about whether to allow mining at all.

In 25 years of political debate on mining issues, one thing has never changed and never will change: our economy remains vitally dependent upon mining. And while most people can understand the need for mining if they think about it for a moment, nobody—absolutely nobody—wants a mine or quarry anywhere near their own home.

Going BANANAS

John Berlau of the Competitive Enterprise Institute recently wrote about the terrible ordeal of Alfred and Barbara Langner, whose car slid off Interstate 87 during a 2007 blizzard in Essex County, New York, and plunged into a snow bank. The couple—cold, scared and tired—were trapped in their car and could not get help. Mr. Langner was an ambulance driver, well trained in such situations. He had a new cell phone, but there was no cell service in the area. That happened because Adirondack area environmental groups had waged a fierce battle against a proposed cell tower on this fifty-mile stretch of road. Verizon Wireless had even offered to build and paint the tower to look like a tree, as the company has often done elsewhere in sensitive areas. The environmental opponents dubbed the proposed tower "Frankenpine" and insisted that it would mar the landscape. In fact, many such towers are all-but invisible when constructed in this manner, but that did not matter to the opponents, who won the battle. So the cell tower was not built. These groups said we should "save" this landscape for our grandchildren, but as Mr. Berlau points out, Alfred Langner never saw his grandchildren. Stranded for 2 days, Mr. Langner froze to death and his badly injured widow was barely saved.

One of the most important energy issues facing the United States actually has nothing to do with energy supply or sources, but with infrastructure. The truth is that while everyone wants the lights to come on when they flip the switch, no one really likes the infrastructure it takes to make that happen. Power plants of any kind–gas, coal, nuclear, or biomass–are unpopular; we hate the site of smokestacks; we don't want substations in our neighborhoods; and most of all, we hate power lines. People who oppose any nearby infrastructure used to be called "NIMBY's" from the acronym that means "Not in My Back Yard." In recent years, though, organizations that fight the construction of power plants and transmission lines do not seem to care whose back yard is involved. Some local officials have now begun to refer to opponents as "BANANA's," based on a new acronym that means "Build Absolutely Nothing Anywhere Near Anything."

In truth, that view probably represents my opinion, too, at least partly. And if you're like most Americans it is your private opinion, as well. We all want things to work, and whether we admit it or not, we all wish we did not have to look at power lines, power plants, or even cell towers. If we could remove every telephone pole from the landscape and still have all the services they bring, of course most of us would wish to do so. For the time being, that is to dream the impossible dream. Of course, we have improved the ability to hide infrastructure over the years. Every city now has miles of cables buried underground that were once very visible eyesores. But getting power from a power plant to homes and businesses requires wires, like it or not. So unless we build power plants in every neighborhood in every city, large power lines must transmit that power, often across landscapes (including public lands) where no one wants to see them. And the cost of burying them underground over long distances averages more than a million dollars per mile, even on flat open land (the U.S. has more than a half-million miles of power lines, so burying them all would cost more than $500 Billion).

Transmission Lines

The ability to transport electricity to homes is as important as the ability to generate it—from whatever source. It is among the most difficult issues facing the environment today, because the resources from which electricity can be generated are so rarely located in the same place where most of the people live. There is no coal in downtown Manhattan, no dependable year-round sunlight in Chicago, no great geothermal reservoir under Denver, nor natural gas under Washington, D.C. These resources must be tapped where they exist, and transported. There are really only two choices: raw resources can be transported to the cities by truck, rail, or pipeline, or the electricity can be generated nearer the coal and gas, and then transported to the cities by power lines. Both choices are unpopular. Almost no one likes power lines or pipelines in their neighborhoods, and few people want them to cross national forests, parks and wilderness areas. No one wants more trucks on the road, nor power plants anywhere.

That political reality made national news in January, 2012 when President Obama decided to deny federal permits for the proposed Keystone Pipeline to bring natural gas from Canada to Texas. At a time when America desperately needed the estimated 20,000 jobs the project would have created, and the energy it would have made available, Administration officials were persuaded by the environmental industry. There are arguments over the number of jobs such projects would really create, or how long such jobs might last, though it is difficult to argue that the project could have quite literally replaced the oil now imported from Venezuela—over 900,000 barrels a day. That could mean an end to the transfer of over \$30 billion dollars annually from the U.S. to Hugo Chavez. And some opponents argue whether that would be the actual outcome—all legitimate debates. But those arguments are not about the environment—the environment is merely the excuse. In truth the White House was playing the political odds, believing a majority of Americans are more opposed to pipelines and power lines than in favor of energy security or job creation.

This is an especially difficult issue in the West, again because so much of the land is federally owned. For instance, in Colorado and Wyoming there are vast reserves of coal on the western side of both states, and clean state-of-the-art mines and power plants. But the massive population growth in desperate need of additional electric power is on the eastern side of the mountains. It is not possible to get power from the plants at Craig or Hayden to Denver or Cheyenne without crossing national forests and BLM lands, a common problem throughout the West. Generating more power in Craig or Hayden would be relatively easy because of the proximity to the coal resources and the strong support of most local residents. But connecting that additional power to the "grid" is a huge problem, not easily solved.

There is no "national power grid" in the United States that connects all the electrical systems. In fact, the continental United States is divided into three main power grids, the Eastern, Western, and Texas systems.

The Eastern and Western grids have very limited interconnections to each other, and the Texas system is only linked to the others by a few lines. Both the Western and Texas grids are linked with Mexico; and the Eastern and Western grids are strongly interconnected with Canada. The systems of all the electric utilities in the mainland United States are connected to other systems through these power grids. Starting with a rivalry between Edison and Westinghouse, the grids evolved differently over decades of time with numerous and varied electrical systems, and are enormously complicated. Today's system is so complex that even the top utility experts in the country cannot avoid power failures, sometimes stunning failures.

Because electricity is often transmitted over vast distances from generating plants (remember the United States has almost a half-million miles of power lines) the grid system depends on dozens of control centers that act as "choke points." These centers reroute electricity to areas of high demand, generally using automatic switches (not people). When a grid's distribution becomes unbalanced or overloaded, a switch interrupts the flow to avoid damaging equipment and the result is a power outage. If the blackout is severe, it can ripple all across the grid, shutting sections down all along the route. Such a system provides hundreds of opportune targets for curious squirrels or fast-growing trees. Even worse, they may appeal to terrorists, because so many of these "choke points" are unmanned and unguarded.

A post-mortem analysis of a series of 1996 blackouts determined that "the cascade of events might have been lessened" had regional electrical utilities communicated better, providing early notice of potential problems. Thus, a multi-million dollar study by federal and state power regulators recommended improved communications among managers. The utilities, power plants and grid operators set up plans to deal with potential blackouts that would give everyone earlier warnings. But the improved communication plan did nothing to prevent another massive blackout in the northeast in 2003. In fact, because of the rapid growth of demand a September, 2008 report by NextGen Energy Council (an association of power companies) called "Lights Out in 2009?" concluded that we have not yet begun to address the problem on the scale needed:

"The U.S. faces potentially crippling electricity brownouts and blackouts... Unless major investments are made immediately in both electricity generation (power plants) and transmission (power lines), the threat of service interruptions will increase."

The demand for electricity in the U.S. is expected to increase 18 percent by 2016, while generating capacity is projected to grow by only 8 percent (and virtually every new power plant proposed anywhere faces stiff opposition). That means more power is needed in the future, but more importantly, transmission lines are needed to make power more portable and flexible. Power lines can be buried and unobtrusive, but at a cost exponentially higher than above-ground lines, especially in isolated rural and mountain areas. Americans simply must come to terms with themselves over the issue of infra-structure somewhere–in someone's back yard.

Alternative Energy

Absent a better understanding of why we need more power plants and power lines, Americans will always suffer from the con-sequences of an under-built system, regardless of which natural resources we use to generate our electricity. Nevertheless, while that problem remains constant, policy makers continue to focus their attention on the issue of fossil fuels versus renewable resources, not on increasing the total supply or addressing the need for better/ more transmission systems. Somehow many leaders have convinced themselves that if only we could stop drilling and start using the sun and wind for our energy needs, these other issues might somehow resolve themselves. But they won't.

No solution to the problems associated with energy generation or mineral extraction can ignore the giant underlying question of whether there exists some better way. Can we power our economy without coal, natural gas, oil, copper, clay, sand, gravel, lead, zinc, gold, cement, iron, aluminum, and salt? Can we build houses that do not require fossil fuels to heat? Can we drive cars that do not need gasoline or even electricity? It is the environmental question of our age, and the next great generation of leaders will emerge from those who find the answers.

Technology is rapidly providing a number of alternative ways to produce energy, especially electricity. Still, contrary to the popular political view of the moment, there remain very significant problems with every "alternate" form of energy. Many of these technologies show great promise and we should continue the research, while working to address the challenges. It is an important priority for the Obama Administration, and is highlighted by governors across the nation, as well, because it is so politically popular to say that our society should "invest" in better ways to power itself. We are doing so, at far greater expense than most Americans know.

The Obama Administration has created a powerful misconception that we are subsidizing "big oil" to the tune of billions, while failing to invest in renewable energy. The idea that tax credits are "subsidies" is disingenuous, of course, since all it really means is letting people keep more of the money they earned—you can only think of tax credits as "subsidies" if you think it is the government's money. But even aside from that academic debate about tax policy, we "spend" exponentially more not only in tax credits, but in direct financial subsidies for renewables, especially compared to the miniscule amount of energy produced. The Institute for Energy Research reports that coal-fired and gas-fired power generation receive 64 cents per megawatt-hour in "subsidies." By contrast, wind turbines get over 56 dollars and photovoltaic solar systems over 775 dollars. The subsidies for renewables continue to rise each year, of course, in light of the massive "investments" made by the Obama Administration. In fact, by the summer of 2012 the Administration had already spent over $90 billion in the renewable energy sector, mostly in direct government grants and subsidized loans.

Has it paid off? Even today only about 9% of the energy consumption in America is produced from all "renewable" sources combined. That number has been growing very slowly for several years and may grow a bit more in the next few years because of the rising price of oil, the growth in research, and the continued growth of state government mandates in over 30 states. The Obama Administration's stated goal is to double America's supply of energy from renewables. But even if that is successful, we will still get 82% of all energy from fossil fuels.

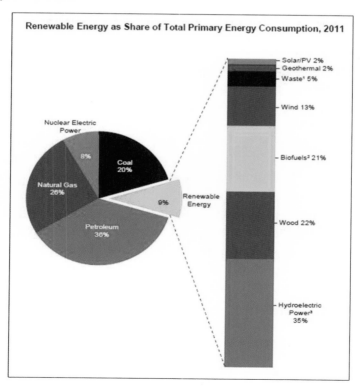

Source: U.S. Energy Information Administration, Annual Energy Review, 2010

The growth of companies selling and installing solar and wind systems has been phenomenal in the past decade, even before the billions in subsidies unleashed by the Obama budgets. We now know, of course, that at some of these companies (such as Solyndra) were subsidized for political reasons, despite poor economic prospects, and the resulting scandal has probably set further development of solar energy back to some degree. Still, thousands of solar and wind companies now operate across the U.S., in addition to hundreds now selling equipment to convert biomass into electricity, small home windmills and pumping stations, and other newer technologies. All this growth has nevertheless been a mere drop in the bucket compared to America's energy use.

Reducing Energy Demand

Many advocates for renewable energy argue that our first step must be reducing demand, and there are ways to do that without reducing our quality of life. We ought to pursue those strategies to the maximum practical extent.

It almost goes without saying that if the demand for energy could be reduced by as much as 50% (which some people think is possible), the economics of producing renewable energy from solar, wind, biomass or other sources would change dramatically. But of course, a significant decrease in energy demand would also drastically reduce the comparative price of oil and gas. Either way, if we can reduce demand that much—without huge expense or drastic declines in our lifestyle—perhaps we should do so.

Reducing our use of energy alone, however, is only part of the solution, and it must be tempered with an understanding that the population is growing, not shrinking. As most politicians advocate, all of the alternative forms of energy should be pursued as part of our national need for energy independence. But all those forms of energy combined still do not represent more than a drop in the bucket compared to our needs—nor will they in the near future. Remember, we still rely on fossil fuels for 91% of the energy our country needs.

To be completely honest with ourselves about this issue, we must acknowledge that the primary focus of the debate must be supply, not demand. Unless you think Americans are about to quit driving cars, stop heating their homes, start going to bed at sunset, and go back to growing their own food, the issue is how to supply the energy they need. Supply still lies at the heart of the matter, and as our economy continues to grow, so do the economies of developing nations around the world. The bottom line is that our future requires more energy, not less. And although biomass, water, wind, solar and geothermal may all be a part of the solution, none of these alternatives can come anywhere close to providing the amount of energy our economy needs and uses.

Back to the Future – Fossil Fuels

America remains dependent for its economic prosperity on oil, gas, and coal–not just as a whole society, but all of us individually, too. Some people think that is a terrible thing, for a variety of reasons, most of them wrong. Generally the arguments against continued use of "fossil fuels" fall into two categories: we're causing global warming, and we're running out of oil. Global warming was discussed earlier, but the issue of "dwindling" supply remains at the heart of the debates between various sources of energy. Americans are concerned, even distressed, to be so dependent on a resource that we are rapidly exhausting, and that we must import from other countries–especially from unfriendly countries.

Every President for the past 40 years has not only expressed concern about our dependence on foreign oil, but made energy independence a vital goal of American foreign policy.

- *"Let this be our national goal: At the end of this decade, in the year 1980, the United States will not be dependent on any other country for the energy we need to provide our jobs, to heat our homes, and to keep our transportation moving."* President Richard Nixon, State of Union, January 30, 1974.

- *"A massive program must be initiated to increase energy supply, to cut demand, and provide new standby emergency programs to achieve the independence we want by 1985."* President Gerald Ford, State of the Union, January 15, 1975.

- *"Beginning this moment, this nation will never use more foreign oil than we did in 1977 -- never. From now on, every new addition to our demand for energy will be met from our own production and our own conservation. The generation-long growth in our dependence on foreign oil will be stopped dead in its tracks right now..."* President Jimmy Carter, Oval Office speech, July 15, 1979.

- *"I have decontrolled oil, which should result in more domestic production and less dependence on foreign oil."* President Ronald Reagan, first televised Oval Office speech, February 5, 1981.

- *"The gulfs and oceans off our shores hold the promise of oil and gas reserves which can make our nation more secure and less dependent on foreign oil."* President George Bush, Speech to Joint Session of Congress, February 9, 1989.

- *"The nation's growing reliance on imports of crude oil and refined products threatens the nation's security because they make us more vulnerable to oil supply disruptions... the Administration will continue its efforts to develop additional cost-effective policies to enhance domestic energy production and to revitalize the U.S. petroleum industry."* President Bill Clinton, Energy Security Statement, February 16, 1995.

- *"We can promote alternative energy sources and conservation, and we must. America must become more energy independent, and we will."* President George W. Bush, State of the Union, February 7, 2001.

- *"For the sake of our economy, our security, and the future of our planet, I will set a clear goal as president: In 10 years, we will finally end our dependence on oil from the Middle East."* Barack Obama, Nomination acceptance speech, August 28, 2008.

During the years represented by these presidential statements, the United States went from using about 15 million barrels of oil per day to over 20 million—and doubled the percentage of it imported (from 35% to nearly 70). Believe it or not, similar statements about the importance of energy independence can be found on the web sites of almost every Member of Congress from every state. Yet despite the almost unanimous lip service given to the policy of weaning our economy from the clutches of foreign oil, our country has done exactly the opposite for two generations.

The short and simple truth is that the U.S. government has steadily pursued policies that encourage our dependence on imported oil, and those policies have been extremely effective. One consequence has been the largest transfer of wealth in human history (from the U.S. to previously-poor Middle Eastern countries). Another is that the American economy is less insulated than at any time in its history. Perhaps that has been a 30-year design accident, or maybe world events have simply not responded to policies the way our leaders expected. Either way, the result is that we now spend upwards of $700 billion per year importing nearly 70% of the oil our nation needs from countries whose supply is unreliable, at best. Not all of the oil we import is from enemies or dangerous dictators (much is from Canada, for example), but enough of it is that Americans ought to be alarmed.

It is worth noting that the import trend has slowed as a result of increased domestic production—almost entirely on private lands—over the past couple years. Still, the Administration's regulatory policy is so heavily weighted against fossil fuel production that over the long-term America will remain dependent on foreign imports for most of its oil until public sentiment changes.

Surprisingly, the same growth in dependence is also predicted for natural gas. A recent forecast by the U.S. Energy Information Administration (EIA) projects that by 2020, America will depend upon imported liquefied natural gas for over 40% of its incremental gas supply (even despite the new large scale production in the northeast). Does any American think that is a good idea?

Less Is Not More

Globally, the demand for energy is projected to grow by 50 percent between now and 2030, as the standard of living continues to increase for more and more of the world's population. Vigorous economic growth and increasing population in developing countries, means more people will have homes with electric lights and other modern conveniences. The EIA says total energy demand will increase by 40% in the United States, and a whopping 95% in developing countries.

That should be seen as a tremendous achievement because it means more of the world's people are finally escaping poverty. Many environmental elitists, however, view it as a looming disaster because they fear all 2.5 billion people in China and India are going to want cars—and that means global warming and other ecological catastrophes. But remember, anyone can wring their hands about how to cope with another billion automobile drivers, but we are not going to stop China and India from producing those drivers, nor have we any right to do so. Real leaders must focus on how to supply the additional energy we, as well as the rest of world, will need.

If the United States maintains the current mix of energy sources, to meet future demand over the next generation the U.S. would need to build 747 new coal and gas power plants, 52 new nuclear plants and 1,000 new hydro-electric dams. I do not know a single leader in either party who believes our nation is prepared to do that.

We are clearly at a crossroads with a major decision to make. The United States already imports nearly three-fourths of its oil, and without a significant change in national policy that will not change. I do not know a single leader in either party who thinks that is acceptable, either. So for those leaders who talk of the need for a different future, it is past time to lead. Giving lip service to a new energy economy based on green jobs—while continuing to say "no" to everything—is not a new policy. Claiming we need an "all of the above" policy while in fact supporting a "none of the above" policy will not fool the public for long. That is not leadership; it is obstruction. More to the point, it does not relieve the dire circumstances of our foreign oil dependency—in the long run it makes them worse.

Out of Gas?

Since the 2008 presidential campaign, numerous candidates in both parties have followed a new rallying cry based on the assumption that America is unavoidably running out of oil. It has become official government policy since the election of Barack Obama. In June of 2010, following a tour of America's Gulf Coast, President

Obama repeated the argument in an Oval Office speech: "We consume more than 20% of the world's oil, but have less than 2% of the world's oil reserve. And that's part of the reason oil companies are drilling a mile beneath the surface of the ocean—because we're running out of places to drill on land and in shallow water." He repeated the theme frequently during the 2012 campaign. And our use of oil might be "unsustainable," if that were true.

It is unequivocally false—not exactly because politicians are lying, but because of the way our government defines "reserves" to exclude oil they don't *want* to produce. When the U.S. government publishes statistics about the oil "reserves," it simply does not include the oil locked in oil shale in the West, nor any of the oil that is deemed off-limits in the Gulf of Mexico, the Pacific Coast or the North Sea, nor any of the many other known oil deposits the government won't allow to be produced (such as ANWR). Nor are companies required to report such holdings among their "reserves" on government reports (they can even get into legal trouble for doing so). In other words, if the government does not want particular oil deposits to be produced in certain areas, it just pretends those deposits are not there.

Officials use technical criteria to make this determination, pretending to verify what oil can be produced economically, versus oil that we might admit is there but claim cannot be produced efficiently. But considering the significant advances in technology (both in discovery and production) in recent years, that claim is disingenuous. Technical issues aside, it is pure fraud to tell the public that the U.S. does not have the oil it in fact has. Voters cannot make intelligent decisions without the facts, so a government determined to lock up America's oil and gas—for political reasons—does not want the public to know how unnecessary that policy is.

Here is the unvarnished truth. The United States has more untapped petroleum than exists in the proven reserves of either Iran (136 billion barrels) or Iraq (115 billion barrels). The U.S. has more than the Energy Information Administration reports are the proven reserves of Russia, Libya and Nigeria combined (137.7 billion barrels). It is more than can be found in Venezuela (80 billion barrels), Kuwait (101.5 billion barrels) or the United Arab Emirates (97.6 billion barrels). And buried in the Green River Formation of

Colorado and Utah is more oil (in shale) than all the known reserves of the entire world.

If you wonder who is keeping all this American oil off the market, you are asking exactly the right question. Is OPEC hording it to keep prices high? No. Are rich "big oil" executives stifling development to fuel their greed? Again, no. It is us. Americans have made the conscious decision to keep our own oil off the market, to lock up most of our own resources from our own use. And this being a democratic republic, the politicians we have elected have responded by blocking development of American oil and gas. The United States has untapped oil under its deserts, its mountains, its forests, and its oceans—enough to make the U.S. completely energy independent—and has decided not to use it.

Some may think it is a simple matter that Americans value the deserts, mountains, forests and oceans more than the energy they contain. But in reality, the "environmental industry" has successfully convinced many Americans, and their political leaders, that producing this oil requires sacrificing these great places. There is a healthy debate about how to require technology that will protect and restore such places as part of the cost of production, especially in light of incidents like the 1989 Exxon Valdez spill or the 2010 BP disaster in the Gulf of Mexico. That is a legitimate concern. But it is *not* a debate about running out of oil.

The Minerals Management Service published a report in 2006 on U.S. offshore oil resources, and determined there were 86 billion barrels of oil and 420 trillion cubic feet of natural gas in American coastal waters. That is a 10-year supply of oil and a 20-year supply of natural gas for the entire nation, just from offshore sources known in 2006. In 2008 the Bureau of Land Management released a similar report, estimating the extent of the other part of America's undiscovered oil—onshore. Even without considering oil shale, this added 53 billion barrels to the total, meaning the U.S.'s known-but-untapped oil resources totaled nearly 140 billion barrels (in 2008). There were also said to be 231 trillion cubic feet of natural gas under onshore federal lands—10 more years of supply for the entire country. The news media took virtually no notice of either report. And several vast discoveries since then have dramatically expanded our supply—buy at least a third!

In fact, the media pays little attention to any news about the quantities of oil and gas being discovered and produced anywhere around the world. Consider one of the most revealing speeches about world oil reserves, given to OPEC in 2006 by the head of the world's largest oil company, Saudi Aramco, and barely mentioned by the news media. CEO Abdallah Jum'ah said:

> *"We are looking at more than four and a half trillion barrels of potentially recoverable oil. That number translates into 140 years of oil at current rates of consumption, or to put it another way, the world has only consumed about 18 percent of its conventional oil potential. **That fact alone should discredit the argument that peak oil is imminent and put our minds at ease concerning future petrol supplies."***
> [emphasis added]

The claim that we are running out of oil is not new, of course. When oil was first discovered in Pennsylvania in 1859 it sparked an "oil rush," but skeptics immediately began to argue against dependence because they thought there was insufficient oil to supply a nationwide market—and that was before the invention of the automobile. In 1919 Secretary of State Robert Lansing, quoting "the best technical authorities," warned that "the peak of petroleum production in the United States will be practically exhausted within a measurable period." A year later the U.S. Geological Survey estimated that America had only 12 years of reserves, and new discoveries were diminishing. By the end of the 1920's the Federal Oil Conservation Board, concerned about the largest year of auto sales yet, announced the impending danger that the country would run out of oil in the near future because of the new mania for cars.

None of today's pessimism is new. But you might think today's leaders would be more impressed with the constant ability of modern technology to locate and produce previously unknown or unreachable resources.

Official Government Policy:

Clearly, the United States is not running out of oil, nor is the rest of the world. However, we might as well be, if we choose to restrict our own access to our own oil. That is precisely the official policy of the U.S. government. That policy for more than 40 years in almost everything related to energy has led directly to restraining energy supply while demand continues to grow, with the obvious impact that has on prices. High energy prices, especially fuel prices, contribute to an economic crisis that Americans simply cannot be expected to tolerate much longer.

Besides driving up the price of nearly everything we buy, high fuel prices and dependence on foreign oil devastate the American economy. And while holding U.S. economic growth down, such policies "have enriched the Middle East, African and Venezuelan oil suppliers," writes national security expert William Weronko. He argues forcefully that "this policy has undermined the security of the United States by weakening the U.S. economically, destabilizing the Lesser Developed Countries by food shortages, and through direct payment 'leakage' to terrorist organizations."

Decisions to restrict America's use of its own resources could hardly be more misguided. They are doubly wrong, though, when couched in terms of environmental protection, a "red herring" if ever there was one. Just as British fugitives once dragged a smelly red herring on a string to confuse the dogs and lure them off the trail, so modern environmental leaders have used environmental causes to lock up public lands and divert attention from their real agenda—which has little to do with environmental protection and everything to do with stopping our use of energy.

Think about this: if someone proposed openly to ban the internal combustion engine, prohibit driving cars, and force everyone to walk or ride buses everywhere they go, that person would not be elected dogcatcher. Even a bit less extreme, if a politician proposed that we should stop producing oil and gas, and Americans should stop using it, such a politician would still not be very popular with most voters who like and depend on their cars. But if someone proposed to protect the deserts, mountains, forests and oceans against destruction by "big oil" tycoons for windfall profits, that person would be seen as a responsible leader who cares about doing the right thing. The policy implication is more or less the same, but a politician taking the latter approach might be elected to any office in the country. That is why almost every politician in the last 40 years has taken the latter approach to environmental issues involving energy and land use. Marketing will always be a critical element in American elections.

Hands Off

The United States may be the only country in the world that purposely bans the use of its own natural resources—resources upon which its economy depends. This is especially ironic when you remember that energy independence is a *clearly stated goal* of every president for the last 40 years. Nevertheless, large areas with vast petroleum reserves, including almost the entire East and West coasts, have been placed off-limits by the Congress and by several of these same presidents.

The BLM report explains the problem clearly. It says there are 279 million acres of federal land "with potential for oil or natural gas resources," and that 60% is off limits to energy production, either by law or administrative policies. Another 23% is open to energy leases, but "with restrictions." What that means is: "lands that can be leased but ground-disturbing oil and natural gas exploration and development activities are prohibited," and "lands that can be leased, but stipulations ... limit the time of the year when oil and gas exploration and drilling can take place to less than three months." In other words, the lands can technically be leased for energy production, but not really, not economically, not in any way that could result in actual production of actual oil and gas. That leaves only 17% of federal land truly open to oil and gas exploration and production—if the lessee can survive the costs and delays of planning, permitting, delays, appeals, and lawsuits. That is a major problem when you consider how much of the country and its energy resources are owned by the federal government.

Wasted Resources

In addition to locking up so much of our energy, the United

States also pursues policies that result in significant waste. For example, there are numerous coal mines in the Rocky Mountain region that produce significant amounts of methane gas, but merely vent it into the atmosphere because capturing and using it would require construction of a road, equipment, and a pipeline in a national forest–and such facilities cannot be permitted under existing forest management. Thus, perfectly usable–even valuable–gas is completely wasted (when some regard methane as the worst greenhouse gas).

A shortage of infrastructure creates similar problems in many oil producing regions. The Iraqi Oil Ministry spent several months in 2008 negotiating with Shell over a joint venture to develop natural gas in southern Iraq. An Iraqi official said that country loses about $40 million worth of natural gas a day associated with oil production because of insufficient means to export the gas or consume it domestically. It is a common problem, and leaders everywhere ought to work with these companies to ensure the proper conservation of these resources.

Drill, Baby, Drill?

During the 2008 presidential campaign when gasoline prices spiked to over $4 a gallon, there was a national outcry for domestic oil production, albeit a brief one. Popular bumper stickers were seen around the country reading, "Drill Here, Drill Now, Pay Less." The McCain-Palin campaign was greeted at rallies with crowds chanting, "Drill, baby, drill!" Though short-lived, it was nonetheless a very enthusiastic "boomlet." A spirited debate ensued about whether to lift the ban on offshore drilling (President Bush lifted an administrative ban, but Congress did not lift the statutory ban). The general response of many Democratic candidates was a fascinating argument against new drilling based on the assertion that oil companies should first drill on lands they already had. As the argument goes, companies seeking access to currently off-limits areas have often failed to produce oil on millions of acres worth of leases they already have. Environmental groups were quick to jump on the same bandwagon, pushing legislation that would actually cancel existing leases if not produced within a short time, a use-it-or-lose-it approach that would discourage domestic production and further drive up gasoline prices. The same argument was used again during the 2012 campaign when Mitt Romney questioned the Obama policies against domestic drilling. Once again, the argument is based on politics, not facts.

Claims that oil companies voluntarily choose to sit on otherwise productive leases are especially absurd with oil prices at an all-time high. The truth is that any serious oil company that is not drilling in a particular area it already paid to lease either has not found recoverable oil there, or has other oil that can be produced less expensively—or even more likely, has not yet completed the dozens of plans and permits needed to allow drilling. It is worth noting that none of the liberal politicians espousing the use-it-or-lose-it policy proposed speeding up the permitting process to allow it. That is because the argument was never intended to spur additional production, but merely to divert attention away from the national outcry for more drilling. Coupled with a reduction in gas prices later that year, and with Americans' notoriously short attention span, the diversion worked, at least for the time being.

In 2009, House Speaker Nancy Pelosi and a number of her colleagues argued that oil companies were "sitting on" 68 million acres of "non-producing" leased land. She proposed to force energy companies to "use" this leased land within ten years—or lose all exploration and drilling rights. She argued that no new public lands should be leased until all the existing leases had been produced and used up. That ignores the fact that lease agreements already require that leased land be used in a timely manner. The current law requires energy companies to comply with lease provisions, and explore expeditiously, or risk forfeiture of the lease. Moreover, the argument is based on the absurd notion that every acre of land leased by the government contains oil. Denying a company the right to any more land until it has spent huge amounts of time and money drilling all current leases would simply mean no more new government leases. Perhaps that was the real intent after all—not to promote new exploration but to cancel existing leases.

As any geologist can attest, finding oil is a difficult, complex, and expensive process. It does not begin with an assurance that oil is present, but with an educated guess about what geologic structures are likely to hold oil or gas. Based on that guess, companies bid on government leases, which are nothing more than agreements that allow them to test their theories, and hopefully find and produce oil and gas from the property. The expensive and complex analysis that follows leasing often shows that the chances are too slim to justify drilling an exploratory well. Companies need to have a fairly strong idea what to expect to spend the $1-5 million it costs to drill a well on land, or the $25-100 million it costs to drill in deep offshore waters. Yet even after that analysis, only one out of every three onshore wells finds enough oil or gas to be profitable. In deep water the risk is even greater, with only one in five wells eventually profitable. That is why only a small percentage of leased federal land ends up producing–federal land is no different than any other in that respect.

That is only the beginning of the process for producing oil, by the way. If a commercial-sized discovery is made, more expensive wells have to be drilled, to find out the extent of the oil and the shape of the oil field. Production facilities and pipelines have to be designed, built, brought to the site and installed–all contingent on planning, studies, permitting, public hearings, lawsuits, appeals, and the rest of the lengthy public approval process. Only after oil or gas is actually flowing does the government consider a lease to be "producing," so the Obama-Pelosi assumption that all other leased land is being wasted is disingenuous, at best.

In one example often mentioned in various blog articles, Shell Oil and several partners in 1997 leased an area in 7,800 feet of water 200 miles off the Texas coast. After five years of exploring and evaluating, the companies drilled several unsuccessful wells, and finally drilled a well in 2002 that hit oil. Over the next three years, three appraisal wells costing $100 million each confirmed the presence of a major oil field, and in 2006 the company ordered a huge floating platform and pipeline system that was installed and began production in mid-2010. In all, the partners invested over $3 billion and 13 years in the project before finally producing oil.

If thirteen years seems like a long time, remember that the legal process, used so effectively by opponents, also adds to the time it takes to produce energy. In the Rocky Mountain region, appeals of lease sales rose from 27% of all leases in 2001 to 81% by 2007. That process is so exasperating to federal land managers that many leasing prospects have never even been offered, because the likelihood of appeals makes the process so difficult and expensive. Some companies express the frustration that opponents once used endangered species as the tool of choice, but now use global warming—as if producing domestic oil causes climate change, but importing oil does not.

Drilling Takes Way Too Long

The other really absurd argument opponents inevitably raise against domestic drilling during gas price spikes is that new drilling takes too long. During the 2008 and 2012 campaigns, politicians opposed to domestic drilling chimed almost in unison that it will take more than ten years for any such new drilling to produce any oil anyway. Therefore, they argued, it is pointless to start. They are wrong on two counts.

First, if we have the resources, and the economy needs those resources, it makes no difference whether it takes two years, ten years or fifty—we should get started. Like many Americans, I harbor some hope that our economy may not be dependent upon oil and gas at all in another generation. But should we bet the farm on it? Thirty years ago leaders were talking about alternative energy and we have indeed made admirable progress. Yet we still use more oil and gas than ever before. The fact that we may not need as much oil 20 years from now is no reason to stop looking for it and producing it. On the contrary, it is irresponsible to stop exploring for more energy without knowing what the next generation may need. At least, we know what we need now.

Second, those who think new oil cannot be brought into production sooner in the midst of a crisis have too little faith in American ingenuity. The Alaska Oil Pipeline took two years, two months, and four days from the first shovel of dirt until oil flowed through the pipe. This engineering feat is a modern wonder of the world—it covers 800 miles, crosses three mountain ranges and 800 rivers and streams. Within 24 months of its completion, the pipeline's deliveries reached 1.5 million barrels per day. The Keystone Pipeline, had the Obama Administration chosen to permit rather than delay it, was scheduled to be completed in less than two years.

Some oil wells have taken as long as 15 years from discovery to production, others as little as two. The actual drilling itself only takes 30-100 days, depending on depth. The rest of the time is involved in planning, permitting (often including lawsuits and appeals), and analysis, so anything the government can do to speed that up might help the economy recover sooner, and might lead to energy independence. But to cite the lead time as a reason *never to start* drilling for oil makes shortages a self-fulfilling prophecy.

Fractured Future

New discoveries of oil and natural gas–and new technologies for accessing previously difficult areas–have begun to change the national debate once again since the election of Barack Obama. Campaign rhetoric about running out of resources is nearly forgotten now, as previously untested reservoirs have changed that perception, especially the oil-rich Bakken formation and the natural gas bonanza known as the Marcellus shale.

The Bakken formation lies under North Dakota and parts of Montana and Saskatchewan, and is now said to contain more than 20 billion barrels of recoverable oil. A friendly business climate in North Dakota (including supportive communities and state tax incentives) has led to an economic boom that is the envy of a nation in recession. Oil produced in the Bakken region went from only 3,000 barrels a day in 2005 to more than 600,000 a day by 2012. In communities like Williston, North Dakota, housing can hardly be built fast enough for the influx of oilfield workers, and some Wall Street investors are now predicting that the U.S. will overtake Saudi Arabia as the world's largest oil producer within a few years.

The Marcellus shale formation is centered in Pennsylvania and stretches throughout the Allegheny Plateau into New York, West Virginia, Ohio, Tennessee, Kentucky, Maryland, and New Jersey. The shale layer is as thick as 200 feet in much of that range, and it is full of natural gas. A decade ago, the U.S. Geological Survey estimated that the Marcellus shale contained about 1.9 trillion cubic feet of recoverable gas, but today the Energy Department says there is more than 260 trillion cubic feet, a good example of how drastically the government underestimated those reserves. For several years there was a raging debate about how much of the gas is actually recoverable, but that debate has simply been overtaken by events. Government geologists once said only about 10% of the Marcellus gas could be recovered, which would represent a two-year supply for the U.S. But enormous long-term investments in the region by all the major oil and gas companies prove that industry experts think otherwise. In Pennsylvania, more than 1,000 wells a year were drilled between 2008 and 2011, and thousands more have been permitted. In Susquehanna County alone, 262 wells were drilled by the summer of 2011 and permits had been issued for 400 more. A Pennsylvania State University study in 2008 concluded that recoverable natural gas reserves in the U.S. had gone up by more than $1 trillion, largely as a result of the Marcellus shale development.

Why are geologic formations like Bakken and Marcellus, which have been known for years, suddenly at the forefront of the energy debate? And why are American companies now producing vast supplies of oil and gas where reserves were previously thought unrecoverable? In a nutshell, the discussion has changed because of the rapid growth in technology, especially in the use of "hydraulic fracturing."

Simply explained, a mix of water (99.5%), sand, and chemicals is pumped under high pressure to create minute cracks in the rock formations thousands of feet below the surface so oil and gas can flow and be extracted–energy that could not previously be accessed without this technology. But rather than celebrate America's new-found riches, or the now-very-realistic prospect of energy independence, or the sudden availability of unfathomable quantities of clean-burning natural gas, environmental organizations instead decided to attack the technology itself. Now, wherever there are projects to recover new oil and gas resources, environmental groups have created a near hysteria about hydraulic fracturing, or "fracking."

The fracking debate ought to be about our energy future. U.S. shale gas resources are now the second largest in the world, according to the U.S. Energy Information Administration. Nationally, the U.S. has over 100 years' supply of natural gas at today's consumption rate, and America's recoverable oil reserves have skyrocketed, largely as a result of fracking, without which much of our own energy simply could not previously be produced.

Fracking has been used since the 1940s. Recent technical advances, along with the recent discoveries of larger deposits of natural gas and oil, have made fracking more common. That has led to new hope for Americans concerned about dependence on foreign oil and high energy prices. And that makes it the target of another negative campaign by alarmists who oppose all uses of energy.

Now a cadre of "environmental protection" organizations has been created for the purpose of turning public opinion against providers that use fracking to access previously unreachable oil and gas. As a result, there are new national debates about the practice, and the threat of new EPA regulation of the practice. Such drilling practices have always been regulated at the State level, so this represents a major new expansion of federal power, part of the regulatory tirade of the current EPA leadership. Predictably, that possibility has led to angry congressional hearings, potential legislation, public hearings, and a rash of speeches and letters–mostly generated by these same environmental organizations.

True to form, these groups and their heavily-funded ad campaigns are creating fear in the minds of thousands of residents, especially in the Marcellus region. The anti-energy crusaders hope that fear among local residents will lead to politicians blocking or limiting oil and gas development. The result could be a morass of burdensome and expensive regulations that are not justified by any reasonable environmental concerns.

Opponents of fracking have trouble explaining any geologic problem to pumping water into the ground, so they instead focus on the minute traces of chemicals added to the water, sometimes resorting to outright falsehoods and distortions. For example, many residents have been told that fracking will cause the contamination of groundwater and poison drinking water. Some extremists have even produced films purporting to show drinking water being set afire because of the sudden presence of natural gas in the water (in fact, flammable water has been observed in some areas for more than a century before the invention of fracking). Even the EPA and the Groundwater Protection Council (composed of state regulators) have issued reports admitting that there is not a single documented example of groundwater contamination caused by fracking.

That does not mean there has never been contamination caused by drilling. But where contamination of drinking water has occurred, the source was not fracking, which takes place at depths far below any drinking water, but the corrosion of well pipes at shallower depths. Ironically, preventing such corrosion is the very purpose of the trace chemicals added to the water and sand–the chemicals opponents use to stir up public fear. If these activists are truly worried about corrosion of pipes and the resulting water contamination, they ought to argue for better or different chemicals. But if the goal is simply to stop all drilling, they are pursuing exactly the right strategy.

In the U.S., more than a million gas and oil wells have used the fracking technique without negative impacts, and we all benefit from the energy they produce. To be clear, there are risks involved in all energy production. That is why there are industry standards and reasonable governmental regulations on such activities–and there should be. But we should approach this issue with an understanding that the promise of energy self-sufficiency and reasonable energy prices can be delivered if the U.S. can produce more of its own resources. Public policy should be designed to encourage that.

Fear can sometimes be useful if it's based on facts and helps avoid dangerous situations. But when it is driven by false agendas, as in the debate about fracking, it can blind our vision on important issues like energy independence.

Drilling Our Way Out

A slogan frequently used by opponents of oil and gas production is the simplistic, "We cannot drill our way out of our energy problems." It is a quick and easy sound bite, and it may sound right at first, but like so many political slogans, it does not really address the issue. Energy is a complex matter, so 10-second answers are not especially helpful, though they always get lots of attention. Clearly, the more energy we produce–from any source–the faster we become independent of foreign oil. We certainly can restrain gas prices and reduce foreign dependence if we develop our own resources instead of blocking access to them. There is simply no reason for us to remain dependent on unreliable foreign governments when we have billions of barrels of our own oil and gas in the United States. Some may think we *should* choose foreign imports over domestic production for various reasons, but make no mistake–*it is a choice.*

Notice that in debates about drilling, environmental leaders always argue about a specific site, never about the nation's need for energy. With that flawed premise, they often argue that the area in question is too small! The theory is that a particular proposed site cannot produce enough energy to justify the environmental risk. This was the excuse in 2009 when Interior Secretary Ken Salazar cancelled 77 recent natural gas leases in Utah. Opponents of those leases had argued that even if fully developed, the area could supply only 0.02% of the nation's oil usage and only 0.5% of its natural gas needs. In other words, if we can only do a little, we should do nothing.

The truth is that the vast majority of Americans will continue driving cars as their primary means of transportation. So long as cars are fueled by gasoline, we in fact *can* drill our way to energy independence. We know we have enough oil in the U.S., and we know we have the technology to produce it responsibly. We need not trust oil companies to operate in a conscientious way–we can require it. That is why we have important environmental regulations, and they must be enforced. But deciding not to produce America's own domestic energy *at all* is counter-intuitive. That decision cannot be justified by the fear that we might run out of oil, nor by a jingoistic view that all oil production is bad for the environment. In fact, Americans have made that decision based on something else altogether.

The Hidden Agenda

Any decision to limit the supply of oil available to Americans inevitably drives up prices. That is no accident. Many environmental leaders argue that is precisely the goal. In an era of rising gasoline prices, our choice is to increase supply, or reduce demand. Reducing our demand for energy in general, and oil in particular, is exactly what environmental leaders want. In their utopian view of the perfect world, most people would live right by their offices, and the few who must commute would always do so by mass transit. Our homes would be smaller and closer together, no one would need cars, and travel would be on buses and trains. This future, they think, can be accomplished by pushing the price of gasoline so high that people will simply have to stop driving. They argue that there is a price at which people will stop driving; we just have not yet found that price point. Is it $7 per gallon? $10 per gallon?

Some environmental "visionaries" will acknowledge, when pressed, that such a solution cannot work in much of rural America (the vast majority of all communities in the U.S.). There will never be a Japanese bullet train connecting Broadwater to Bayard in rural Western Nebraska. I do not know how many people routinely drive from Broadwater (population 140) to Bayard (population 1,247), but the number is not zero. Yet residents of those small but vibrant agricultural communities would be put completely out of business by fuel prices in that range. Does it make sense to obliterate the economy of Middle America in order to persuade people in the metropolitan areas to give up automobiles? Would urban dwellers think their lives were a perfect utopia if their food had to be imported (along with their oil)?

Clearly such a solution cannot work in the real world. Like so much of the misinformation and false premises spread by the environmental lobby, the real agenda cannot be admitted because the public would not support it. Al Gore argued in his first book (*Earth in the Balance*, 1992) that the internal combustion engine should be eliminated, yet even 2 decades later his strongest allies in Congress have never once tried to do that. Gore himself never proposed such legislation during his 24 years in Congress, or his 8 years as Vice President. He has argued for years that significantly higher gas prices would be a good thing, yet he and his supporters have never proposed legislation to add $4 more to the price of gasoline–which government could easily do through taxes. He and his crowd always stop short of proposing actual policies to implement their rhetoric, because they know how unpopular such policies would be.

Thus, modern environmental organizations seek more indirect and clever ways to change public behavior. Locking up America's oil and gas supply, and blocking access to minerals, trees, water and other natural resources, is easier because it is incremental and sounds nobler. If Americans were asked whether it would be a good idea to lock up their own oil on lands they own, forcing perpetual dependence on foreign imports, they would of course resoundingly say no. But when confronted with the environmental "horrors" of developing a specific resource in a specific area where the case can be made locally, people will often (usually) opt for further environmental protection. In this way, one small piece at a time, we have steadily locked away *more than 80%* of all the oil reserves under the United States, and *nearly all* our offshore oil–without the public ever having consciously decided to do so.

Americans need to make a simple decision to use their own energy first, before relying on foreign sources. Congress ought to make domestic production a high priority, and remove the legal barriers it has erected. Such production can and should be done according to carefully designed standards to protect the environment, but such concerns should no longer be permitted to stop production the country so desperately needs.

The Rock That Burns

Ironically, even the most impressive oil and gas statistics do not include the largest known oil reserves in the world–oil shale. The term "oil shale" is a bit misleading because the sedimentary rock is not really shale and the kerogen it contains is not technically oil. But heat drains hydrocarbons from the rocks in liquid form and it can be easily processed into oil, gasoline, diesel fuel, kerosene, naphtha and other high-demand petroleum products. Best of all, there is enough of it in one state to make the U.S. independent of the Middle East and alter the nature of foreign affairs.

A Rand Corporation study calls it the largest known oil shale deposit in the world. There are somewhere between *1.5 and 2.1 trillion barrels of oil* stored in the rocks of the Piceance Basin, part of the 16,000 square mile Green River Formation that covers Western

Colorado, Eastern Utah, and Southern Wyoming. In other words, the total oil stored in that region's oil shale exceeds the entire known oil reserves of the entire world, now estimated at 1.317 trillion barrels. And 80% of the oil shale is on federal lands, so it belongs to the public.

Oil shale has been known, though poorly understood, for centuries. It exists in varying quantities throughout the world, though not generally in commercially viable amounts. The greatest exception to that was discovered by accident in the early 1880's when settlers arrived in Western Colorado. Local Utes told of the "rock that burns" around Rifle and Parachute Creeks, though most settlers assumed they were confusing it with coal. A Parachute Creek settler named Mike Callahan built his first home in 1882, using local logs for the walls and the attractive rocks he picked up around his ranch for the fireplace and chimney. He invited all his neighbors to a "house-warming" party, an important tradition in those days, and built a raging fire in the fireplace. As the festivities continued, the fireplace and chimney caught fire, and before the inferno could be extinguished, the new home had burned to the ground. Mike Callahan is often credited by locals for "discovering" oil shale, though he was never particularly amused by the story. His find was not properly identified for several years, though others soon started to mine what they called "lignite coal" and sell it as fuel.

Several attempts have been made over the years to perfect a technology that could economically and profitably convert oil shale to oil. Major investment caused temporary booms during the 1920's and 1950's, both times resulting in eventual collapse because the technology could never quite compete with cheap crude oil pumped out of the ground elsewhere. Several technologies have recovered marketable oil from the rocks, but never quite cheaply enough to make it competitive.

The people of Western Colorado have a love-hate relationship with oil shale. It has helped create some of the most robust economic booms in local history, and without a doubt the most spectacular economic bust. Local residents understand that the resource is badly needed by the entire nation; Coloradans dislike high gas prices, too. They also know it can bring thousands of high paying jobs, add tax base to local governments and finance infrastructure across several counties. These same local residents also share a healthy skepticism about the potential impact of large-scale commercial development on a fragile environment. Worse, most locals still have a bad taste in their mouths about the oil shale bust of the 1980s.

The Past is Prologue

The extraordinary economic boom started with the Carter Administration's reaction to a world energy crisis touched off by the 1974 Arab oil embargo. President Carter created several new agencies and programs intended to subsidize America to energy independence. The first plan, which seems especially bizarre in retrospect, was to declare Northwest Colorado a "National Sacrifice Area", and to create an Energy Mobilization Board with power to override federal, state and local environmental and land use laws. That plan became a major source of friction between Carter and political leaders from the West, and it stalled in Congress because of the combined opposition of western senators and the environmental lobby.

Instead, Carter and Congress settled on the $88-billion Synthetic Fuels Corporation, with $15 billion in price guarantees for oil shale. Oil companies were promised that the "Synfuels Corp" would ensure that the price of oil would remain high enough to guarantee profits to companies that would develop the oil shale right away. And oil companies responded with a dozen major projects in the Piceance Basin.

The promises were extravagant. Exxon distributed a now-famous "white paper" in 1980 suggesting that there would be a population increase of one-million in the region by 1990, requiring at least 700 new schools and other improvements. Various estimates suggested that nearly all the construction workers in United States would be needed if all the companies proceeded as planned. Based on the promise of massive government funding to guarantee prices, oil companies invested billions developing huge projects to extract oil from the shale–including several projects with yet-unproven experimental technologies.

Exxon invested over $5 billion in its "Colony" project, including construction of the entire town of Battlement Mesa for employee housing. Tenneco and Occidental invested in a gigantic joint project called Cathedral Bluffs, while Unocal built its own massive mining and refining facility, and a consortium of 17 oil companies (called Paraho) leased the government's facilities at Anvil Points. Every major oil company was involved in one way or another.

The region had never seen such prosperity and growth, from Grand Junction to Denver. Local and international investors alike poured money into construction projects, new housing developments, shopping centers and businesses. Lots of local businesses made lots of money, but it was all based on high global oil prices that did not last. In 1982 oil demand fell and prices plummeted, and the promises of the Carter Administration to guarantee profits vanished into the woodwork.

In Western Colorado, May 2, 1982 will always be remembered as "Black Sunday," the day Exxon pulled the plug without warning and touched off a decade-long recession across the entire Rocky Mountain region. An Exxon executive called Colorado Governor Richard Lamm at home that Sunday to warn him, but local people–including 2,000 employees–received no advanced notice. Workers showed up Monday morning to find locked gates.

Over the next few months, all the other projects were systematically mothballed, as well, although Unocal hung on for a few more years at constantly decreasing levels of investment, employment, and production. The recession hit hard, bankrupting hundreds of families, causing thousands of home foreclosures, shuttered businesses, and shattered dreams. Towns like Parachute and Rifle were almost entirely boarded up for several years, tumbleweeds blowing down Main Streets. More than 15,000 people moved away from Mesa and Garfield Counties alone, and the bust had ripple effects across the nation. It took Colorado's economy well over a decade to recover, and many families never did.

Typically, Congress overreacted and shut down virtually all oil shale research programs, despite recommendations from many experts that research and development, at least, should continue. The

Synfuels Corporation was abolished in 1986, but that was not the end for oil shale. Despite the disastrous results of a failed national experiment, one simple fact had not changed–there is still a massive quantity of oil in the region, and there remains a dire national need for it. The issue could not stay buried for long.

Another Boom, Anyone?

With encouragement of the government, the global oil-shale industry began to revive at the outset of the 21st century for three reasons. First, some companies had never abandoned private research, and some major technological advances changed the economics of oil shale production. Second, the U.S. government restarted an oil-shale development program in 2003, though this time it was based on leasing lands, not on subsidies or price guarantees. Third, another round of oil price increases around the world starting in 2004 rekindled a strong national push for energy independence.

One project in particular, a series of tests conducted by Shell at its Mahogany site, finally cracked the technological barrier. It eliminated the largest expense and the most significant environmental problems of all the previous attempts by avoiding mining. Previous projects were mostly based on digging up the rocks and extracting the oil by melting it in large retorts (massive furnaces that "melt" oil out of the rock). Like all mines, that left holes in the mountains, massive piles of left-over material, and petroleum by-products with the inevitable disposal problems. The Shell technology is based on heating the rocks where they are–deep underground–and pumping the oil to the surface with systems more like traditional oil wells than mines. Thus, there are no permanent scars on the surface or holes in the mountains, and no piles of sludge to be reclaimed. At three different test sites over a ten-year period, Shell quietly demonstrated that this technology could not only produce oil efficiently, but profitably. That break-through resulted in renewed calls for the government to make its lands available for oil shale leasing (remember, the government owns nearly all the oil shale lands).

Under direction from Congress in 2005, the BLM introduced a commercial leasing program, encouraging the development of technologies for extraction of oil from shale on federal lands. The new

BLM regulations provided rules on which private investors could rely in determining whether to invest in oil shale projects.

Oops, We Changed Our Minds

Immediately, the environmental groups churned up strong opposition, however, so barely two years after directing Interior to proceed with oil shale leasing, Congress essentially barred the Department from doing so. A rider was tacked onto the Department's annual appropriations bill barring the agency from finalizing or publishing the proposed rules–thereby blocking commercial exploration for oil shale on public lands. The moratorium expired, then was added again, then expired again. But in the Obama Administration a temporary moratorium has become long-term policy. This on-again-off-again uncertainty naturally led to yet another slow-down by the industry and its investors (Shell put its commercial plans on hold), and leaves a still-uncertain future for America's largest energy supply.

Even as the price of gasoline hovered between $3.50 and $4.50 per gallon during 2009, and with alarms sounding about the impact of escalating fuel costs on a deep recession, Congress chose to listen instead to the environmental lobby. By a margin of six votes, an amendment to Interior's appropriations bill effectively locked away the world's largest oil reserve, in our own back yard, a lock that remains in place still. Why would Congress do such a thing at such a time?

The Loyal Opposition

Opponents of oil shale development have used several tactics in the recent debate, including the emotional plea to Western Colorado residents not to let themselves be a "sacrifice zone" again. Of course, Jimmy Carter is no longer president and no government official has proposed such an extreme course again. Nor do Colorado residents have any intention of sacrificing anything–they won that battle in 1979 and would certainly win it again. Today, local governments in the area have numerous legal protections in place to mitigate economic impacts, and the state administers its own regulatory program–funded with energy industry severance taxes that did not exist during the previous boom/bust–to guard against abuses and to fund energy impacts. State regulations also protect wildlife habitat and other environmental values better than ever. In short, the dangers of the previous abuses have been foreseen, the technology to preclude a "sacrifice zone" situation is at hand, and the current political climate is very different than that of the 1970's.

Nevertheless, environmental organizations advance several arguments to stop any further discussion of oil shale:

- There is not enough water,
- Groundwater might be polluted,
- Every previous attempt has resulted in an economic bust,
- Power plants and pipelines would be needed,
- It takes a lot of oil shale to produce oil,
- It takes a long time to develop.

There is not enough water – Energy companies saw this fight coming decades ago, and all the major companies now own sufficient water rights for massive industrial operations. Using that much water would affect other water users, of course, but it cannot credibly be argued that the oil companies do not have the water they need. In fact, energy companies control more than 25% of the flow and 55% of the storage of all water in the four-state Upper Colorado River Basin. Of course, as with all *water use*, very little is *used up*, and nearly all river water returns to the river at the end of the process. But in the West, when you threaten water, you get people's attention instantly, so the rhetoric is quite effective. As we have seen, there is plenty of unused water available in the West, so for this purpose it is a hollow argument. The oil companies paid dearly for senior water rights, which they now own and have a clear right to use for oil shale development.

Groundwater might be polluted – This may actually be the most misleading argument of all, because there is virtually no groundwater that matters in that area, and because any water that is pumped to the surface could be treated and used to replace water lost from the rivers–if that were legal. Some environmental lobbyists have argued that the Shell project, for example, might "contaminate ground-water" and even that it "could allow high-salinity groundwater to mix with low-salinity groundwater." Think about that last point–if salinity in groundwater is a bad thing, surely diluting it with "low-salinity groundwater" would be an improvement! In any case, here is the truth about groundwater in the oil shale formations of the Piceance Basin: water at that depth is held in underground "pools" that do not move in geologic time, and such water is not tributary to any domestic water source anywhere. It does not flow into any other water that people or animals use, ever. Shell has invested a fortune in a new technology to preclude any degradation of the groundwater at that depth, not because there is any real danger of polluting anyone's water, but because the company saw this argument coming and had to address it. Such arguments purposely add to the cost of produced oil, but they have little to do with mitigating any real environmental impacts.

Every previous attempt has resulted in an economic bust – This is the most important reason given by members of the Colorado congressional delegation who sought to block any future use of oil shale in 2008. In a guest editorial printed during the congressional debate, one Senator wrote:

> *"It is no easy task, and past efforts have failed miserably… Sometimes it seems that we are getting close to overcoming these barriers. But each time we near a boom, we bust. The last bust, the infamous "Black Sunday" of 1982, left Western communities holding the bill long after the speculators, Beltway boosters and energy companies had taken off."*

In other words, the Senator argued, we should not allow exploration and development of the world's largest oil reserve because past efforts failed. But oil is being produced every day in places where the technology did not exist a few short years ago. It is contrary to the innate nature of Americans to give up on something important just because their first attempts fail. That is a good reason to move cautiously with oil shale and make sure we get it right; it is not an excuse to stop trying.

Power plants and pipelines would be needed – Indeed, if oil shale is to be heated underground so oil can be pumped to the surface, electric heaters require electric power. Any oil produced would require pipelines to get it to market. But some people remain horrified at the prospect of more power plants, transmission lines, pipelines, and other infrastructure. Still, there is no other way–at least not yet–to get energy from its source to your house and car. This is just as true for wind and solar power as it is for tidal power, wave power, oil and gas, and oil shale. As with all forms of energy, most people do not like such facilities, but it is not a realistic reason to stop the development of America's energy resources–from whatever source. Instead, we should spend the time and resources making sure such facilities are built and operated in the most efficient, responsible and sustainable manner.

It takes a lot of oil shale to produce oil – Numerous opponents have used this argument, completely ignoring the vast quantities available there (especially in comparison to other sources the U.S. already uses). The same 2008 guest editorial made this comparison: "It would take around one ton of rock to produce enough fuel to last the average car two weeks." But how much oil shale is a ton? It sounds like a lot when making a political argument, but of course, it is not. In fact, one ton of solid shale is less than half a cubic yard. A rock the size of a file cabinet weighs a ton. And the available resource occupies several counties, several thousand feet deep, literally an area larger than many states. Even more important, remember that with today's technology, the rock would still be in place after the oil is melted out, so the volume is actually irrelevant.

It takes a long time to develop – This is the same argument Congressional leaders used to continue the ban on offshore drilling, even with unprecedented gas prices. Some leaders claim that oil shale development could not produce oil earlier than 2020 at the earliest. Even assuming that is true, is it really a legitimate argument against getting started? Should we continue to lock away the largest oil reserve in the world just because it might take us a while to get to it? On the contrary, there is nothing wrong with taking our time and proceeding slowly, cautiously, making sure other environmental values are protected every step of the way. This is what political leaders say they want. Beginning that process with an absolute moratorium, however, can do nothing but create skepticism about the real agenda. One who wants to proceed cautiously does not begin by locking the door and not proceeding at all.

Let There Be Light

The bottom line to all debates about all forms of energy must be that the growing demand will be met one way or another. The question is at what price. Those who expect future generations to lower their standard of living are bound for disappointment, as Americans will rebel against attempts to limit their use of modern conveniences. Many environmental leaders are counting on people not noticing when price increases accomplish the same thing, but Americans *have* noticed, and cannot be expected to tolerate it much longer.

Consider the plight of energy providers and leaders in Arizona—perhaps the best example of the dilemma we all face. Penn State and Arizona State economists presented a study called "Powering Arizona: Choices and Trade-Offs for Electricity Policy," at a Phoenix conference in 2008, reviewing the state's energy options. The picture it painted was not pretty. It concluded that providing energy to Arizona in future years will become "a lot more challenging, and potentially a lot more expensive." With a projected 1 million more households by 2018, utilities face daunting choices without new infrastructure. Without an increase in supply, prices will increase dramatically.

The report mentioned numerous challenges the state faces finding new sources of energy. Coal-fired power plants, for years the major source of power in the state, may actually be shut down because of the fear of global warming. In the past decade, Arizona utilities have used natural-gas for all new power generation, but continued growth of natural gas will result in energy prices rising 60% by 2030, if current price trends continue. Arizona has added no nuclear power, and no renewable source generates enough energy to be very helpful. So what is Arizona to do now and in the coming decade?

The report said that solar power plants might generate less-expensive electricity by 2030, but at the moment they still cost more, not less, to build. That presents an unlikely solution to more immediate energy demands, so the report actually suggests waiting until 2020 or later to try commercial solar technology.

No solution recommended or discussed in the report offered any hope for the million new people moving to Arizona and needing electricity for their homes, other than paying much higher prices. For most Americans, that is not a solution. Energy must be produced from a variety of sources, including those we know are most reliable and abundant, or Americans everywhere will begin to face costs beyond their ability to pay. I do not believe they will accept the latter outcome, knowing there are other more immediate–if more conventional–solutions.

A place called the Roan Plateau contains an estimated 9 trillion cubic feet of natural gas–enough to heat 4 million homes for 20 years. It is owned by the government, of course, and the Bureau of Land Management will allow drilling on no more than 1% of the plateau's surface at any time. The BLM administers the area with such severe restrictions for one simple reason: it is what the public wants. The debate about the region raged for ten years, with environmental organizations making a national cause of it, much like the Alaska National Wildlife Refuge (ANWR), and with proponents working to produce alternatives allowing carefully regulated drilling. The opponents won, so yet another major energy source is effectively locked away.

Specific areas often become major national causes, and participating in that game plays right into the hands of an "environmental industry" with other agendas. The ANWR debate is not really about that area for many environmental groups; it is about raising money by convincing people the sky is about to fall. And conservatives who try to make a cause of opening the area to drilling only help their opponents raise more money. They might be smarter to give up on ANWR and drill in any of the thousands of other promising areas where we know there is oil and gas to be found. In fact, modern directional-drilling technology probably even makes it possible to get oil from *under* ANWR without drilling *within* ANWR. Strategic use of modern technology might finally defeat dishonest politics.

Opponents use extreme rhetoric to convince Americans that big oil executives want to kill polar bears and devastate the last great places. Too often, supporters counter by denying the outrageous claims, and arguing that we can produce energy without harming polar bears or devastating the last great places. It is a losing battle because it is fought on the opponents' turf, as futile as Pickett's Charge trying to take the high ground at Gettysburg. Real leaders concerned about our energy future should choose their own high ground, and frame the argument on issues of more direct personal interest to the audience. They ought to argue that such zealots are causing higher gas prices and higher home utility bills–issues on which they might have a chance of winning public support.

A More Realistic Choice

Not surprisingly, opponents of energy production never mention technological improvements in the oil and gas business. Entrepreneurs and creative minds get very little credit for new discoveries or improvements in the process. Directional drilling was a technological breakthrough of colossal importance, allowing the extraction of oil from entire regions previously unavailable. So was hydraulic fracturing. Development of ways to burn fossil fuels without emitting harmful pollutants is light years ahead of all previous generations. Automobiles now burn gas and emit almost nothing into the air.

Despite all the recent technological advances, the oil and gas industry is still often portrayed as an evil empire, run by Neanderthals who care nothing about the very Earth we inhabit. In reality, the industry has invested hundreds of billions in making energy cleaner, more efficient, less expensive, and more readily available to millions. Far more investment in environmental improvement has come from industry than from any other source, including government and environmental groups. Yet these groups expect us to assume that there is no chance for further improvement, no possibility that the various problems associated with fossil fuels can ever be addressed. Some of the zealots who run these organizations might actually be that myopic, but most Americans are not, nor should they be. We have every reason to expect that the march toward safer and cleaner energy will continue unabated into the foreseeable future. However, placing vast resources off-limits, adding major energy taxes, or eliminating incentives for further investment in the area where we actually get most of our energy, is a poor plan for continued improvement.

Americans have always relied on constantly increasing technology to improve their lives, and their faith in the private enterprise system has never failed to produce advances in every generation. It will continue to do so, and we should continue to insist on it. We need not rely on pure faith to produce such progress; we invest billions in it every year, and we require constant improvement on the part of industry. The profit incentive for development of newer and better systems is powerful and will lead to even better lives for future generations–if we resist the temptation to stop everything now just because we don't like the looks of power plants, drill rigs, or telephone poles.

Americans have an almost pathological tendency to blame themselves for everything and to criticize everything they do. That's why the famous 1990 Greenpeace ad in the New York Times was so effective, scolding, *"It wasn't the Exxon Valdez captain's driving that caused the Alaskan oil spill. It was yours."* We love to psycho-analyze ourselves, and we tend to believe the worst. So when someone accuses us of destroying the planet by driving to work, we don't take offense, rare back and say, "How dare you!" More often, we say to ourselves, "Oh, oops, we'd better stop doing that."

If only we could find a way to make the equipment and facilities needed to produce energy completely invisibly, many of these political battles would never need to be fought. Perhaps the next generation of leaders can focus as much time and energy on that as today's leaders spend arguing about where–if anywhere–to allow anything.

CHAPTER 8

Descent Into Extremism

I was never ruined but twice—once when I lost a lawsuit,
and once when I won one.

—Voltaire

The growth of the environmental industry since the 1980's has been nothing short of astonishing. Though their stated goals have not changed much, the nature of these groups has changed radically. They learned techniques from other non-profit organizations in other fields (charities, health care groups, educators, unions), became extremely sophisticated and professional, and began raising unprecedented amounts of money. An in-depth analysis by the *Sacramento Bee* found that by the year 2000, foundations and corporations in America were giving to environmental organizations at the rate of $9 million a day. A decade later, the industry is bigger than ever.

If there remains any doubt that the environmental lobby has become one of America's largest "industries," consider some raw numbers.

- The Nature Conservancy's 2012 annual report listed total assets of $6 billion and annual revenues of over $870. The organization contributes some $12 million per year to employee retirement plans.

- The Sierra Club (which does not publish its financial reports) says it has over 750,000 members, annual revenues (2008) of over $87 million, and over 500 paid staff members.

- The Sierra Club Foundation also reported total assets (2011) in excess of $100 million, and revenues of over $40 million.

- The Environmental Defense Fund (EDF) reported 2012 assets

of over \$156 million and revenue of \$116.5 million, a budget increasing at around 30% per year over the last 5 years–less than 7% of it from actual membership dues (more than third came from a single wealthy donor in 2010). The EDF has over 300 employees in 9 cities, including its Manhattan headquarters on Park Avenue. In 2009 EDF reported a single foundation grant of almost \$50 million.

- The World Wildlife Fund reported 2011 net assets of nearly \$270 million and annual revenue of \$238 million.

- The Wilderness Society reported assets of over \$45 million and annual revenue of \$23 million.

- Trout Unlimited claims over 140,000 members in 450 chapters across the country, and reported 2010 revenue of \$20.4 million.

- The Natural Resources Defense Council (NRDC) reported annual income for 2011 of over \$107 million, assets of almost \$245 million, and boasts a membership network of 1.3 million "members and online activists."

- Annual revenues of Greenpeace International are around \$80 million;

- The National Wildlife Federation took in \$107 million in 2011;

- World Resources Institute brought in \$41 million;

- Earth Justice, the legal arm of the Sierra Club, raised \$46 million;

- Defenders of Wildlife brought in another \$31 million.

Today there are hundreds of environmental organizations spending billions of dollars in what has become one of the largest segments of the non-profit sector worldwide.

An interesting footnote is that many environmental organizations decline to list their members, or even report how many they actually have. Note that NRDC lumps "members" into the same category as people who participate in its web site activity. Most others put "members and donors" into the same category for required financial reporting, making it virtually impossible to question their statements about how many people they actually represent. In truth, many of these groups do not actually have members who pay annual dues, but include all donors, visitors to their websites, and attendees at their meetings when reporting their impressive "members and supporters" lists. Thus, these groups can claim to represent millions— and have the financial clout to show for it—when in fact many have very few actual dues-paying members, especially at the local chapter level.

In late 2012 the Audubon Society created a new website called the "American Eagle Compact," which asks visitors to sign a simple statement that conservation is not partisan, and asks to "send our leaders a message: stop playing politics with the planet." The document does not say what politics are deemed offensive, nor what policies are being advocated, yet more than 65,000 people signed on within a few weeks. Rest assured that eventually those 65,000 people will be counted as Audubon Society supporters who back some policy position—without their actual participation or permission.

In Colorado I have often dealt with new organizations with clever names like "Friends of the Canyon" or "Concerned Citizens of the Valley," who would refuse all requests for information about membership, because in fact they had no members at all (just a grant from some larger group). It is a clever technique that has helped fuel the growth, activity, involvement, awareness, credibility and clout of the environmental industry.

The environmental movement has grown not just in the size and scope of these major organizations, but also in their number. Every subcategory of natural resources has seen the evolution of a host of conservation groups specializing in related issues. For example, protection of national parks is one area near and dear to the hearts of conservationists, but it is only one area. Nevertheless, at least 52 national environmental organizations spend a considerable portion of their energies on national parks issues. A similar cadre of organizations can be found swirling around endangered species protection, forest health, energy development, agriculture, transportation, waste management, urban sprawl, global warming, ocean protection, clean air and water, open space protection, and wildlife. In each of these categories, more than a hundred dedicated national and international organizations can readily be identified.

You can check their web sites for more information, if you can figure out which sites to check. There are at least 19 web sites in 40 countries operated by GreenPeace, at least 27 Sierra Club sites, 6 for Friends of the Earth, 10 for EarthFirst!, 10 for the Natural Resources Defense Council (NRDC), and several thousand more. A Google search for "environmental organizations" finds over 200,000 web sites.

Attempts to keep track of this vast and rapidly growing industry are doomed from the start—even the groups themselves cannot monitor their own ever-changing numbers. The World Directory of Environmental Organizations was created in 1972 in one attempt to keep track. By 2006 its online version organized groups into over 350 web pages with literally tens of thousands of links around the world. Designed to be the definitive global guide in this field, it was produced by InterEnvironment (part of the California Institute of Public Affairs), in cooperation with the World Conservation Union and the Sierra Club. Its growth was so costly and overwhelming the effort was finally abandoned in 2008. The "Environmental Yellow Pages," headquartered in Florida, boasts over 350,000 listings worldwide.

Although there is no complete list of environmental organizations (such a list would be outdated almost daily), one website called the EnviroLink Network makes perhaps the best attempt. It lists thousands of organizations, including 347 dedicated to wildlife issues, 176 working on global warming, 588 involved in energy, 156 concerned about oceans, 46 involved in forest management issues, 65 anti-population groups, 48 urban environment groups, 245 concerned with "sustainable agriculture," and over 450 air quality and 705 water quality groups. Altogether the EnviroLink site monitors thousands of conservation organizations and "resources" and admits to barely scratching the surface.

"Citizen Groups"

Perhaps the biggest story, though, has been almost completely missed by the media and other observers of the movement over the past generation. The speed and professionalism with which the movement spawns new organizations is not just an impressive phe-nomenon—it is a carefully developed strategy.

Twenty-five years ago (1987) the Rockefeller Family Fund put together a "retreat" for other foundations whose donations help fund the conservation movement. They formed the Environmental Grantmakers Association (EGA), originally with twelve member foundations in the United States. Today, the association's members represent over 225 foundations from North America and around the world, including virtually all of the major funding sources of the environmental industry. These foundations have fingerprints on the annual reports of all of the largest environmental organizations, and their assets are vast:

- Ford Foundation ($10.7 billion),
- William and Flora Hewlett Foundation ($6.8 billion),
- David and Lucile Packard Foundation ($5.7 billion),
- Heinz Endowments ($1.2 billion),
- Joyce Foundation ($773.6 million),
- Rockefeller Brothers Fund ($729 million),
- Park Foundation ($321 million),
- Overbrook Foundation ($127 million),
- Johnson Family Foundation ($76 million)

Those are just a few examples; so much for the image of little neighborhood conservation groups fighting the big evil corporate giants.

The EGA foundations continue to meet at annual "retreats" during which strategies are developed to maximize the impact of donations. By the late 1980's the group began to discuss better ways to influence environmental policy at the local, state and national levels, and hit upon a more grass-roots-based strategy. Many Americans had grown weary of the constant involvement, especially in local decisions, of out-of-state environmentalists. Opponents had begun fighting back with accusations about constant Sierra Club "meddling" in local matters, and editorials regularly invited "eastern elites" to "stay out of our back yard."

It didn't take long for the EGA foundation members to figure out that local citizen groups are more effective than the national office of the Sierra Club or Friends of the Earth. Local citizen groups do not have same history, baggage, or questionable reputations as older and larger national organizations. So the EGA developed a new strategy for dealing with new issues as they arose: new organizations, based in the local communities affected by new problems, and composed of local citizens, not national leaders. If usable local organizations didn't exist, they would be created and quickly funded, even professionally staffed, in ways that could not easily be traced to outsiders.

For example, when it looked like the Interior Department might actually begin construction of the long-halted Animas-La Plata water project near Durango, Colorado, "Taxpayers for the Animas River" and the "Four Corners Action Coalition" suddenly appeared with lots of "members" ready to write letters, show up at public hearings, and file lawsuits, the costs of which the local "members" could not possibly afford. Of course, these organizations were neither local nor independent, despite their local-sounding names. They were subsidiaries of California-based EarthJustice, the legal defense fund established by the Sierra Club in 1971.

As soon as 23-year-old Adam Werbach was elected president of the Sierra Club in 1996, he gained national attention by advocating "decommissioning" Lake Powell and Glen Canyon Dam. A blaze of controversy ensued, with leaders throughout the West arguing the importance of the lake—not only because of its enormous recreation and economic value, but because the delicate balance of Colorado River law cannot be administered without it. Angry state officials insisted that the kid from California didn't know what he was talking about, and demanded that the Sierra Club stay out of local matters.

Almost overnight, the "Glen Canyon Institute" appeared like a flash flood, heavily funded and with slick brochures, handouts, and websites—even with 8 scientific studies on the impact of the dam, studies that could not have been completed locally within such a short time frame. But based in Salt Lake City, it could not be called an "out-of-state" interest group and was immediately given credibility by a carefully selected board of westerners, a highly professional staff, and plenty of press coverage. How could such a large coalition have been created so quickly? Simply put, it was founded by David Brower, the 27-year board member and former executive director of the Sierra Club, and one of the original opponents of the dam's construction. Glen Canyon Institute is not an independent and spontaneously created group of local people. It is a "branch" of the Sierra Club—it just doesn't look like it on paper.

Flush with success, the phenomenon quickly swept across the nation. In California when Louisiana-Pacific proposed new timber cuts in a place called Enchanted Meadow, the old Albion River Watershed Protection Association and Earth First! suddenly spawned "Friends of Enchanted Meadow" and the "Coastal Land Trust." A Forest Service discussion about the historic impacts of Lake Chelan in Washington was suddenly joined by the local group, "People for Lake Chelan." The National Park Service began a serious study of the health of Jamaica Bay in New York City's Gateway National Recreation Area because of new studies issued by "Jamaica Bay Ecowatchers." Almost overnight meetings were being attended by "Friends of the Gateway," part of the "Tree Branch Network" of local citizen groups. The story is now familiar to nearly all watchers of public policy debates—the sudden emergence of local groups that locals had never heard of before, and government agencies granting them "official stakeholder" status (in much the same way courts determine a person's legal "standing"). Clearly, states, counties, landowners whose property is affected by management decisions, and residents of the local community have a direct "stake" in the outcome of such decisions. But the agencies frequently grant equal weight to the opinions of these new groups, whose members and backers may or may not have any "stake" at all, and who may or may not live in the area.

In fact, federal land management agencies, when required to consider and publish conclusions about several different alternatives, sometimes even refer to one submitted by these groups as the "citizen alternative"—whether or not most local citizens actually share that opinion. It is especially ironic when the "citizens" proposals differ from those of local elected officials who were actually elected by actual citizens. Still, adopting the same language used by these groups and their EGA foundation funders adds further credibility for federal land managers and the practice is routine.

This grant of official status to such groups is rarely questioned, but in some cases locals have raised the concern that these groups are often comprised of people who don't really have a "stake" in the outcome (at least not in the same way community members and landowners have), but to no avail. The simple reality is that public policy must be conducted in public. Including "public" groups in the official process is not a difficult choice for government agencies—especially if their employees happen to agree with the environmental groups' position. Thus, the EGA foundation members' strategy has paid off in a big way.

Today literally hundreds of new local groups are official "stakeholders" helping to push environmental decisions across the nation and dealing with nearly all major natural resource agencies at every level of government. It is a subversion of the public process. The National Environmental Policy Act (NEPA) created this required public hearing and comment procedure with a very noble and simple idea–before agencies make major management decisions, they ought to get input from the people whose lives would be affected. It was never intended to be a tool for activists from elsewhere (or wealthy foundation donors) to influence these decisions by pretending to be involved "local citizens." That does not mean people from all over the country have no right to be heard on federal land management issues—of course they do. But their opinions could be more accurately considered if it were more clear who they were. That is a clarity they do not want.

A careful examination of the budgets and financial statements of many of these "local" organizations reveals their secret. As mentioned before, they generally lump income sources together under a category such as "memberships and donations" to make it appear that most of the funds come from membership dues–even in cases where they have few members at all. While most funding appears in this "memberships and donations" category, of course, it is mostly from donations, not memberships. And they are not required by any law to disclose who those donors are, or how many there are. So a heavily funded professional group might show a million dollars in revenue from members and donations, even though in fact it may be entirely funded by one grant from one foundation.

One good example is the Western Colorado Congress (WCC), a key player in influencing environmental debates in that state since 1980. It is a loose coalition of smaller local groups in the region (Grand Valley Citizens Alliance, Yampa Valley Community Alliance, Uncompahgre Valley Association, and several others), but few people have ever paid actual membership dues to the WCC. Nevertheless, it has a budget larger than any similar organization in the region, and in some years has listed over a dozen paid staff members in four offices, though several of them commonly identify themselves in public as staff of these smaller local groups. Remember, the EGA strategy is based on an understanding that local is more effective than regional, just as regional is more effective than national. The bulk of WCC's funding does not come from membership dues, but from grants. They come from national foundations that are part of the EGA: The Norman Foundation (NY), Norcross Wildlife Foundation (NY), Hewlett Foundation (CA), Wyss Foundation (DC), Kenney Brothers Foundation (CA), Public Welfare Foundation (DC), Further Foundation (CA), Patagonia (CA), Ben and Jerry's (VT), Peradam Foundation (CA), New-Land Foundation (NY), and others.

For 30 years a steady, dependable flow of funds has made WCC professional, sophisticated, visible, and successful. Most local governments now readily accept the group's involvement in public policy, though to this day no reporter has ever succeeded in obtaining a list of its actual members, much less a detailed donor list (few reporters have ever asked). The group can't afford to make such lists public; they would show relatively few members and the bulk of funding from outside the state, which would undermine a local reputation 30 years in the making. Today, there are thousands of "local" organizations just like WCC throughout the nation, and they did not appear spontaneously. They were a tactic.

In addition to the creation of new organizations, another technique proved equally effective for the grant makers—generating involvement by local "individuals." Few things can have a stronger impact on public officials sitting through late-night public hearings than a parade of local citizens airing their distress about decisions that could ruin their lives, jeopardize the health of their children, or destroy the quality of life in their communities. County commissioners and city council members increasingly see just that, often from new people they have not seen before at such public hearings. Local TV stations are now regularly treated to highly emotional interviews with young parents holding their crying babies, and demanding to know "how many more children must be put at risk for corporate profits?!" Officials listen to the testimony of local residents who describe their decision to move to the area because of its beauty and rare peaceful lifestyle, only to find out later about planned developments—developments about which they were never warned before buying property.

Since the early 1990's, individuals showing up at public hearings to testify against permits and zoning changes and public land leases have often identified themselves only as "John Doe, concerned citizen," not identifying with any organization at all. In many cases, such witnesses are actually being paid to be there, frequently transported from elsewhere for the purpose of packing the hearings, but no law requires disclosure of those facts. In numerous cases they are even paid staff members of environmental organizations funded by the EGA foundations, but they do not have to say so. So why should they? The technique is extraordinarily effective, as evidenced by the outcomes in countless federal decisions where public involvement is required. And they are rarely questioned about it.

As a member of a governing commission, I once had a chance publicly to question the growth of these so-called "citizen groups." During a regulatory hearing of the Colorado Wildlife Commission, a witness identified himself as "President of the Progressive Citizens Alliance" and began lecturing the board on behalf of his "members." Cross-examination is common practice on that board, so I interrupted to ask him what that group was (I am a native of the area and had never heard of it). The man assured me that the PCA was a citizen-based, grass-roots organization involved in quality-of-life issues throughout the Grand Valley.

I asked, "How many dues-paying members do you have?" He responded, "We represent several thousand members, donors and activists throughout the region." I asked how much the membership costs, and he replied, "Our supporters pay varying amounts, depending on their ability and interest. Why?" I repeated, "How many people actually pay dues to belong to the PCA?" He was squirming uncomfortably and began steadily raising his voice as we continued the colloquy, "We do not release our membership lists to the public," he said. "Why do you want to know?" I explained that for the benefit of the hundreds of people in the audience, the other board members and the press, "I am trying to get a sense of who you represent when you identify yourself as president of an organization with which we are not familiar. So what exactly is your annual budget and where does it come from?" He became openly hostile and said, "Our budget is not public information, nor is our membership. I don't see what difference it makes."

These seemed to me like obvious questions that other local observers wanted to ask, too. So finally, I said, "You claim to represent lots of people but you won't tell us if anyone actually pays dues to belong, whether you're being paid to be here today, how big your group is, or anything about it. Can you tell us anything to show you in fact represent anyone besides yourself?" To which he thundered, "Why are you asking me all these questions?!"

It is worth noting that the practice of creating local organizations without disclosing their real funding sources is not universally accepted as proper conduct. Indeed, the practice is specifically prohibited by the code of ethics of the Public Relations Society of America. Former Senator Lloyd Benson coined a now-common term for such groups; he called them "Astroturf," because their grassroots appearance is really artificial. People or organizations that use the technique are often said to be "astroturfing." Ethical or not, the practice is a key weapon in the arsenal of today's environmental industry.

From local meetings in Middle America to board rooms on Wall Street, these groups have developed a remarkable degree of sophistication. One anecdote from the pages of the New York Times is illustrative. As Thomas Friedman wrote, the Texas power giant, TXU, announced a plan in 2006 to build 11 new coal-fired power plants and the ensuing controversy reached a new level of intensity from Austin to Manhattan. Environmental Defense Fund president Fred Krupp asked to meet with TXU chairman John Wilder but was refused. So EDF and the Natural Resources Defense Council (NRDC) launched a web site (StopTXU.com), published electronic newsletters, built a national constituency and filed a lawsuit. It paid off when the large buyout firms of Kohlberg Kravis Roberts and Texas Pacific Group collaborated to buy TXU in the largest leveraged buyout in history ($45 billion)—but only on the condition that EDF and NRDC approved the deal! The buyers simply would not risk the investment with unpopular proposals and lawsuits hanging over it.

The resulting plan cut the number of new power plants from 11 to 3, and the company agreed to spend $400 million on energy-efficiency programs, double its purchase of wind power, and publicly support a U.S. cap on greenhouse gas emissions. EDF hired the Wall Street firm of Perella Weinberg Partners to negotiate the fine print and the deal is now history. In short, a group without a dime at stake sat at the table on Wall Street and dictated details of the largest deal of its kind in business history.

Clearly, the conservation movement has achieved a level of sophistication which rivals that of the world's largest companies and exceeds that of most government agencies. Its ability to adopt strategic plans and implement tactical campaigns is second to none. It employs some of the brightest and best educated minds in the world, and can react almost instantly to new events, threats and opportunities.

The Litigation Nation

In addition to the strategy of creating new grass-roots organizations, the other major shift in direction and policy of the environmental industry over the past two decades has been its focus on litigation. While Americans in general sue each other at a rate unparalleled in human history, few economic sectors can compare with the environmental industry in the skill, scope, and sheer magnitude of the lawsuits.

Nearly all of the major national conservation groups have established separate legal arms for the sole purpose of filing lawsuits.

Often called "Legal Defense Funds" or "Legal Foundations," these branch organizations often operate under different tax laws than their non-profit "parent" organizations, with different disclosure rules and with the protection of the lawyer-client privilege that makes monitoring their activities more difficult for outside observers. Nor must they report statistics on all of their total legal action or budgets. That makes tracking their exact activities thorny, but clearly the growth of lawsuits on environmental issues has been staggering. It is now a regular part of the cost of doing business in every industry related to natural resources.

The Sierra Club's original legal arm, EarthJustice, lists 129 federal lawsuits it filed between February, 2001 and February, 2007, nearly all of them against federal agencies. In other words, the group found something so egregious as to justify a lawsuit against the government twenty times a year, almost twice a month for nearly a decade. Similar legal branches have been created all over the country by environmental organizations large and small, at nearly every level. The $4 million-a-year Environmental Working Group has a separate legal arm ("EWG Action Fund"); so do smaller regional and local groups like the Wisconsin Lakes Association ("legal action fund") and the Chesapeake Bay Foundation ("Chesapeake Bay Watershed Litigation Project"). Sometimes they are created specifically to fight specific government actions, as in the case of Free Our Forests and its separate "Fee Demo Legal Challenge Fund," created to fight the U.S. Forest Service's demonstration project charging fees for recreational users of public lands. In most cases, they are created and funded the same way as many of the new "local" organizations. The Chesapeake Bay Watershed Litigation Fund, for example, was created for the sole purpose of filing lawsuits, with a $1.25 million grant from Philadelphia's Lenfest Foundation, one of the newer foundations (2000) mentioned earlier.

This course of intimidating federal agencies through lawsuits is played out every day at the local level, in communities across the country. A Pennsylvania group called the Community Environmental Defense Fund brags on its website about its success in banning mining near the Blaine Township.

"Thanks to their civic-minded actions Blaine Township became the first municipality in the country to ban corporations from mining, the third to recognize that natural ecosystems independently possess enforceable rights within the community, and the fifth to strip corporations of legal and constitutional protections."

Across the country each year, the scale of this legal activity is so staggering it can hardly be measured. One impressive attempt to get a handle on the statistics was undertaken by Professors Theodore Eisenberg and Kevin Clermont at Cornell Law School. Eisenberg is one of the foremost authorities on legal system empirical data and has advised the Justice Department on the need for better data on lawsuits and the legal system. The Cornell Law School database resulting from his work tracks around 260,000 civil lawsuits by type and disposition, showing the alarming expansion of Americans' litigious tendencies. The total number of such lawsuits increased over 9.2% between 1987 and 2000. But lawsuits related to environmental matters, during the same period, increased by a whopping 65% (from 555 in 1987 to 914 in 1999 and over 1,000 in 2000 and every year since). In other words, *three environmental lawsuits are filed in the United States every day.*

Some civil actions are also filed by government agencies in their enforcement capacity, but *the bulk of them* are lawsuits filed by environmental organizations, companies and "concerned citizens." More than a third of all environmental lawsuits are filed against the federal government. Annual Reports of the Bureau of Justice Statistics show that *an environmental lawsuit is filed against the government every 36 hours.* Considering the cost of legal fees in the modern era, every one of these lawsuits costs thousands of dollars to pursue, and some run into the millions. There has been very little discussion of the massive resources available to an environmental industry practicing routine litigation on that scale.

In fact, one of the best kept secrets in Washington is the extent to which taxpayers not only pay to defend the government in these lawsuits, but also pay the costs of the environmental groups filing them. In 1980, Congress passed the Equal Access to Justice Act (EAJA) to help individuals, small businesses and non-profits with limited budgets to "seek judicial redress against the federal government." It allows plaintiffs who sue the federal government to recover their attorney's fees and costs (from tax dollars) if they prevail in the case—or if they settle out of court. Two recent studies have shown that despite the intent to help small organizations, large environmental groups are actually the major beneficiaries of EAJA payments. A 2011 GAO report found that nearly $5 million—more than a fourth of the legal fees paid out by EPA—went to EarthJustice (the legal arm of the Sierra Club) and another 9% to the Sierra Club itself and the Natural Resources Defense Council. Those are, of course, three of the world's largest environmental organizations, hardly strapped for cash or unable to file lawsuits without the government's help.

The Clinton Administration stopped the government's tracking and reporting of these payments in 1995, so the growing use of the EAJA program to fund environmental group lawsuits has been mostly secret since then.

According to recent research by a Wyoming law firm, the 14 major environmental groups it studied have brought over 1,200 federal lawsuits in 19 states and the District of Columbia, and collected over $37 million in federal funds to pay their expenses. Those numbers do not include settlements and fees that are sealed from public view by court orders (as in most out-of-court settlements). Another independent study from Virginia Tech discovered similar results in a comprehensive Freedom of Information Act request of five federal agencies. The Virginia Tech study also revealed that two of the five agencies could provide absolutely no data on EAJA payments (since they are no longer required to track or report such payments). There is no question that the taxpayers are spending billions of dollars defending the actions of the federal government. If they are also to be charged for the expenses of the environmental industry filing these lawsuits, then without question taxpayers are entitled to more discussion about these organizations, where their resources come from, and who directs them.

While these numbers help show the level of priority given this strategy by the conservation movement, the problem with this escalation in lawsuits goes far beyond the simple numbers, or even the cost to taxpayers. It is a problem that also causes an actual counterproductive paradox. It is that litigation has become a colossal impediment to implementing the very national environmental policies we as a nation have agreed upon. It changes the priorities and in far too many cases actually cripples efforts to protect or improve the environment.

The inescapable conclusion is that lawsuits, the fear of lawsuits, court actions and court orders have become the primary factors in determining environmental policy—in place of and often in direct contradiction of the responsible and honorable will of the people of the United States. For instance, the U.S. Fish and Wildlife Service, charged with primary enforcement of the Endangered Species Act, told Interior Secretary Bruce Babbitt in the late 1990s that it faced so many court orders it had no remaining budget for any other activities. By 2000 the situation progressed to the point that public announcements had to be made explaining the problem. As one story went,

> *"Employees last week were told to stop working on studies about adding species to the endangered and threatened list and focus instead on completing court-ordered work on labeling habitat for species already on the list, Fish and Wildlife spokesman Hugh Vickery said. The decision means that about 25 species being considered for the endangered list will have to wait past the end of this fiscal year on Sept. 30, 2001, Vickery said. The agency will make exceptions for species in imminent danger of becoming extinct." (AP, 11-23-2000)*

In other words, federal courts had taken operational control over the agency away from the executive branch. No court purposely decided to do so, of course, but the number of court orders issued as lawsuit settlements had simply overwhelmed the remaining ability of the agency to plan or implement anything else. The same dilemma, in varying degrees, affects the Bureau of Land Management, National Park Service, U.S. Forest Service, National Marine Fisheries Service, Army Corps of Engineers, and many state environmental protection agencies.

There is another less obvious cost to all this litigation, a cost borne by every American. Consider the costs of defending these lawsuits. When a federal agency is the target of the suit, tax dollars pay the enormous cost. But when corporations are the target, consumers pay the costs, passed along in higher prices. That cost is larger than you may think. For instance, a 2006 survey by the law firm of Fulbright and Jaworski found that the average energy company faces 364 separate pending lawsuits in U.S. courts. The survey found that energy companies spend an average of $13.5 million a year on litigation. Seventy-seven percent of energy companies retain at least 6 outside law firms (in addition to their own in-house lawyers), and 29% hire more than 20 such firms. Corporate executives do not pay these costs—energy consumers do. It is hard to know how much of the cost of a gallon of gas pays for lawyers, but clearly *some of it does*. For the environmental industry, legal action has trumped the democratic process.

To be clear, the court system, including adversarial lawsuits, has a place of honor in a democratic society. The judicial system represents free citizens' right to justice when society turns a deaf ear. After all, poor people accused of crimes were not guaranteed the right to an attorney until Clarence Gideon wrote his famous lawsuit using a pencil and prison stationery.

Some environmental lawsuits have helped call attention to serious ecological problems, and have helped force recalcitrant government agencies to do something about them. For example, an environmental lawsuit in 2002 (accompanied by significant congressional pressure) finally forced the federal government to limit its dumping of toxic sludge into the Potomac River, which is now cleaner than any time since World War II, with plants and fish recovering quickly. Prior to the lawsuit, the Corps of Engineers and the D.C. government had routinely ignored the Clean Water Act and Endangered Species Act. They even tried to justify the double standard with an EPA memo claiming the toxic sludge helped save fish by forcing them to leave the D.C. area. The leak of that hypocritical memo (imagine anyone but the federal government itself trying to make that claim) prompted the lawsuit, a rash of congressional hearings, and what will eventually be over $2 billion in improvements to the government's water treatment systems.

Similarly, citizen lawsuits have occasionally helped correct heavy-handed agencies abusing their authority in the name of the environment. David Lucas bought two lots on a barrier island near Charleston, but the South Carolina Coastal Commission later change the zoning laws and prohibited the two houses he had planned to build. His 1992 lawsuit went all the way to the Supreme Court and re-affirmed the 5th Amendment prohibition against government taking private property for public purposes without just compensation—even when the "taking" is of the land's value, rather than its actual title.

Unfortunately, such "regulatory takings" remain commonplace elsewhere. Contrast that outcome of the Lucas case in South Carolina with that of Jim Wickstra, a Michigan developer in a similar situation. He bought a 3-acre parcel on Lake Michigan, intending to build a valuable beach home for resale. But a few months later, the Legislature approved the Michigan Sand Dune Protection Act, designed to stop development along the lakefront. Mr. Wickstra applied for the required permit, but was denied by the state Department of Natural Resources, even though he offered several alternate plans to protect the dune and to build an environmentally sensitive home. The State tax agency ruled that the property was worth $200,000 with a building permit and only $500 without it. Yet he spent more than a decade fighting to get compensation for the loss of his property value. One bureaucrat reportedly told Mr. Wickstra that he would never win the battle, saying "I will bleed you white," and that is exactly what happened. The Michigan Court of Claims Judge rejected Mr. Wickstra's property rights lawsuit, ruling that $195,500 was an insufficient decline in value to justify compensation. Mr. Wickstra says the ordeal not only cost him the total value of the land, but also $170,000 in legal fees, to no avail.

The legal system failed Mr. Wickstra where it had aided Mr. Lucas. That inconsistency is a complex problem, but it does not obscure the vital purpose of our legal system. There are many examples of citizens and organizations using the legal process to gain justice when all else fails—on both sides of environmental debates.

However, the growth of the modern lawsuit industry has perverted this noble purpose and actually made it much more difficult for courts to perform this vital function, by clogging the dockets of the court system and monopolizing the budgets and staff time of the agencies. Thousands of these lawsuits are not filed as a last resort when other avenues have failed. Rather, they are the first choice of groups organized for the sole purpose of using the court system to delay, impede, and stop activities they oppose. It is the tool of first choice for many of these groups precisely because the public is not on their side, and they cannot win their battles in the normal democratic process. They have simply found another way, and used it with staggering effectiveness.

As environmental organizations have become increasingly shrill in their approach, government agencies empowered to implement environmental laws have also shifted their focus away from conservation and onto enforcement, often to the exclusion of common sense. A businessman named Fred Grange, who owned a construction company in San Rafael, California, found that out the hard way. As reported by the International Society for Individual Liberties and several other websites, an employee accidentally spilled a barrel of oil on a vacant lot. A law abiding citizen, Mr. Grange knew he was required to report the spill to the EPA, although it was small and easy enough to clean up. So he reported the accidental spill to the EPA and to local agencies as required under California state law. Over a dozen agencies, from both the state and federal governments, including state and local police forces, swooped down upon the business, sending several hundred investigators. Mr. Grange had the audacity to be angry about the over-reaction—after all, he had voluntarily done the right thing, cleaned up the mess and filed the reports—and he made some admittedly harsh remarks about how ridiculous all these investigations seemed. So he says the agencies made an example of him and imposed fines of over $20 million, forcing the business to close and costing all the employees (not just the one who had the accident) their jobs.

While the environmental movement has become enormously successful, in membership, money and influence, something far more important has been lost. The environmental "movement" has become intellectually bankrupt. That is, these gigantic organizations have virtually no answers for the nation's most pressing environmental problems. As if still fighting the battles of 30 years ago (burning rivers and belching smokestacks), their reaction to nearly every single project being proposed is to *stop it*.

In the modern era, the constant chorus calling for stopping everything is simply irrational. It provides no answers for the economy's most complex and difficult questions (consider the complete inability of environmental leaders opposing oil and gas drilling to offer any meaningful solution to high gas prices). Indeed, the environmental lobby has become so successful that it doesn't even require much effort to stop major projects.

Today, advocates of energy production, new refineries, factories, sawmills, and water projects often stop short of even proposing new projects, because of the assumption that environmental opposition will make success impossible. Opponents of such developments are powerful, well-funded, and politically connected. That's why many western states have built no new water projects in decades despite unprecedented droughts. It's why no new refineries have been built in the United States for 30 years. And it is one reason numerous overcrowded highways remain overcrowded instead of expanded. Some water solutions do not involve new dams, and some energy solutions do not require new refineries. Yet many local governments, special districts, and resource companies have stopped even proposing major new projects because they are weary of the cost of fighting environmental opposition. For environmental activists with a goal of stopping everything, that must seem like the definition of success. But it supplies no answers to problems of drought, energy supply, or transportation needs—all of which have a direct impact on the environment.

The most difficult challenges facing the modern world have very little to do with *stopping* human activity. The real challenge that should excite today's environmental leaders is how to provide the natural resources required to sustain a prosperous civilization—in a manner that is responsible, sustainable, environmentally friendly, and available to future generations. Simply *stopping* activity actually has the opposite effect. It provides no resources, no answers, and sometimes even damages the environment or hinders environmental improvement. The real challenge—providing resources responsibly—is complex, difficult, and a potentially exciting career for future leaders. There is a serious difference between obstructionism and leadership, and many modern environmental organizations have flatly lost track of that difference.

We are in a quagmire of partisan politics, divisive bickering, and lawsuits. Opposite sides of this contentious battle cannot talk to each other across a conference table, much less a coffee table, because they continually face each other across a courtroom table. It's Republicans vs. Democrats, liberals vs. conservatives, East vs. West, North vs. South, urban vs. rural, young vs. old, ecology vs. economy, and environmentalists vs. corporations. For so many of these players, the game is all about the minutia, the lawsuits, the meetings, the process itself–that's how they get paid. But this is not a game, or at least it shouldn't be. Americans have loved their environment from the very beginning and worked hard to conserve and improve it. That noble legacy has been hijacked, and it is time to recover it.

CHAPTER 9

FROM ROAD BLOCKS TO ROADMAPS

"Truth is incontrovertible; ignorance can deride it, panic may resent it, malice may destroy it, but there it is."
—*Winston Churchill*

Taking back the high ground on environmental issues requires one and only one clear strategy–doing the right thing for the environment. All the rest is nonsense, hidden agendas, money-changing, and phony political posturing. The trouble is that all this noise often makes it difficult for today's leaders to know what is right for the environment. "Doing the right thing" sounds good, but what is the right thing?

When listening to the often rancorous debates about environmental policy, there is a very simple test for sorting it all out. Next time you hear a contentious disagreement about some proposal, ask yourself one simple question: will this actually improve the environment?

Here is one example: there is a current debate underway in several states about proposals to tax ranchers for the gas emitted by their cows, sheep, and pigs. It is an issue because some fanatics think animal flatulence is a significant cause of global warming. In response, several state legislatures are discussing proposals to levy a tax, in some cases as much as $175 per animal, on ranchers with more than 200 farm animals. The simple test in this case is to ask ourselves this question: will a tax on ranchers keep animals from passing gas? The answer is: of course not. The animals won't actually know whether their owner has paid the tax or not (cows don't even know they have an owner). So what would the actual result of such a proposal be? Either there would be fewer animals, and thus a smaller and more expensive food supply for Americans, or a larger percentage of our food would have to be imported (like our oil), or the number of animals would stay the same and government revenues would increase. None of those scenarios have anything whatsoever to do with the environment; they're all about money. Unless we all quit eating meat, there are going to be farm animals passing gas on this planet—but these advocates are *not* proposing a vegetarian requirement to ban meat-eating. Why not? If legislators really believed animal flatulence was causing unacceptable air pollution and endangering the universe, the right solution for the environment would be to ban cows, sheep and pigs. Instead, they want to raise money.

Similar examples are found everywhere if you look for them. The *Merced Sun Star* newspaper ran afoul of the San Joaquin Valley Air Pollution Control Authority in 2008 because its owners had the bad judgment to *upgrade* their printing presses without first getting permission from all the right bureaucrats. One employee had left and another, suddenly in charge of installing the new equipment, proceeded without knowing about a local permit requirement. He found out the next time the Authority sent an inspector on his regular rounds. Keep in mind that nobody ever suggested the printing press *upgrades* polluted the air, emitted any more chemicals or smells than before, or in any way hurt the environment. Nevertheless, after two years of hassle, the company was forced to pay a $2,250 fine, and promise never again to commit such a horrible offense as failing to ask permission to update its equipment. The local Air Pollution Control Authority was created to control air pollution, but clearly is being used to generate county revenue through permits and fines.

This same simple test can apply to nearly all environmental questions. The case of methane gas from cows is a good example of what has become the most common outcome of such clear and easily applied analysis. We find that in far too many cases, the proposed "solution" would contribute nothing to improving the environment, but would generate money or power for someone, somewhere.

With that in mind, think about the various environmental disputes that have become so contentious over the past few years. We as a nation are debating: whether to close roads and ban human activity in areas that may someday be habitat for animals that do not actually live there; whether a power plant in Arizona may lead to extinction of polar bears in Alaska; whether we should allow air to contain 5 or 10 parts per trillion of completely natural elements; how much of the world's food supply we should burn to change the source of our electricity; whether to clear brush and overgrowth from dead and dying forests or simply let wildfires burn and destroy everything in their path; and whether there is any place for the public on public lands. And we turn to government for every detail of these debates—we now expect government to determine:

- the means of extraction and use of all minerals
- the apportionment of privately-owned land between food crops and energy crops
- the location and permitting of windmills and solar panels on both public and private land
- the manner of combustion of all minerals and biomass
- the means of transport and disposal of all wastes
- the effects of combustion and nuclear reaction
- the route of transport for all energy around the nation
- the location and design of power plants, mines, and drill rigs
- the design of cars and trucks, the distribution of fuel to power them, and the construction of roads to drive them on
- the detailed design of all houses and buildings, and
- the content, processing and preparation of our food.

Some people even seem to think government can alter the effects of weather, the earth's variable orbit around the sun, and the air and ocean currents driven by the sun and moon. Do we really believe government is more powerful than the sun, moon and stars?

All of these are false debates. In the final analysis they are about stopping people from doing what they want to do—and they do not offer solutions for real environmental problems. None of them are really about improving the environment. They are clever diversions from the real agenda—a quest for money and power, to expand the size and scope of government, and to regulate human behavior and economic activity.

We have seen how the overwhelming success of the environmental industry in recent years has created a climate in which any dedicated opponent can stop almost anything. That represents hardly any challenge at all; the tactics have become formulaic. But such efforts to stop human activity also offer no path for the future, because they do not supply the goods and services a prosperous society requires. Nor do they offer solutions to environmental challenges—challenges increasingly brought about by these very tactics.

The challenge for tomorrow's leaders is how to supply what we need in a responsible manner that is good for the environment and sustainable for future generations. That challenge is complex, difficult, and exciting. Those who come up with the answers, and persuade people to accept them, will be the real conservation leaders and the new heroes of the environment in this century.

Words Matter

Perhaps the first step in changing this contentious debate is to change the language. There is certainly no shortage of hype and spin in the world of environmental politics, but that generally creates more heat than light. Politicians, reporters and lobbyists hurl accusations cloaked in the most outrageous terms. One side calls the other "enviro-nazis" and "wackos." They respond by accusing opponents of "pillaging" or even "raping" the environment (I myself have been called a "bulldozing wilderness rapist" and worse). Such abusive language causes people on both sides to dig in their heels, raises the level of anger, and in the end makes it more difficult to achieve consensus. We need to turn down the volume and admit to ourselves, and to each other, that we *all* care deeply about the treasures of the environment we live in.

Even on the positive side, the words are so often abused that the public can only be confused. Advertisers now toss out terms like "green," "environmentally friendly," and "sustainable" with such frequency that those terms are quickly losing all meaning. For instance, consider how frequently you hear products called "green." Programs on HGTV commonly refer to "green" approaches like "sustainable" bamboo flooring. Just because bamboo grows faster than other trees, is it really more "sustainable," especially if it has to be transported 3,000 miles? One episode actually referred to Astroturf as "environmentally friendly"—compared to actual grass (Astroturf is made from oil!). Another refers to plastic decking as "green"—as if it is better to drill for oil, which takes thousands of years to replace, than to cut a tree, which takes about twenty.

Products and practices that remind us of the importance of environmental consciousness are a good thing, but there is a danger that people begin to tune out if the hype is so overblown that it simply rings false. Travelers are used to seeing signs in hotel rooms encouraging them to re-use towels, for example. But look at the different approach of these two hotel signs:

Note that the sign on the left quite properly suggests that re-using towels "helps the environment" by saving soap and water, whereas the sign on the right says doing so will "SAVE OUR PLANET"! Save it from what? Does the hotel management mean to suggest that using a few gallons of water and a cup of soap can destroy the Earth? Regrettably, the sign on the right is more common in hotels today than that on the left, and eventually people will simply ignore the over-hyped language. To the extent that they do so, and ignore the request, that hyperbole might actually harm the environment. Over-exposure weakens even a good idea, or as the old adage goes, "familiarity breeds contempt."

An even worse—and much more pervasive—example of misleading enviro-advertising has caused an explosion in the sale of bottled water. The Beverage Marketing Corporation says worldwide sales went from 2.2 billion gallons in 1990 to 9.1 billion gallons by 2011. It is a $12 billion industry and growing almost 10% per year, according to the trade group. But not only is the water less regulated (could it be less healthy?), the bottles are unquestionably bad for the environment.

The Container Recycling Institute says the amount of plastic bottles being recycled increased from around 775 million pounds in 1995 to about 1.2 billion pounds in 2005. But during that same decade, plastic bottles sent to landfills skyrocketed from 1.2 billion to 3.9 billion pounds—and the bottles take over 1,000 years to degrade. Even more ironic is the wasted water these bottles cause. Dr. Todd Jarvis, of the Institute for Water and Watersheds at Oregon State University, calculates that it takes about 72 billion gallons of water a year, worldwide, just to make the empty bottles. Treating, filtering and bottling tap water wastes even more, since Jarvis says it takes about two gallons of water to make every gallon sold in bottles, not including the water used to make the bottle itself. In short, everything about bottled water is bad for the environment, even though the skyrocketing sales are a direct result of pro-environment advertising.

One brand of "young natural artesian water" says it is "nature's gift." Another company calls its plastic bottles "low environmental impact packaging." One is so creative that it sells bottles of its "living water" in brown paper bags and calls it "raw water" from "one of the last true free flowing" springs in the country. Yet another is said to be "the essence of purity" and the "spring of life" itself. Bottled water is so popular in Hollywood that one producer created his own brand, Bling, so the beautiful people could have even more prestigious water from even prettier bottles. Virtually all brands have labels depicting beautiful mountains, waterfalls, streams, forests or meadows (no pictures of their bottling plants). And they all promote a lifestyle they call "sustainable."

As with all forms of advertising where the public has developed a healthy skepticism, words like "green" or "sustainable" should always prompt us to wonder. Is it real, or is it just another slogan meant to influence our thinking—in politics or in business. Anything made of wood is sustainable, so long as we are not cutting wood faster than it grows (as we have seen, we are not even close to that threshold). Energy is sustainable forever if produced from the wind, sun, oceans, or gravity (hydro-power). Even fossil fuel use is sustainable well beyond foreseeable generations.

What cannot be sustained is an environmental protection movement whose power and influence are based upon convincing the public that the sky is about to fall. If policies are based on an understanding that irreversible global warming will destroy the Earth by some particular year, what happens when that year comes and goes without such destruction? Indeed, we already see signs that the public is weary of the whole concept, as the past decade has shown no further increase in average global temperatures, and as advocates of the theory have been caught doctoring the science. For most people genuinely interested in improving the world—and that does describe most people—there is a limit to gullibility. And there is absolutely a limit to people's willingness to pay more, earn less, live in smaller homes, travel less, and tolerate inconveniences—especially if they do not believe the underlying premise.

Recognizing Good News When We See It

It does not suit the purposes of the "sky is falling" crowd to celebrate, or even acknowledge, improvements in the environment. In fact, doing so may serve to weaken their future arguments. I remember the Colorado Division of Wildlife being justifiably proud of the recovery of the greater prairie chicken, nearly extinct in the 1930's but so thoroughly recovered that hunting was again permitted by 2002. But leaders of the environmental industry were not among those who praised the Division for a half-century of excellent work. We now know that was because they intended to use the "endangered" bird as a tool for stopping the growth of wind power on the Eastern Plains in later years–a battle well underway today. No such environmental accomplishment is ever touted as "complete" by the major environment groups, because that would deprive them of an important tool that could be useful later. And of course, people write checks to help stop outrageous abuses, not to express thanks for a completed task.

Real conservation leaders have no reason to be shy about achievements, however–because for real leaders, conservation is not about persuading people to write checks. In fact, the public is far more likely to continue supporting a movement that seems to be heading in the right direction, and accomplishing something along the way. There is no question that environment regulations cost the public money, but most people are willing to bear that burden *if* they think it is worthwhile. Thus, it becomes extremely important to recognize progress, and to talk about improvements. Future conservation efforts depend on it.

No environmental improvement in history is as obvious as the air we breathe. From the Middle Ages well into the 20th Century, nearly every major city in the world was choked with black smoke from the coal and fuel oil used for heating and cooking. Millions died from lung diseases, acid ate away at bricks and mortar, and soot discolored historic landmarks and buildings. Here is the way London's air was described by a 17th Century writer:

> *"And what is all this, but that Hellish and dismall Cloud of SEACOALE? So universally mixed with the otherwise wholesome and excellent Aer, that her Inhabitants breathe nothing but an impure and thick Mist accompanied with a fuliginous and filthy vapour..." FUMIFUNGIUM: or the Inconvenience of the Aer and Smoake of London Dissipated, John Evelyn, 1661*

By the 1970's coal had been replaced by oil as the primary source of energy in the industrialized world and thick black smoke gave way to brown clouds called "smog," perhaps even deadlier in some ways. It was so bad that California comedians once joked about rural America, "Who wants to breathe air you can't see?!" Former Congressman Paul Rogers, writing about a 1970 Clean Air Act debate, wrote that:

One of my colleagues quoted a small town mayor, who (in expressing the previous conventional wisdom that environmental protection and economic growth were not compatible) is reported to have said: "If you want this town to grow, it has got to stink."

Most of that kind of thinking is now anachronistic. Gone, too, is most of smog that prompted it. People in most of the United States generally enjoy air of a pre-industrial quality. It is an astounding success story that is barely ever mentioned in the popular media–and never by the environmental industry. There is no better example than the nearly-complete disappearance of Denver's notorious "brown cloud" between 1970 and 2002.

When the EPA developed its first national ambient air quality standards in 1970, Denver was designated as a "non-attainment" area for all 6 regulated air pollutants. The area was found to have violated the new air quality standards 200 days in 1970. But by 2002, it had violated the standards only 15 days of the year and was re-designated as an "attainment area" (having met the federal standards) for particulate pollution, ozone, and carbon dioxide. Today Denver has brown air only intermittently, not constantly. In fact, such pollutants have been declining nationwide for more than 40 years.

The brown clouds in Denver, Los Angeles and scores of other cities were caused partly by automobiles and to an even larger degree by dust–in Denver's case dust from sanding roads during icy weather was a major contributor. When cars were first invented, they were terrible polluters, though no one noticed until there were millions on the roads. But science and engineering, spurred by EPA regulations and strong public demand, brought us better cars that pollute less. As Jack Coleman wrote in a recent guest editorial:

"Better exhaust and ignition systems, catalytic converters, fuel injectors, better engineering throughout the engine and reformulated gasoline have all contributed to a huge reduction in the exhaust emissions from today's cars. Their goal then was to only exhaust carbon dioxide and water vapor, two gases widely accepted as natural and totally harmless."

The result was dramatic improvement in air quality throughout the country. But rather than tout this astonishing achievement, environmental industry leaders now demand regulation of carbon dioxide—strong evidence that these new efforts are about something other than clear air.

For many of these environmental organizations, the battle is much more important than the war. It is the effort (not the goal) that brings money, notoriety, and power. Even Aldo Leopold once said, "We shall never achieve harmony with land, any more than we shall achieve absolute justice or liberty for people. In these higher aspirations, the important thing is not to achieve but to strive." As admired as Aldo Leopold is, the important thing, in fact, *is to achieve*. When we do so, we ought to be proud of it, look for ways to duplicate that success, and emulate those who achieved it. We must never stop working for greater improvement, so "to strive" also matters, but the effort itself cannot become so important that we lose sight of the goal.

Birth of a Notion

A new era of respect is crucial to the future of the conservation movement, and new leaders must seize every opportunity to create it. Those who use harsh accusations, lawsuits, and insults to push their agenda will be marginalized by their own behavior, by the public's revulsion at a never-ending array of bad news, and by new leaders that talk in more realistic and respectful terms.

Respect for people with differing viewpoints is an important part of the formula for success. Rather than working to demonize each other and claim the high ground by yelling louder, we ought to recognize that reasonable people can disagree while seeking the same goal. *The key is to articulate the goal, make sure the public knows what the issue is, and marginalize those whose goal is something different.*

Respect for people with hands-on experience is perhaps even more critical. The environmental industry has so successfully demonized all the natural resource businesses that it is difficult to consider consulting oil companies, for example, about environmental issues. But make no mistake, the world's foremost experts on energy work for them. The top experts in forestry work for the timber industry, not the government. No government regulator or environmental activist understands more about generating electricity than those who make their living at it. So treating such experts as pariahs not to be trusted is virtually the same as not consulting them at all. And how can they be expected to react to such treatment, except to consider political opponents as absolute enemies?

Another vital part of the new approach must be respect for the science upon which all decisions should be based. The notion of "settled science" is offensive to real scientists and it should not be tolerated by leaders who genuinely want to do the right thing. Science is based on ongoing observation, not speculation. So to the maximum extent possible, decisions ought to be based on actual facts observed in an objective way, not computer "modeling" subject to whatever interpretation the programmer wanted. If we wonder how many prairie dogs remain, we should count them, not give grants to university computer modelers. If we need to know how much water we lose to evaporation from overgrown forests, we need to measure it. If we want to know whether the globe is warming, we should read thermometers, not academic treatises.

Environmental decisions ought to be based on facts, not political agendas—of any stripe. To be sure, facts are elusive, sometimes frustratingly so. In the minds of many of today's politically active scientists, it is easier to express opinions—especially those shared by a majority of colleagues, or those desired by grantors who control the funding—than to wait for conclusions from a scientific process that may take decades. Scientists are human, and they are entitled to opinions like all of us. Just remember, the fact that an opinion is held by a scientist does not make it science.

The same concept must underlie our actions, as well as our studies. Actual field work should always trump theoretical discussions and committee meetings. If we want to remove tamarisk from the river banks, we should pay companies with the equipment to cut them, not think tanks to study them. If we want to restore forests to save endangered watersheds, we must send people into the forest to remove dead trees and plant new trees, and no congressional oversight hearing will ever accomplish that. If we want to recover fish in the rivers, someone has to put fish back in the rivers—establishing government programs, publishing documents and blocking all water projects *will not* achieve it.

Mission Creep

It is crucial that we de-politicize the agencies empowered with managing and regulating our environment. The U.S. Forest Service ought to be staffed by professional foresters, just as the National Weather Service needs trained climatologists. NASA doesn't hire rocket scientists without the required college degrees, nor should the EPA hire clean water regulators without education and training in that field. In the same way all agencies must give preference in the hiring and promotion process to veterans, the Forest Service ought to give hiring and promotion preference to people with degrees in forestry from credible forestry schools—not degrees in wildlife biology like that held by one recent agency chief.

Long-time veteran workers in agencies from the National Park Service to the Bureau of Land Management lament the loss of a "professional class" of trained land managers they once had. They fear these agencies have more recently been populated (some say taken over) by political activists, not trained professionals. They are at least partly right, but it is not the fault of the activists for wanting these jobs; the system should be changed to hire, promote and reward professionals with directly relevant education and training. We need to rebuild a class of professional civil servants with the needed expertise, whose opinions, advice, and program plans can be trusted—so politicians, courts, the media and interest groups can let them do their jobs without undue interference.

Sadly, we are still headed in exactly the opposite direction in the staffing and operation of many environmental protection agencies, at every level of government. Rather than focus on a specific mission with employees who are trained experts in that field, many have expanded their role to fit available employees and funding. There is a common term for this phenomenon in government: *mission creep*. It describes the tendency of bureaucracies to constantly grow and expand their roles, sometimes beyond the point where the original purposes can even be recognized. In the administration of the nation's environmental laws, it can be counterproductive, duplicative, wasteful and even destructive.

Sometimes the result is an agency in search of a mission. Remember how the Bureau of Reclamation, for instance (created to build water projects and "make the desserts bloom") no longer builds water projects, but now administers water systems across the country like a mega-utility, systems whose function is primarily local and regional, not federal. If the government no longer builds water projects on a scale requiring federal help, why is the Bureau larger than ever before, with more money and staff than at any time during its heyday? Because, put simply, bureaucracies never shrink; they always grow.

This "mission creep" can cause confusion and duplication and make decisions more difficult. For example, the U.S. Geological Survey (created to map the nation and its geological resources) now has dozens of biologists conducting studies of endangered species–a clear mission of the U.S. Fish and Wildlife Service (USFWS). So when the USFWS and the Secretary's office were about to take the Preble's Meadow Jumping Mouse off the endangered list, they were blind-sided at the last minute by a conflicting study from USGS–a costly duplication of effort and contradiction of purpose that has made a rational decision on the mouse impossible to this day.

An examination of all the agencies charged with administering our environmental laws shows examples everywhere of bureaus spending time, money, and human resources on issues other than those for which they were established.

- The U.S. Forest Service manages the national forests, but also finds itself administering biomass energy grants to create new jobs, a duplication of efforts authorized and liberally funded at the Department of Energy.

- The Army Corps of Engineers, whose historic mission was vital to military progress (building pontoon bridges to get armies across rivers), now issues permits for virtually all construction that involves any riverbank.

- The Bureau of Land Management (created to administer multiple use lands that were not forests or parks) still issues mineral leases, but now also manages wilderness areas and parks, much the same as the National Park Service and the Forest Service.

- The Council on Environmental Quality was created to oversee the National Environmental Policy Act (NEPA), because it applies to numerous agencies. But because CEQ was created as a White House office, it has also been used by several presidents to oversee the activities of all the other natural resources agencies and all their missions. Today even that CEQ function is duplicated by President Obama's environmental "czar" in the White House.

- The EPA still regulates air and water pollution, but today is also poised to begin regulation of virtually all activity that generates carbon dioxide (now classified as a pollutant), creating potential jurisdiction over everything from logging and cattle grazing to highway construction and our driving habits.

- In state governments across the country, the same growth has plagued resources agencies. In nearly all state natural resources departments, for instance, more than half the employees can be found in the state headquarters offices–not in state parks and other field offices. They perform some important administrative functions, but also run numerous projects not directly related to parks, forests, wildlife, energy, or water.

Perhaps most onerous of all is a new proposal to radically expand the mission of the EPA to include regulation of stormwater runoff, irrigation ditches and any place that is wet. The Clean Water Act asserted federal authority over the "navigable waters" of the U.S., since rivers plied by cargo vessels are involved in interstate commerce. But federal agencies and the courts have constantly expanded the definition of what water is "navigable" to the point of absurdity over the last 30 years. The government uses this authority to regulate all activities affecting any and all rivers, streams, and brooks, whether or not they are large enough to float a canoe. Still not satisfied, liberals in Congress are now pushing to completely remove the word "navigable" from the law, which would result in federal authority over all "waters of the United States," without any limit to what that means. Thus, EPA could then regulate rain water runoff, including the construction of streets, curbs, gutters, parking lots, and roofs all across America (without the slightest pretense of constitutional authority under the interstate commerce clause–or any real environmental threat).

The trouble with the constantly expanding roles and missions of these agencies is that it diminishes their ability to preserve and protect the environment. Just as lawsuits absorb time, attention and funds, so do these other continually growing functions. Is it any wonder that the Forest Service has trouble managing national forests when we also expect it to spend staff time figuring out how to cool the globe, rebuild the economy, create new jobs, and protect the homes of everyone who lives in the mountains? We have added "climate change" to the official mission of nearly every agency, yet we expect them all to continue their specific–and important–roles. That is expecting too much.

The Main Thing

In the early 1990's government agencies, school districts and corporations (always fond of sending staffers to facilitated retreats with flip charts and break-out sessions) began using a new slogan to describe their vision of the future. It was jingoistic and came from the same academics who coined terms like "paradigm shift" and "thinking outside the box." This new "vision" was expressed by the redundant-sounding expression, *"The main thing is to keep the main thing the main thing."* Agencies across the country adopted it as the title of their strategic plans, and the media often made fun of it–easy enough to do. The idea behind it seems so obvious that repeating it sounds almost silly. That is, if not reminded constantly, people can get so caught up in the details that they literally forget "the main thing."

It is actually a very apt way to describe, in a nutshell, the right policy for rebuilding credibility on environmental issues—the way to take back the high ground from these groups that have hijacked the conservation movement. When we focus on the actual environmental issue, it smokes out those with a different agenda, focuses attention on genuine environmental improvement, and most important, puts leadership back where it belongs—with those whose conservation agenda is genuine. That requires one very simple strategy—make the environment "the main thing." It is preposterous for anyone to argue against recovering endangered species, or removing them from the endangered list once they have actually been recovered. It is equally absurd to oppose rebuilding healthy forests by removing dead trees and allowing new ones to grow.

Whether the issue is clean air, water supply, public lands, endangered species or energy, if we do the right thing for the environment, the environmental industry will usually be left behind—precisely because they seek some other outcome. Remember, solving problems is contrary to the best interests of these groups because they depend on boogeymen to scare donors into giving more and more money, and to scare politicians into ceding more and more power. The last thing they want is an actual solution, an actual improvement in the environment. That "Achilles heel" provides strength to new, reasonable and courageous leaders who are genuine problem-solvers.

The public can only be pushed so far, and I believe the American people are near the breaking point in their patience with our political system. The environmental lobby is pushing people closer to the edge all the time, and the public is ready to push back. But do not mistake this *frustration* for *ambivalence* on environmental issues. People care as much as ever about leaving the world better than we found it. They simply no longer believe most of the "green" rhetoric they hear will accomplish that. So it is up to a new generation of political leaders to win back that confidence and respect—not just respect for the leaders (that comes naturally if they are genuine) but for their cause. Public confidence in the conservation movement is at an all-time low, but can be rebuilt quickly when people believe the agenda is genuine, progress is being made, and the honest costs are affordable.

If that seems like an uphill battle, of course, it is. There is nothing to be gained by underestimating the power and resources of the environmental industry, or the lengths to which its leaders will go to discredit anyone they view as a threat. That is why so many politicians are so hesitant to take these people on, to wonder aloud why the emperor has no clothes. No one wants to be seen as anti-environment, and that accusation is made every single time any official disagrees with the environmental lobby–*every single time*. Thus, it takes courage to "speak truth to power." But it is possible, and one leader can make an enormous difference in beginning that process. As Margaret Meade once wrote,

"Never forget that a small group of thoughtful citizens can change the world; indeed, it is the only thing that ever has."

The Backlash

In the end, it is not enough to build *roadblocks*. Anyone can do that. We need *roadmaps*. We need new ways to provide the resources our society requires, while protecting and improving our environment. That is not always easy; leadership rarely is. But it is necessary, indeed essential.

Americans are not about to give up their standard of living–nor lower it–just because of the implausible and unfounded accusation that we are destroying the world by eating, drinking, breathing, working, traveling, and minding our business. Americans can be gullible at times, but they are not *that* gullible. They can be pushed only so far before demanding that these extremists mind their *own* business.

We are already in the midst of this backlash, though many of today's political leaders do not yet recognize it. That is because political shifts of this magnitude do not come as a sudden rapture, and they never begin with a unanimous consensus. We are nevertheless in the midst of a vitally important shift in national politics, beginning with an irate public sentiment that says "enough is enough."

That is why so many Americans today are more inclined to join the land trusts (The Nature Conservancy, the Trust for Public Lands, the Conservation Fund, and local land trusts) than the Sierra Club or Friends of the Earth–because they "put their money where their mouth is." That is, instead of spending so much time filing lawsuits, they protect beautiful places by buying them–so that they can legitimately control such lands, rather than denying the use of land to its owners through regulation. Groups that raise money to save land from development are far more likely to earn public sympathy today than groups that raise money to stop human activity.

This new political reality does not mean Americans will turn their backs on legitimate activities to protect and improve the environment. Rather, it means they will look for leadership somewhere other than today's intellectually bankrupt environmental industry. They will look to a new generation of leaders whose agenda is genuine, and whose plans include improving our standard of living, not downgrading it. The shift will help encourage the rise of new leaders whose work will lead to a more prosperous future, with an even cleaner and healthier environment for the next generation.

Those who seek to be leaders of a new conservation movement must talk openly and clearly about environmental issues. They must propose environmental policies that are good for people, recognizing that people are part of the environment, not a threat to it. Most important, they must put natural resources atop the priority list–above membership, grants, dollars, politics and power.

As Mark Twain put it, *"Do the right thing. It will gratify some people and astonish the rest."*

THE END

ACKNOWLEDGMENTS

"If you copy from one author, it's plagiarism. If you copy from two, it's research." This and similar quotes have been attributed variously to Wilson Mizner, John Burke, Dwight Eisenhower, Ambrose Bierce, Thomas Lehrer, Paul Gaugin, and even comedian Steven Wright. It is unclear who first said it—perhaps they all plagiarized each other. There are very few truly new ideas on a subject as broad as environmental policy, on which so much has been written for so long. Nor could I claim complete originality on most of the material in this book. Indeed, I am indebted to hundreds of other thinkers, writers, speakers, public officials, professors, and others whose work has helped inform mine.

I have always been an avid reader, especially of non-fiction works on important issues, and of history. I am not a big fan of the footnotes that sometimes bog down the flow of a good book, and interrupt thoughts not yet completed. In this case there are so many facts, numbers, and details that our attempts to footnote the material resulted in dozens of notes per page, and would have left a manuscript with 300 pages of text and 400 pages of footnotes. So I elected not to footnote the material in this book for that reason, and because it was never my intent to write an academic treatise that would be used in college classrooms. Rather, my only intent was to make common sense of a very complex set of issues, and make rational conclusions accessible to any reader, whether or not they are experts on the subject. To whatever extent that may have been accomplished, it required use of much existing literature and numerous websites, the suggestions and ideas of many activists and officials I have known, factual and technical analyses of other writers, and many of my own experiences in government and business.

Rather than specific footnotes attributing every detail, fact, or idea, I opted instead to include a fairly extensive bibliography of sources I consulted in researching this book. That included several hundred books and articles, and dozens of web sites and Internet-based resources. The latter are difficult to include in a bibliography because web sites change constantly, and material I reviewed may or may not remain online very long. Still, it should be clear that I did not invent any of the facts or technical analyses in this book, nor was I the first to use many of these concepts, terms, phrases, jargon, or examples. Where I relied heavily on other sources for stories or anecdotes I tried to let the reader know where they can check, or make clear that I appreciated the work of others. With apologies for any instances where I neglected to do that well enough, I believe any reader who examines the bibliography will understand the heavy influences of others, on both sides of these issues, on my own thinking.

If anything here is new, it is an application of original conservation principles to the specific issues of the modern era, a way to approach these issues that will actually improve the environment, while causing less disruption of human activity. Without claiming this approach has never been contemplated before, I can attest that it is rare. We have created a system in which the best solution for the environment is seldom the outcome, and that must change. How to make that change, on a series of specific issues, is my attempt at originality. For the underlying science and expertise, and for many examples, I am completely indebted to others. For instance, the National Center for Public Policy Research has published several editions of its book of atrocities committed in the name of the environment, called the National Directory of Environmental and Regulatory Victims, and I used several anecdotes based on their excellent research and writing. Much of my own experience was gained in the family orchard and produce business, and especially through the patience and encouragement of the many friends with whom I worked in the office of Senator Bill Armstrong, the Cabinet of Governor Bill Owens, the Colorado Department of Natural Resources, and the great Colorado organization, Club 20.

For help in preparing the book itself, I will always be indebted to another avid reader with a superb sense of clarity, my brother Tom, who spent countless hours early in the process reading, rereading, and tossing ideas back and forth. My close friend and former colleague at the Colorado DNR, Tim Pollard, also read the first draft and helped check my memory on the details of issues and incidents. The editing assistance of American Tradition Institute colleague Dr. David Schnare was brilliant. The unwavering and unconditional encouragement of my dear wife, Diana, has made this and everything else in my life possible. And finally, for moral support to me, and financial assistance to the American Tradition Institute during this process, we are forever grateful to Helen Krieble and the Vernon K. Krieble Foundation, without whom this would not have been published.

BIBLIOGRAPHY

Books:

Almasi, David et.al. *Shattered Dreams: 100 Stories of Government Abuse (National Directory of Environmental and Regulatory Victims), 5th Edition*. Washington, D.C.: National Center for Public Policy Research, 5th Edition, 2007

Andrus, Cecil. *Cecil Andrus: Politics Western Style*. Seattle: Saquatch Books, 1998

Arnold, Ron. *At the Eye of the Storm: James Watt and the Environmentalists*. Chicago: Regnery Gateway, 1982

——*Ecology Wars: Environmentalism As If People Mattered*. Belevue, WA: Free Enterprise Press, 1998

——*Freezing in the Dark: Money, Power, Politics and the Vast Left Wing Conspiracy*. New York: Merrill Press, 2007

——*Undue Influence: Wealthy Foundations, Grant Driven Environmental Groups and Zealous Bureaucrats That Control Your Future*. Bellevue, WA: Free Enterprise Press, 1999

Arrowood, Janet C. *Living With Wildfires: Prevention, Preparation, and Recovery*. Denver: Bradford Publishing, 2003

Audubon, John James. *Delineations of American Scenery and Character*. New York: G.A. Baker & Company, 1926.

Avery, Dennis. *Saving the Planet With Pesticides and Plastic: The Environmental Triumph of High-Yield Farming*. Washington: Hudson Institute, 2000

Babbitt, Bruce. *Cities in the Wilderness: A New Vision of Land Use in America*. Washington: Island Press, 2005

Baden, John A. and Noonan, Douglas S. *Managing the Commons, Second Edition*. Indianapolis: Indiana University Press, 1998

Bailey, Ronald. *The False Prophets of Ecological Apocalypse*. New York: St. Martin's Press, 1993

——*Global Warming and Other Eco Myths: How the Environmental Movement Uses False Science to Scare Us to Death*. Washington: Competitive Enterprise Institute, 2002

Barrows, Pete and Holmes, Judith. *Colorado's Wildlife Story*. Denver: Colorado Division of Wildlife, 1990

Bate, Roger. *All the Water in the World*. Australia: Southwood Press, 2006

Bates, Sarah F., et al. *Searching Out the Headwaters: Change and Rediscovery in Western Water Policy*. Washington: Island Press, 1993

Baur, Donald C. and Irvin, William Robert. *Endangered Species Act: Law, Policy and Perspectives*. Washington: American Bar Association, 2009

Benson, Delwin, Shelton, Skip, and Steinbach, Don. *Wildlife Stewardship and Recreation on Private Lands*. College Station: Texas A&M University Press, 1999

Benson, Maxine (ed.). *From Pittsburgh to the Rocky Mountains: Major Stephen Long's Expedition, 1819-1820*. Golden: Fulcrum Publishing, 1988

Berlau, John. *Eco Freaks: Environmentalism is Hazardous to your Health!* Nashville: Thomas Nelson, 2006

Berry, Wendell. *Another Turn of the Crank: Essays by Wendell Berry*. Washington: Counterpoint Publishers, 1995

Botkin, Daniel B. Discordant Harmonies: A New Ecology for the Twenty-first Century.

New York : Oxford University Press, 1990.

Brick, Philip D., ed. *A Wolf in the Garden: The Land Rights Movement and the New Environmental Debate.* Lanham, MD: Rowman & Littlefield, 1996.

Brower, David and Chapple, Steve. *Let the Mountains Talk, Let the Rivers Run.* San Francisco, Harper Collins West, 1995

Brower, David Ross. *For Earth's Sake: The Life and Times of David Brower.* Layton, UT: Gibbs Smith, 1990.

Brower, David and the Sierra Club (eds.). *Wilderness: America's Living Heritage.* New York: Gillick Press, 1961

——*Work in Progress.* Layton, UT: Gibbs Smith, 1991

Brown, Michael H. *Laying Waste: The Poisoning of America by Toxic Chemicals.* New York: Pantheon Books, 1980.

Bryson, Bill. *A Walk in the Woods: Rediscovering America on the Appalachian Trail.* New York: Harper Collins, 1998.

Cade, Thomas (ed.). *Peregrine Falcon Populations: Their Management and Recovery.* Boise: The Peregrine Fund, 1988

Carlisle, John. *National Directory of Environmental and Regulatory Victims.* Washington, D.C.: National Center for Public Policy Research, 2000

Carson, Rachel. *Lost Woods: The Discovered Writing of Rachel Carson.* Edited and with an introduction by Linda Lear. Boston: Beacon Press, 1998.

——*Silent Spring.* Boston: Houghton Mifflin Company, 1962.

Cawley, R. McGreggor. *Federal Land, Western Anger: The Sagebrush Rebellion & Environmental Politics.* Lawrence: University Press of Kansas, 1993.

Chief Standing Bear, *Land of the Spotted Eagle.* Boston: Houghton Mifflin, 1933

Clark, Tim W. *Averting Extinction: Reconstructing Endangered Species Recovery.* New Haven, CT: Yale University Press, 1997.

Cohen, Michael P. *The History of the Sierra Club, 1892-1970.* San Francisco: Sierra Club Books, 1988

——*The Pathless Way: John Muir and American Wilderness.* Madison: The University of Wisconsin Press, 1984.

Colinvaux, Paul. *Why Big Fierce Animals are Rare: An Ecologist's Perspective.* Princeton: Princeton University Press, 1978

Committee on Energy and Natural Resources, U.S. Senate. *Contempt of Congress: Report on the Congressional Proceedings Against Interior Secretary James G. Watt.* Washington: GPO, 1982

——*Hearings on the Nomination of James G. Watt, Part 1, January 7-8, 1981.* Washington: GPO, 1981

Corsi, Jerome R. and Smith, Craig R. *Black Gold Stranglehold: The Myth of Scarcity and the Politics of Oil.* Los Angeles: WND Books, 2005

Daily, Gretchen and Ellison, Katherine. *The New Economy of Nature: The Quest to Make Conservation Profitable.* Washington: Island Press, 2002

Davies, Gilbert W. and Frank, Florice M., eds. *Forest Service Memories: Past Lives and Times in the United States Forest Service.* Hat Creek, CA: History Ink Books, 1997.

deBuys, William. *Salt Dreams: Land and Water in Low-Down California.* Albuquerque: The University of New Mexico Press, 1999.

——*Seeing Things Whole: The Essential John Wesley Powell.* Washington: Island Press, 2001

de Roos, Robert. *The Thirsty Land: The Story of the Central Valley Project.* Stanford, CA: Stanford University Press, 1948.

Dolnick, Edward. *Down the Great Unknown: John Wesley Powell's 1869 Journey of Discovery and Tragedy Through the Grand Canyon.* New York: Harper Perennial, 2002

Driessen, Paul. *Eco-Imperialism: Green Power, Black Death.* Bellevue, WA: Free Enterprise Press, 2003

Duda, Mark Damian; Bissell, Steven J. and Young, Kira C. *Wildlife and the American Mind: Public Opinion on and Attitudes toward Fish and Wildlife Management.* Harrisonburg: Responsive Management, 1998

Duncan, Dayton and Burns, Ken. *National Parks: America's Best Idea – An Illustrated History.* New York: Knopf, 2009

Dunlop, Becky Norton. *Clearing the Air: How the People of Virginia Improved the State's Air and Water Despite the EPA.* Arlington, VA: Alexis de Tocqueville Institution, 2000

Edmonds, Carol. *Wayne Aspinall: Mr. Chairman.* Denver: Crown Point, 1980

Ehrlich, Paul. *The Population Bomb.* New York: Ballantine Books, 1968.

Farmer, Jared. *Glen Canyon Dammed: Inventing Lake Powell and the Canyon Century.* Tucson: The University of Arizona Press, 1999.

Flader, Susan. *Thinking like a Mountain: Aldo Leopold and the Evolution of an Ecological Attitude Toward Deer, Wolves, and Forests,* 1974.

Flippin, J. Brooks. *Conservative Conservationist: Russell E. Train and the Emergence of American Environmentalism.* Baton Rouge: LSU Press, 2006

Fox, Steven. *John Muir and His Legacy: The American Conservation Movement.* Boston: Little, Brown, 1981.

Fumento, Michael. *Science Under Siege: Balancing Technology and the Environment.* New York: Harper Collins, 1993.

Gates, Paul W. *History of Public Land Law Development.* Washington: GPO, 1968.

Gilbert, Janice Dee. *James G. Watt's Department of the Interior.* Monticello, IL: Vance Bibliographies, 1983

Gingrich, Newt. *A Contract with the Earth.* Baltimore: Johns Hopkins University Press, 2007

Goddard, Donald. *Saving Wildlife: A Century of Conservation.* New York: Harry N. Abrams, 1995.

Goklany, Indur M. *Clearing the Air: The Real Story of the War on Air Pollution.* Washington: CATO Institute, 1999

Goodman, Doug, and Daniel McCool, eds., *Contested Landscape: The Politics of Wilderness in Utah and the West.* Salt Lake City: University of Utah Press, 1999.

Gore, Al. *An Inconvenient Truth.* New York: Rodale Press, 2006

Earth in the Balance: Ecology and the Human Spirit. Boston: Houghton Mifflin, 1992

——*Our Choice: A Plan to Solve the Climate Crisis.* Emmaus, PA: Rodale Books, 2009

Gottlieb, Alan and Arnold, Ron. *Politically Correct Environment.* New York: Merrill Press, 1998

Grayson, Melvin J. and Shepard, Thomas R. *The Disaster Lobby: Prophets of Ecological Doom and Other Absurdities.* Chicago: Follet, 1973

Greve, Michael S. and Smith, Fred L. *Environmental Politics: Public Costs, Private Rewards.* Santa Barbara: Praeger Publishers, 1992

Gulliford, Andrew: *Boomtown Blues: Colorado Oil Shale, 1885-1985.* Boulder: University of Colorado Press, 1989.

Hage, Wayne. *Storm over Rangelands: Private Rights in Federal Lands.* Bellevue, WA: Free Enterprise Press, 1989

Hayward, Steven F. *Index of Leading Environmental Indicators 2009.* Fourteenth Edition. San Francisco: Pacific Research Institute, 2009

Heinz Center for Science, Economics and the Environment. *Dam Removal: Science and Decision Making.* Washington: Heinz Center, 2002

Helms, Douglas, and Susan L. Flader (eds.). *The History of Soil and Water Conservation.*

Berkeley: University of California Press, 1985.

High Country News, *Western Water Made Simple*. Washington: Island Press, 1987

Hodel, Donald P. and Dietz, Robert. *Crisis in the Oil Patch: How America's Energy Industry Is Being Destroyed And What Must Be Done To Save It*. Washington: Regnery, 1993

Hollander, Jack M. *The Real Environmental Crisis: Why Poverty, Not Affluence, Is the Environment's Number One Enemy*. Berkeley: University of California Press, 2003

Holmes, Steven J. *The Young John Muir: An Environmental Biography*. Madison, WI: University of Wisconsin Press, 1999.

Horner, Christopher C. *Red Hot Lies: How Global Warming Alarmists Use Threats, Fraud, and Deception to Keep You Misinformed*. Regnery Publishing, 2008

——*The Politically Incorrect Guide to Global Warming and Environmentalism*. Washington: Regnery Publishing, 2007

Huber, Peter and Mills, Mark. *The Bottomless Well: The Twilight of Fuel, the Virtue of Waste, and Why We Will Never Run Out of Energy*. New York: Basic Books, 2005

Hundley, Norris, Jr. *Water and the West: The Colorado River Compact and the Politics of Water in the American West*. Berkeley: University of California Press, 1975.

Idso, Craig D. and Idso, Sherwood B. *The Many Benefits of Atmospheric CO_2 Enrichment*, Pueblo West: Vales Lake Publishing, 2011

Innis, Roy. *Energy Keepers, Energy Killers*, Bellevue, WA: Merril Press, 2008

Jacks, G.V. and Whyte, R.O. *The Rape of the Earth: A World Survey of Soil Erosion*. London: Faber and Faber, 1939.

Jensen, Derrick and McBay, Aric. *What We Leave Behind*, New York: Seven Stories Press, 2009

Jensen, Derrick, and Draffan, George, *Railroads and Clearcuts: Legacy of Congress's 1864 Northern Pacific Railroad Land Grant*, Sand Point, ID: Keokee Co. Publishing, 1995

Jones, William C. and Jones, Elizabeth B. *William Henry Jackson's Colorado*. Boulder: Pruett, 1975

Kania, Alan. *John Otto: Trials and Trails*. Niwot: University Press of Colorado, 1996.

Klaus, Vaclav. *Blue Planet in Green Shackles: What is Endangered: Climate or Freedom?* Washington: Competitive Enterprise Institute, 2007.

Klyza, Christopher. *Who Controls Public Lands? Mining, Forestry, and Grazing Policies, 1870-1990*. Chapel Hill: University of North Carolina Press, 1996.

Kohm, Kathryn A. (ed.). *Balancing on the Brink of Extinction: The Endangered Species Act and Lesson for the Future*. Covelo, CA: Island Press, 1991

Lamar, Howard Roberts. *The Far Southwest: 1846-1912: A Territorial History*. New York: W.W. Norton, 1970

Lamm, Richard D. and McCarthy, Michael. *The Angry West: A Vulnerable Land and Its Future*. New York: Houghton Mifflin,1982

Lamm, Richard D. and Imhoff, Gary. *The Immigration Time Bomb: The Fragmenting of America*. New York: Truman Talley Books, 1985

Lear, Linda J. *Harold L. Ickes: The Aggressive Progressive, 1874-1933*. New York: Garland, 1981.

Lear, Linda J. *Rachel Carson: Witness for Nature*. New York : Henry Holt, 1997.

Leopold, Aldo. *For the Health of the Land: Previously Unpublished Essays and Other Writings*. Washington: Island Press, 2000.

——*Round River, from the Journal of Aldo Leopold*. Edited by Luna B. Leopold. New York: Oxford University Print, 1953.

——*Sand County Almanac*. New York: Oxford University Press, 1949.

Levitt, Steven and Dubner, Stephen. *Freakonomics: A Rogue Economist Explores the Hidden*

Side of Everything. New York: William Morrow, 2006.

——*SuperFreakonomics: Global Cooling, Patriotic Prostitutes and Why Suicide Bombers Should Buy Life Insurance*. New York: William Morrow, 2009.

Lewis, Merriwether, and Clark, William. *The Journals of Lewis and Clark*. Edited by Frank Bergon. New York: Viking, 1989.

Limerick, Patricia. *Desert Passages: Encounters with the American Deserts*. Albuquerque: University of New Mexico Press, 1985.

——*The Legacy of Conquest*. New York: Norton, 1987.

Lomborn, Bjorn. *Cool It: The Skeptical Environmentalist's Guide to Global Warming*. New York: Knopf, 2007

——*The Skeptical Environmentalist: Measuring the Real State of the World*. Cambridge: University Press, 2001

Lowenthal, David. *George Perkins Marsh: Prophet of Conservation*. Seattle: University of Washington Press, 2000.

Maddox, John. *The Doomsday Syndrome*. New York: McGraw-Hill, 1972

Mason, Alpheus. *Bureaucracy Convicts Itself: the Ballinger-Pinchot Controversy of 1910*. New York: Viking Press, 1941

Maxwell, Robert and Yates, Scott. *The Future of Water: A Startling Look Ahead*. Denver: American Water Works Association, 2011

McClelland, Peter D. *Sowing Modernity: America's First Agricultural Revolution*. Ithaca, NY: Cornell University Press, 1997.

McCool, Daniel C. *Waters of Zion: The Politics of Water in Utah*. Salt Lake City: University of Utah Press, 1995.

McCullough, David. *Mornings on Horseback: The Story of an Extraordinary Family, a Vanished Way of Life and the Unique Child Who Became Theodore Roosevelt*. New York: Simon and Schuster, 1981

McKibben, Bill. *The End of Nature*. New York: Random House, 1989.

Mecham, Leonidas Ralph, *Judicial Business of the United States Courts: Annual Report of the Director (Reports for 1997-2005)*, Washington: Administrative Office of the U.S. Courts, 2006

Meine, Kurt. *Aldo Leopold: His Life and Work*. Madison: University of Wisconsin Press, 1987.

Meiners, Roger; Deroches, Pierre; and Morriss, Andrew (editors). *Silent Spring at 50: The False Crises of Rachel Carson*. Washington: Cato Institute, 2012

Melosi, Martin V. *Coping with Abundance: Energy and Environment in Industrial America*. New York: Knopf, 1985.

Meyer, Stephen M. *End of the Wild*. Cambridge.: MIT Press, 2006

Miller, Brian; Reading, Richard P. and Forrest, Steven. *Prairie Night: Black-footed Ferrets and the Recovery of Endangered Species*. Washington: Smithsonian Institution Press, 1996

Miller, Char. *Fluid Arguments: Five Centuries of Western Water Conflict*. Tucson: University of Arizona Press, 2001

——*Gifford Pinchot and the Making of Modern Environmentalism*. Washington: Island Press, 2001

Mitchell, Johnny. *Energy and How We Lost It*. Houston: Gulf Publishing Pacesetter Press, 1979

Morris, Edmund. *Theodore Rex*. New York: Harper Collins, 2002

The Rise of Theodore Roosevelt. New York: Coward, McCann & Geoghegan, 1979

Morris, Julian (ed). *Sustainable Development: Promoting Progress or Perpetuating Poverty*. London: Profile Books, 2002

Morriss, Andrew. *The False Promise of Green Energy*. Washington: Cato Institute, 2011

Muir, John. *My First Summer in the Sierra*. Boston: Houghton Mifflin, 1911.

——*Steep Trails: California, Utah, Nevada, Washington, Oregon, the Grand Canyon*. Boston: Houghton Mifflin, 1918.

——*The Yosemite*. New York: Century Company, 1912.

Murray, Iain. *The Really Inconvenient Truths: Seven Environmental Catastrophes Liberals Don't Want You to Know About--Because They Helped Cause Them*. Washington: Regnery Publishing, 2008

Nash, Roderick. *Wilderness and the American Mind*. Revised edition, 1973. Fourth edition, 2001. New Haven, CT: Yale University Press.

National Association of Home Builders. *Developer's Guide to Endangered Species Regulations*. Washington: Home Builders Press, 1996.

National Center for Public Policy Research. *Shattered Dreams: 100 Stories of Government Abuse, 4th Edition.* Washington, D.C.: National Center for Public Policy Research, 2003

National Reclamation Association. *Reclamation: The Development of the West* (Proceedings of the 8th Annual Meeting, National Reclamation Association: Salt Lake City, Utah, November 2,3,4, 1949). Washington: National Reclamation Association, 1949

National Wilderness Institute, *Conservation Under the Endangered Species Act: A Promise Broken*. Washington: National Wilderness Institute, 1997

Noon, Marita Littauer. *Energy Freedom: The Role of Energy ion Your Life & How Environmentalists Control its Use*. Peoria, AZ: Intermedia Publishing Group, 2011.

Norris, Scott (ed.). *Discovered Country: Tourism and Survival in the American West*. Albuquerque: Stone Ladder Press, 1994

Opie, John. *Nature's Nation: An Environmental History of the United States*. Fort Worth, TX: Harcourt Brace College Publishers, 1998.

Osborn, Fairchild. *Our Plundered Planet*. New York: Little, Brown, 1948

O'Shaughnesy, Michael Maurice. *Hetch Hetchy: its Origin and History*. San Francisco: Recorder Printing and Publishing Co., 1934

Pendley, William Perry. *It Takes a Hero: The Grassroots Battle Against Environmental Oppression*. Bellevue, WA: Free Enterprise Press, 1998

——*War on the West: Government Tyranny on America's Great Frontier*. Washington: Regnery, 1995

Pinchot, Gifford. *Breaking New Ground*. New York: Harcourt Brace, 1947.

The Fight for Conservation. New York: Doubleday, Page & Company, 1910.

Porter, Eliot. *The Place No One Knew: Glen Canyon on the Colorado*. Edited by David Brower. San Francisco: Sierra Club, 1963.

Powell, John Wesley. *The Exploration of the Colorado River and Its Canyons*. Edited with an introduction by Wallace Stegner. New York: Penguin, 1987.

——*Report on the Arid Region of the United States*. Edited by Wallace Stegner. Cambridge: Harvard University Press, 1962.

Ray, Dixie Lee, *Environmental Overkill: Whatever Happened to Common Sense?* Washington: Regnery, 1993

——*Trashing the Planet: How Science Can Help Us Deal With Acid Rain, Depletion of the Ozone, and Nuclear Waste (Among Other Things)*. Washington: Regnery, 1990

Reisner, Marc. *Cadillac Desert: The American West and Its Disappearing Water*. New York: Viking Penguin, Inc., 1986.

Righter, Robert W. *Wind Energy in America: A History*. Norman: University of Oklahoma Press, 1996.

Robbins, Roy M. *Our Landed Heritage The Public Domain, 1776-1970*. Second Edition.

Lincoln: University of Nebraska Press, 1976

Roman, Joe. *Listed: Dispatches from America's Endangered Species Act.* Boston: Harvard University Press, 2011

Roosevelt, Theodore. *Theodore Roosevelt's America: Selections from the Writings of the Oyster Bay Naturalist.* Edited by Farida A. Wiley. New York: Devin-Adair, 1955.

Russell, Edmund. *Peaceful Warfare: Fighting Humans and Insects with Chemicals from World War I to Silent Spring.* New York: Cambridge University Press, 2000.

Sampson, R.Neil. *Farmland or Wasteland, A Time to Choose: Overcoming the Threat to America's Farm and Food Future.* Emmaus, PA: Rodale Press, 1981

Sanera, Michael and Shaw, Jane S. *Facts, Not Fear: A Parent's Guide to Teaching Children About the Environment.* Washington: Regnery, 1996

Schulte, Steven C. *Wayne Aspinall and the Shaping of the American West.* Boulder: University Press of Colorado, 2002

Schwartz, Joel M. and Hayward, Steven F. *Air Quality in America: A Dose of Reality on Air Pollution Levels, Trends, and Health Risks.* Washington: AEI Press, 2008

Shallat, Todd A. Structures in the Stream: *Water, Science, and the Rise of the U.S. Army Corps of Engineers.* Austin: University of Texas Press, 1994.

Smith, Frank E. *The Politics of Conservation: The First Political History of the Conservation & Development of America's Natural Resources.* New York: Random House Pantheon, 1966

Smith, Robert J. *Earth's Resources: Private Ownership vs. Public Waste.* Washington: Libertarian Party, 1980.

Spencer, Roy W. *Climate Confusion: How Global Warming Hysteria Leads to Bad Science, Pandering Politicians and Misguided Policies that Hurt the Poor.* New York: Encounter Books, 2008

Starrs, Paul F. *Let the Cowboy Ride: Cattle Ranching in the American West.* Baltimore: Johns Hopkins University Press, 1998.

Stegner, Wallace. *Beyond the Hundredth Meridian: John Wesley Powell and the Second Opening of the West.* Boston: Houghton Mifflin, 1954

——*Where the Bluebird Sings to the Lemonade Springs: Living and Writing in the West.* New York: Random House, 1992

Sterba, James P. *Nature Wars: The Incredible Story of How Wildlife Comebacks Turned Backyards into Battlegrounds.* New York: Crown Publishers, 2012

Stout, Joseph A., Jr. and Faulk, Odie B. *A Short History of the American West.* New York: Harper and Row, 1974.

Stratton, David H. *Tempest Over Teapot Dome: The Story of Albert B. Fall.* Norman: University of Oklahoma Press, 1998.

Subcommittee on Resource Conservation, Research, and Forestry (Agriculture Committee), House of Representatives. *Private Property Rights Protection*: Hearing, February 15, 1995. Washington: GPO, 1995

Sussman, Brian. *Climategate: A Veteran Meteorologist Exposes the Global Warming Scam.* Los Angeles: WND Books, 2010

Taylor, Ray W. *Hetch Hetchy; the Story of San Francisco's Struggle to Provide a Water Supply for Her Future Needs.* San Francisco: Ricardo J. Orozco, 1926

Thoreau, Henry David. *Walden, or Life in the Woods.* Boston: Ticknor and Fields, 1854

Train, Russell E. *Politics, Pollution, and Pandas: An Environmental Memoir.* Washington: Island Press, 2003

Truettner, William H. and Wallach, Alan (eds.). *Thomas Cole: Landscape Into History.* New Haven: Yale University Press, 1994.

Turner, Frederick Jackson. *The Significance of the Frontier in American History.* Edited by

Martin Ridge. Madison, WI: Silver Buckle Press, 1994.

Udall, Stewart L., Wilkinson, Charles F. and Limerick, Patricia Nelson. *Beyond the Mythic West*. Layton, UT: Gibbs Smith, 1990

——*The Quiet Crisis*. New York: Holt, Rinehart and Winston, 1963.

Underwood, Kathleen. *Town Building on the Colorado Frontier*. Albuquerque: University of New Mexico Press, 1987

Vandenbusche, Duane and Smith, Duane A. *A Land Alone: Colorado's Western Slope*. Boulder: Pruett Publishing, 1981

Vandenbusche, Duane. *The Gunnison Country*. Gunnison: B&B Printers, 1982

Wagenknecht, Edward. *The Seven Worlds of Theodore Roosevelt*. New York: Longmans, Green & Co., 1958

Warnke, Martin. *Political Landscape: The Art History of Nature*. Cambridge: Harvard University Press, 1995.

Watt, James G. *The Courage of a Conservative*. New York: Simon and Schuster, 1985

Weeks, W. William. *Beyond the Ark: Tools for an Ecosystem Approach to Conservation*. Washington: Island Press, 1996

Werbach, Adam. *Act Now, Apologize Later*. New York: Harper Perennial, 1998.

Western, Samuel. *Pushed Off the Mountain and Sold Down the River*. Moose, W: Homestead Publishing, 2002

Whorton, James. *Before Silent Spring: Pesticides and Public Health in Pre-DDT America*. Princeton, NJ: Princeton University Press, 1974.

Wilkinson, Charles F. *Crossing the Next Meridian: Land, Water, and the Future of the West*. Washington: Island Press, 1993

Wolfe, Linnie Marsh (ed.). *John of the Mountains: The Unpublished Journals of John Muir*. Madison: The University of Wisconsin Press, 1979.

Worster, Donald. *Rivers of Empire: Water, Aridity, and the Growth of the American West*. New York: Pantheon, 1985.

Yergin, Daniel. *The Quest: Energy, Security, and the Remaking of the Modern World*. New York: Penguin Books, 2012.

Articles:

Anderson, Steven. "Overzealous EPA Hazardous to Freedoms." *Cavalier Daily, University of Virginia* (November 30, 1993): 3

Asma, Stephen T. "Green Guilt." *The Chronicle of Higher Education* (January 10, 2010).

Babbitt, Bruce. "Age-Old Challenge: Water and the West." *National Geographic* 179, No. 6 (June, 1991): 2-4.

Baird, W. David. "The American West and the Nixon Presidency, 1969-1974." *Journal of the West* 34 (April, 1995): 83-90.

Borelli, Tom. "Bankrupting the Coal Industry." *American Coal* (Issue 2, 2011): 39.

Crichton, Michael, "Aliens Cause Global Warming." Speech: *California Institute of Technology* (January 17, 2003).

Coate, Charles. "'The Biggest Water Fight in American History: Stewart Udall and the Central Arizona Project." *Journal of the Southwest* 37 (Spring, 1995): 79-101.

Dean, Robert. "Dam Building Still Had Some Magic Then" Steward Udall, the Central Arizona Project, and the Evolution of the Pacific Southwest Water Plan, 1963-1968." *Pacific Historical Review* 66.1 (February, 1997): 81-99.

Driessen, Paul. "Affordable Energy: The Foundation of Human Rights and Economic Justice." ALEC, *The State Factor* (April 2010): 1-33.

——"Charles Manson Energy." Website article, *Committee for a Constructive Tomorrow* (January 16, 2012).

Entine, Jon. "Future Energy: Natural Gas Fracking – Who Blew Up the Bridge to the Future?" Website article: *AEI.org* (December 13, 2011)

Gobster, Paul H. "Aldo Leopold's `Ecological Esthetic': Integrating Esthetic and Biodiversity Values." *Journal of Forestry* 93 (February, 1995): 6-10.

Goldberg, Carey. "Sierra Club Gets a New Young Face." *New York Times* (June 2, 1996)

Hardin, Garrett. "Ethical Implications of Carrying Capacity." *The Garrett Hardin Society* (1977)

——"The Tragedy of the Commons." *Science* (December 13, 1968): 1243-1248

Hayward, Steven F. "A Sensible Environmentalism." *The Public Interest* (March 22, 2003).

——"Cooled Down." *National Review* (January 31, 2005)

——"Don't Worry, Be Happy." *Tech Central Station* (April 22, 2004)

Hayward, Steven F. and Green, Kenneth P. "Energy Independence, Security? How About Energy Realism." *Washington Examiner* (September 20, 2009)

Hayward, Steven F. "Gore on the Rocks." *National Review Online* (March 21, 2007).

——"Happy Earth Day." *Human Events Online* (April 22, 2008)

Kaufman, Leslie. "Study Finds a Tree Growth Spurt." *Proceedings of the National Academy of Sciences* (February 2, 2010)

Kuehn, Robert R. The Coastal Barrier Resources Act and the Expenditures Limitation Approach to Natural Resources Conservation: Wave of the Future or Island Unto Itself? *Ecology Law Quarterly, University of California, Berkeley* (Vol. 11, 1984) 583-670

Kreutzer, David. "The Economic Case for Drilling Oil Reserves." Web Memo, *Heritage Foundation* (October 1, 2008)

Lieberman, Ben. "Expanded Offshore Drilling should Be a Part of U.S. Energy Policy." Web Memo, *Heritage Foundation* (February 10, 2009)

——"The Waxman-Markey Global Warming Bill: Is the Economic Pain Justified by the Environmental Gain?" Testimony, *Third International Conference on Climate Change, Washington, The Heartland Institute* (June 2, 2009)

Lloyd William Forster (Oxford, 1833). "Two Lectures on the Checks to Population." Reprinted:

Population and Development Review (September, 1980):473-496.

Luce, Bob. "Wild Times for Ferrets." *Wyoming Wildlife* (October, 1992).

Makower, Joel. "Adam Werbach's Autopsy on Environmentalism's Death." *GreenBiz.com* (December 19, 2004)

Miller, Char, and Sample, V. Alaric. "Gifford Pinchot: A Life in Progress." *Journal of Forestry* 97 (January, 1999): 27-32.

Miller, Char. "Sawdust Memories: Pinchot and the Making of Forest History." *Journal of Forestry* 92 (February, 1994): 8-12.

Miller, M. Catherine. "Who Owns the Water?: Law, Property, and the Price of Irrigation." *Journal of the West* 29 (October, 1990): 35-41.

Patterson, Matt. "Environmentalists Are Bad for the Environment." *The Washington Examiner*, (January 3, 2012)

Pinchot, Gifford, "The Relation of Forests and Forest Fires." *Forest History Today* (Spring, 1999): 29-32.

Prinn, Ron and Wang, Chien. "Wind Turbines Could Cause Temperatures to Rise." *Atmospheric Chemistry and Physics* (February 22, 2010).

Rotella, Carlo. "Travels in a Subjective West: The Letters of Edwin James and Major Stephen Long's Scientific Expedition, 1819-1820." *Montana the Magazine of Western History* 41 (Autumn, 1991).

Russell, Edmund P. "Lost Among the Parts Per Billion: Ecological Protection at the United States Environmental Agency, 1970-1993." *Environmental History* 2.1 (January, 1997): 29-51.

Sarewitz, Daniel. "The Voice of Science: Let's Agree to Disagree." *Nature* 478, No.7 (October 5, 2011).

Scheer, Robert. "Who Needs Divine Intervention?" *Los Angeles Times* (January 6, 1996)

Smith, Fred L., Jr. "Eco-Socialism: Threat to Liberty Around the World." Paper, *Mont Pelerin Society Regional Meeting*, Chattanooga, Tennessee (September 30, 2003).

Scott Streater. "Colorado County Wants Public Lands Opened to Shale Developers." *Energy Wire*, Colorado Springs (April 10, 2012)

Thomas, Heather Smith. "History of Public Land Grazing." *Rangelands* 16 (December, 1994): 50-55.

Utley, Jon Basil. "The Case for Increasing Domestic Oil Production: Why America Can and Must Produce More Oil." *Reason* (March 30, 2011).

Weronko, William. "Energy 2008: The Coming Economic Meltdown." *Intellectual Conservative* (April 15, 2008).

Worster, Donald. "Landscape with Hero: John Wesley Powell and the Colorado Plateau." *Southern California Quarterly* 79 (Spring, 1997): 29-46.

ILLUSTRATIONS

INDEX